CROSS

TATTOOS

JOHNNY KARP

Cross Tattoos
by Johnny Karp

ISBN 978-0-9866426-4-7

Printed in the United States of America

Copyright © 2010 Psylon Press

Other Books in the Series

- Butterfly Tattoos
- Angel Tattoos
- Skull Tattoos
- Fairy Tattoos
- Zodiac Tattoos
- Lettering Tattoos
- Scorpion Tattoos
- Hummingbird Tattoos
- Dragonfly Tattoos
- Kanji Tattoos
- Dolphin Tattoos
- Cherub Tattoos

Other titles are in preparation.

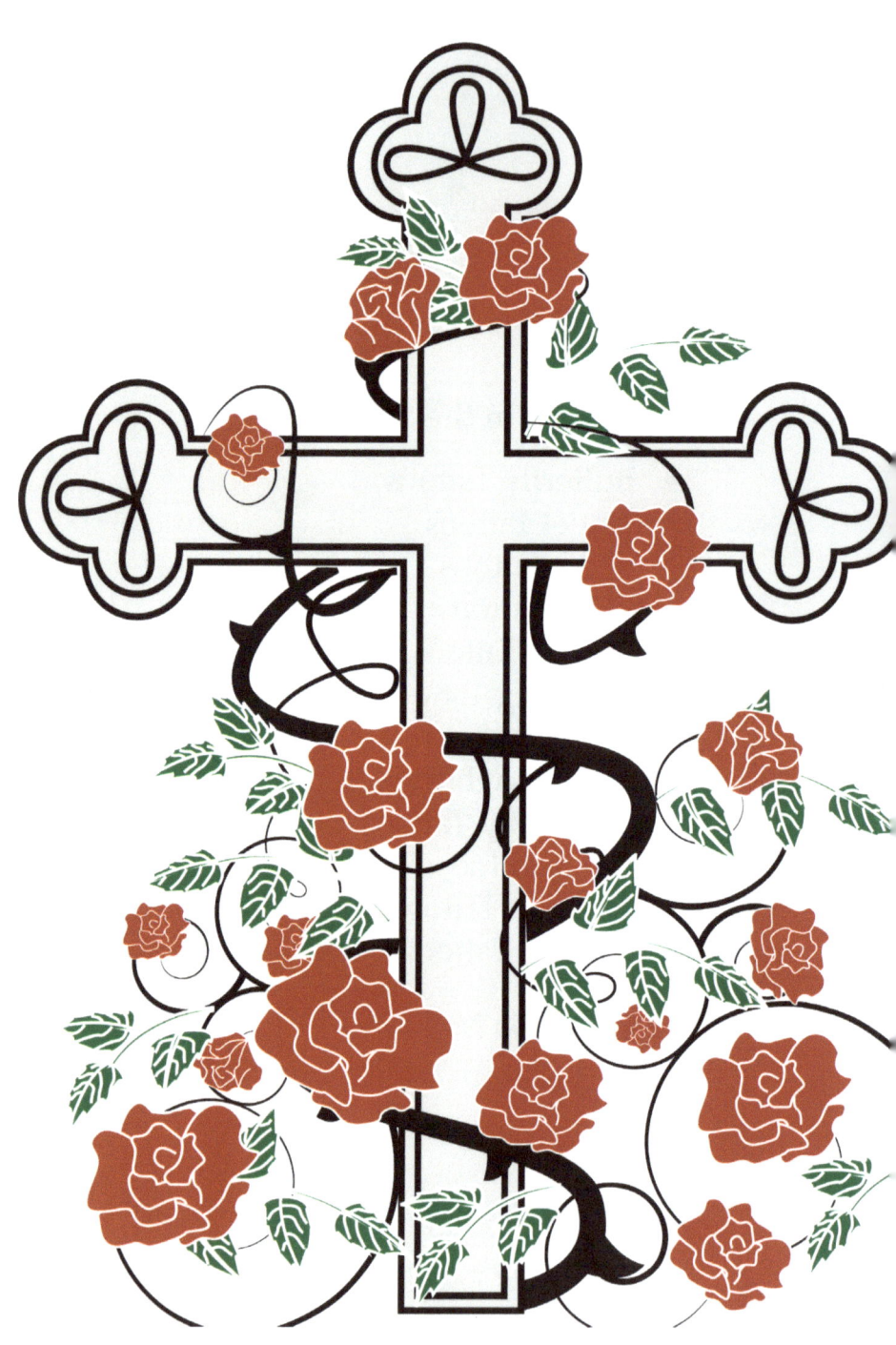

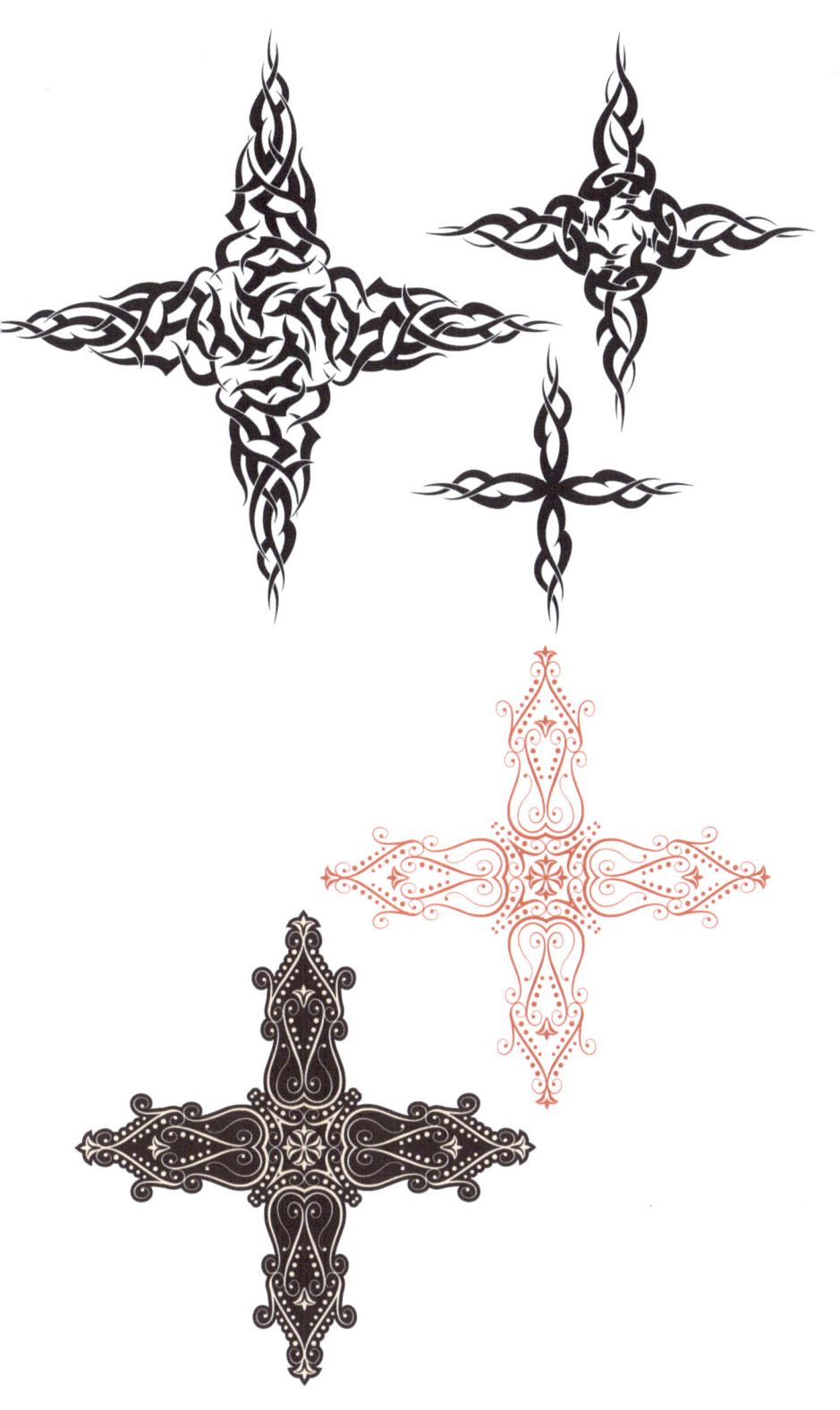

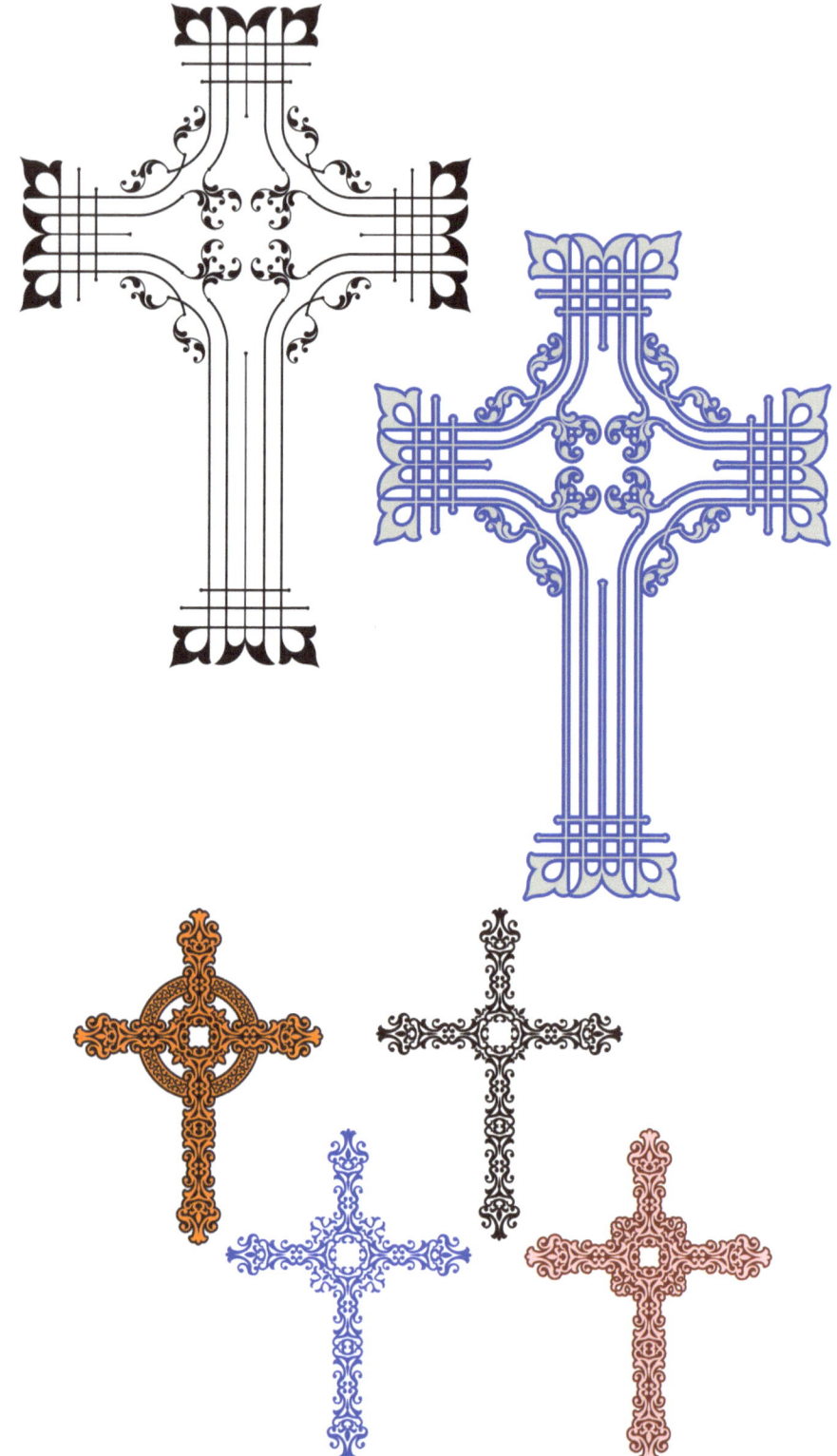

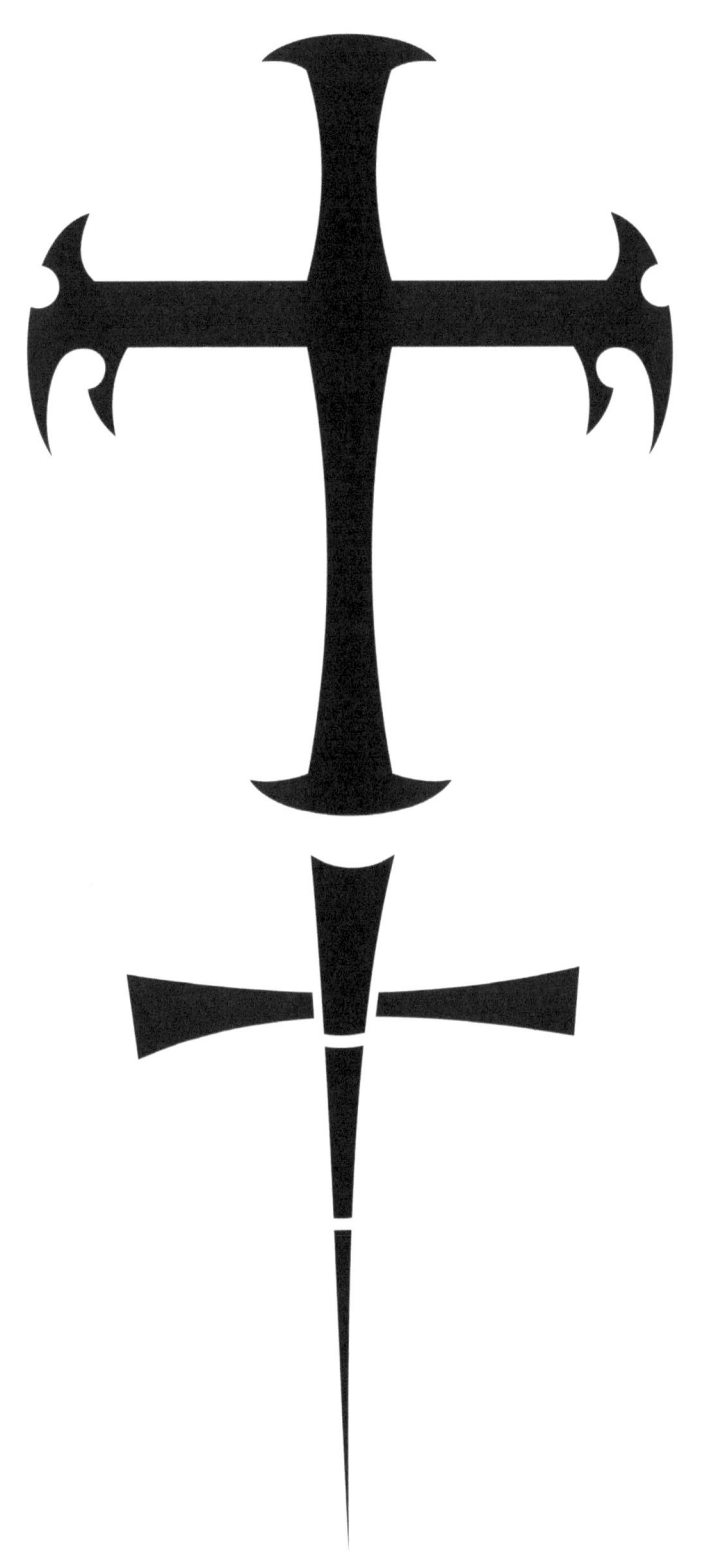

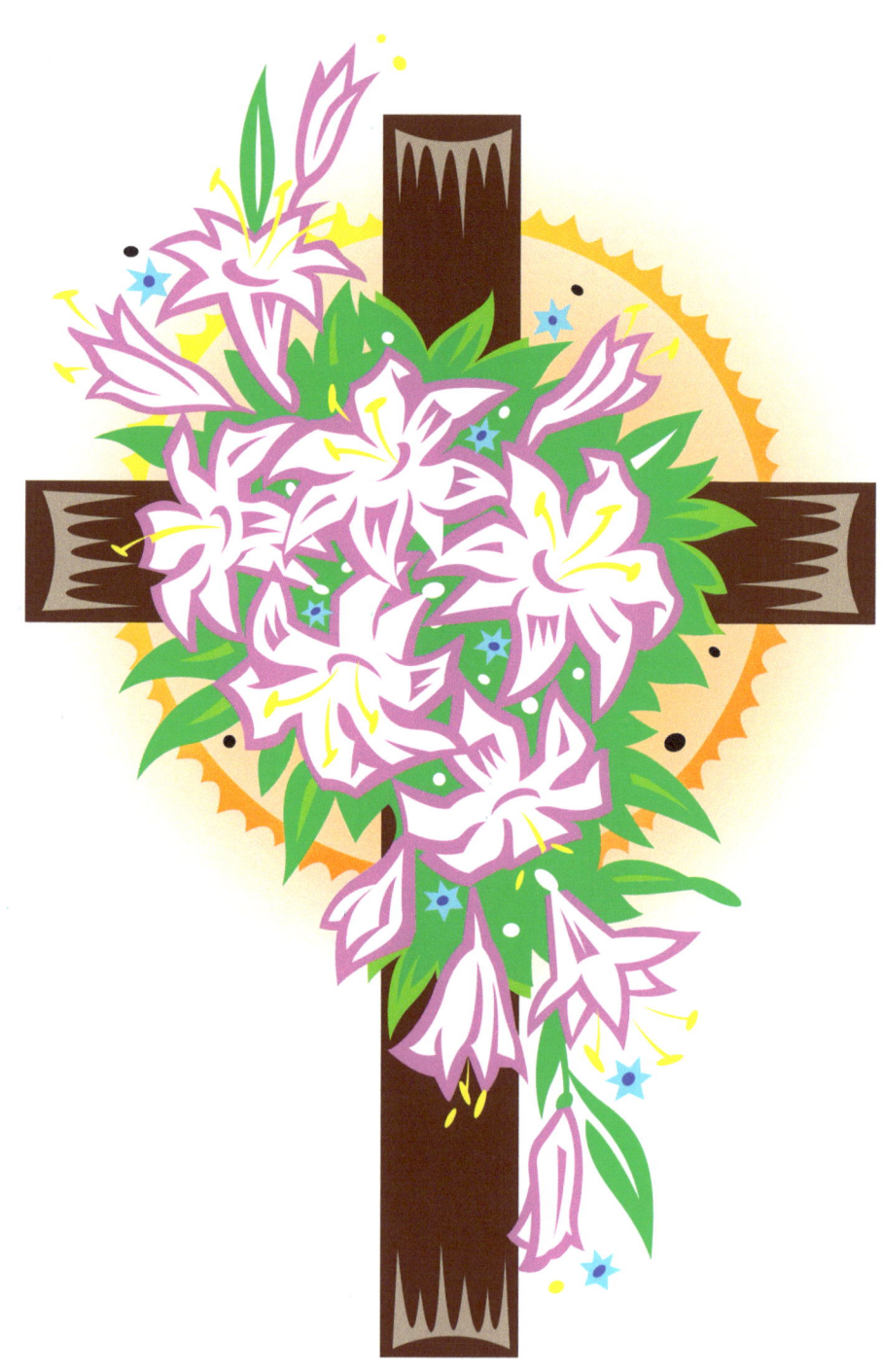

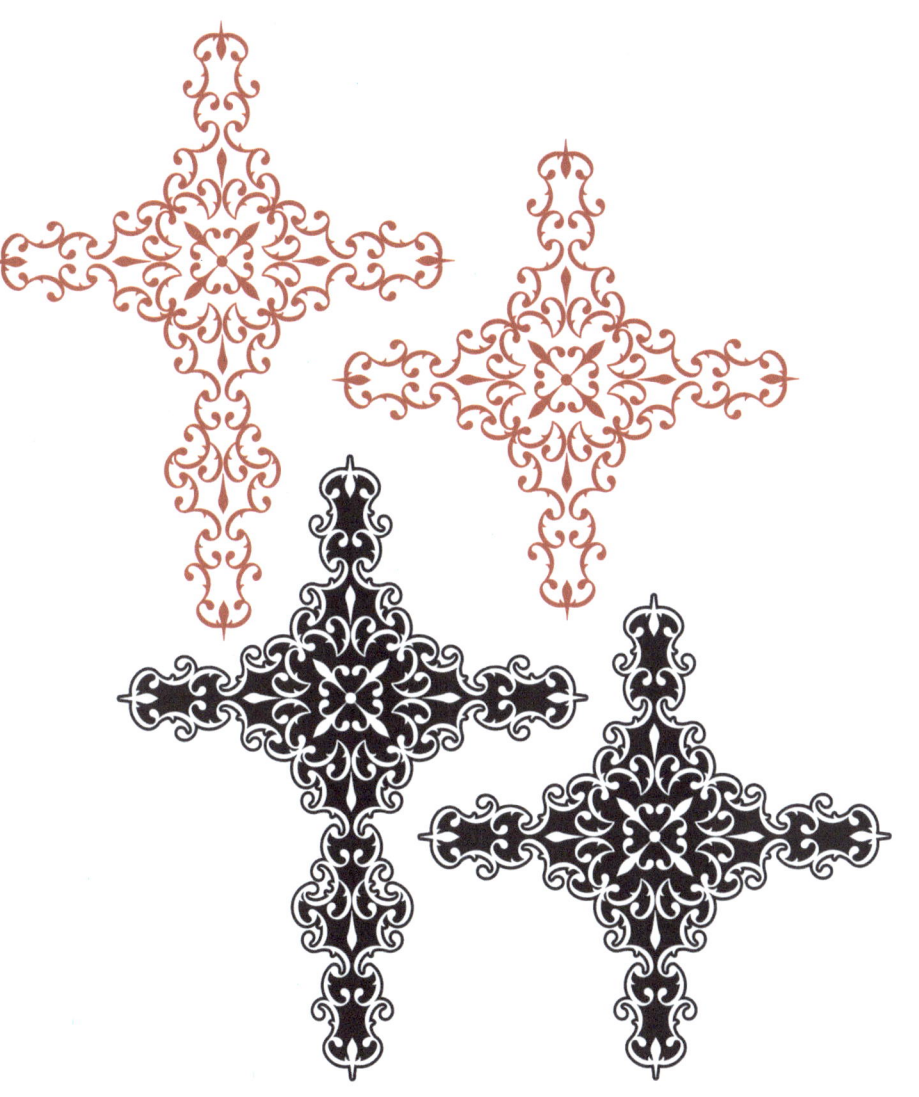

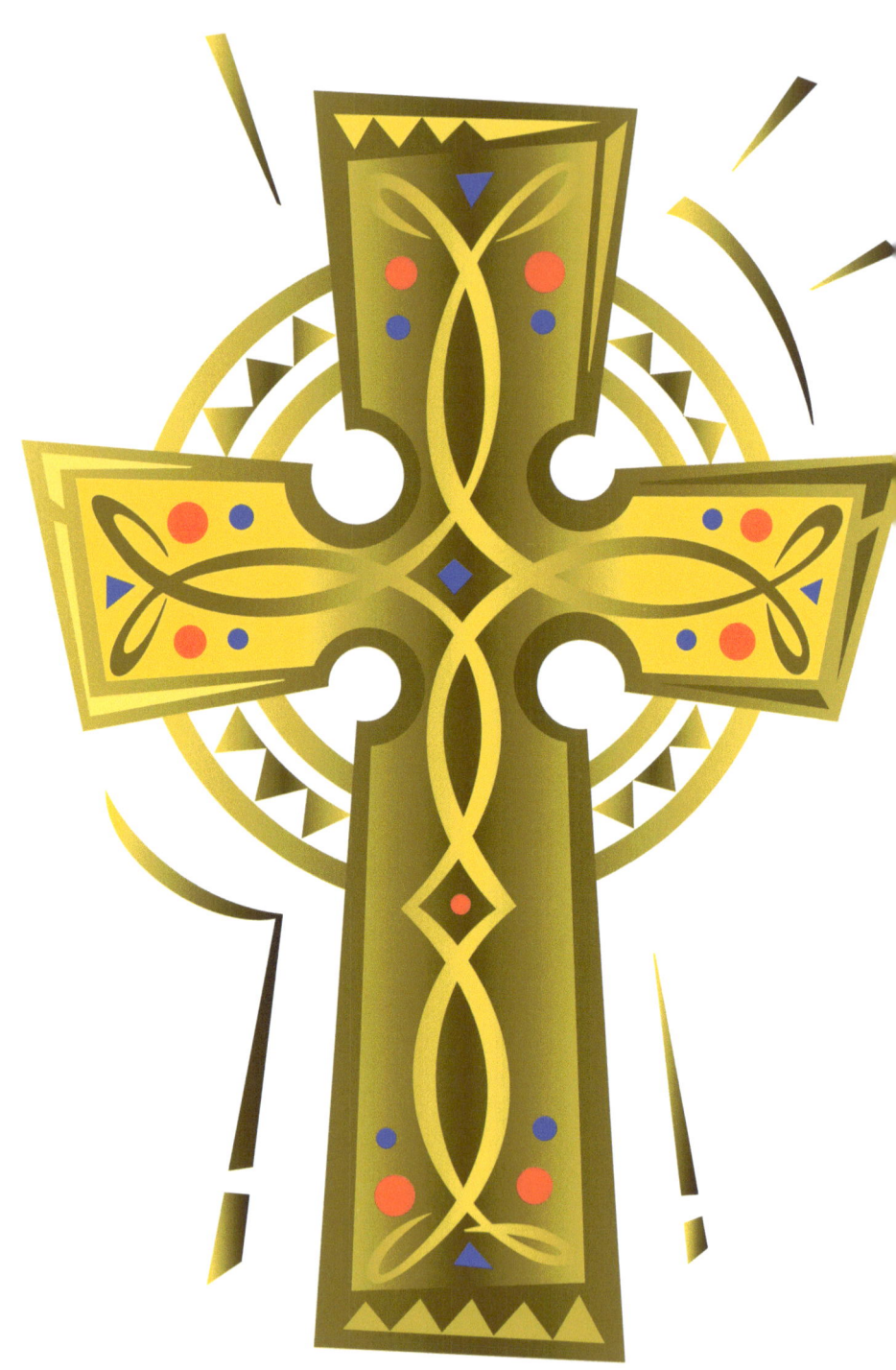

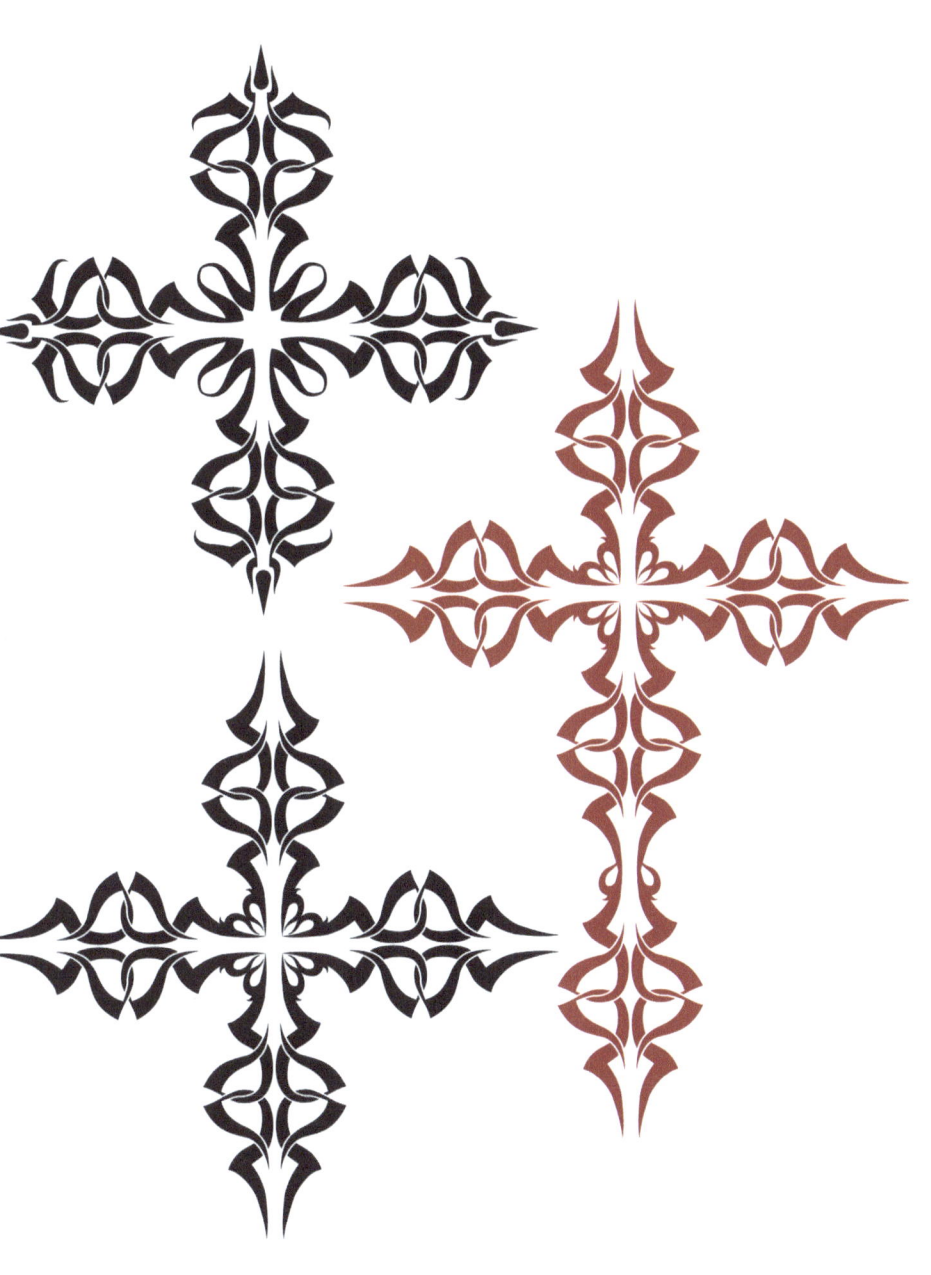

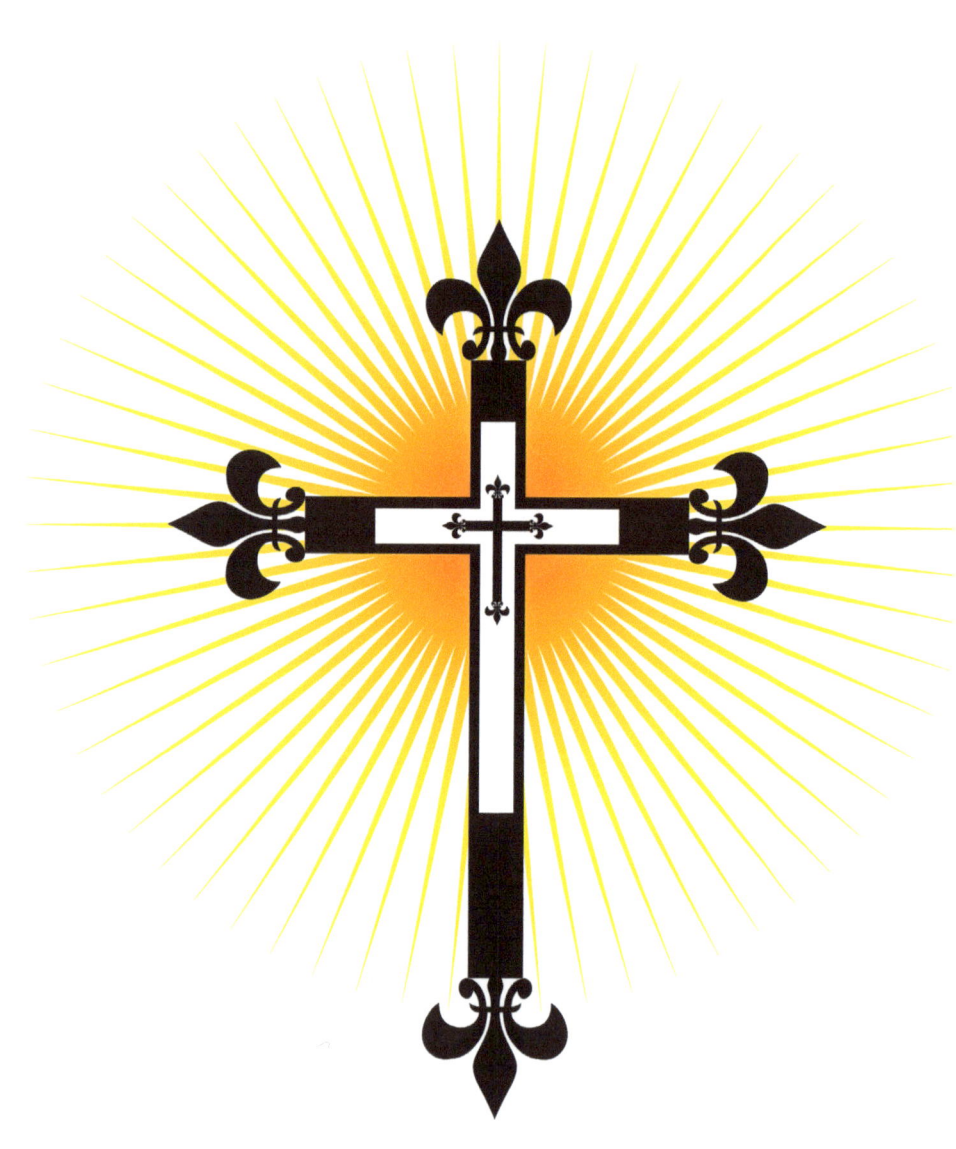

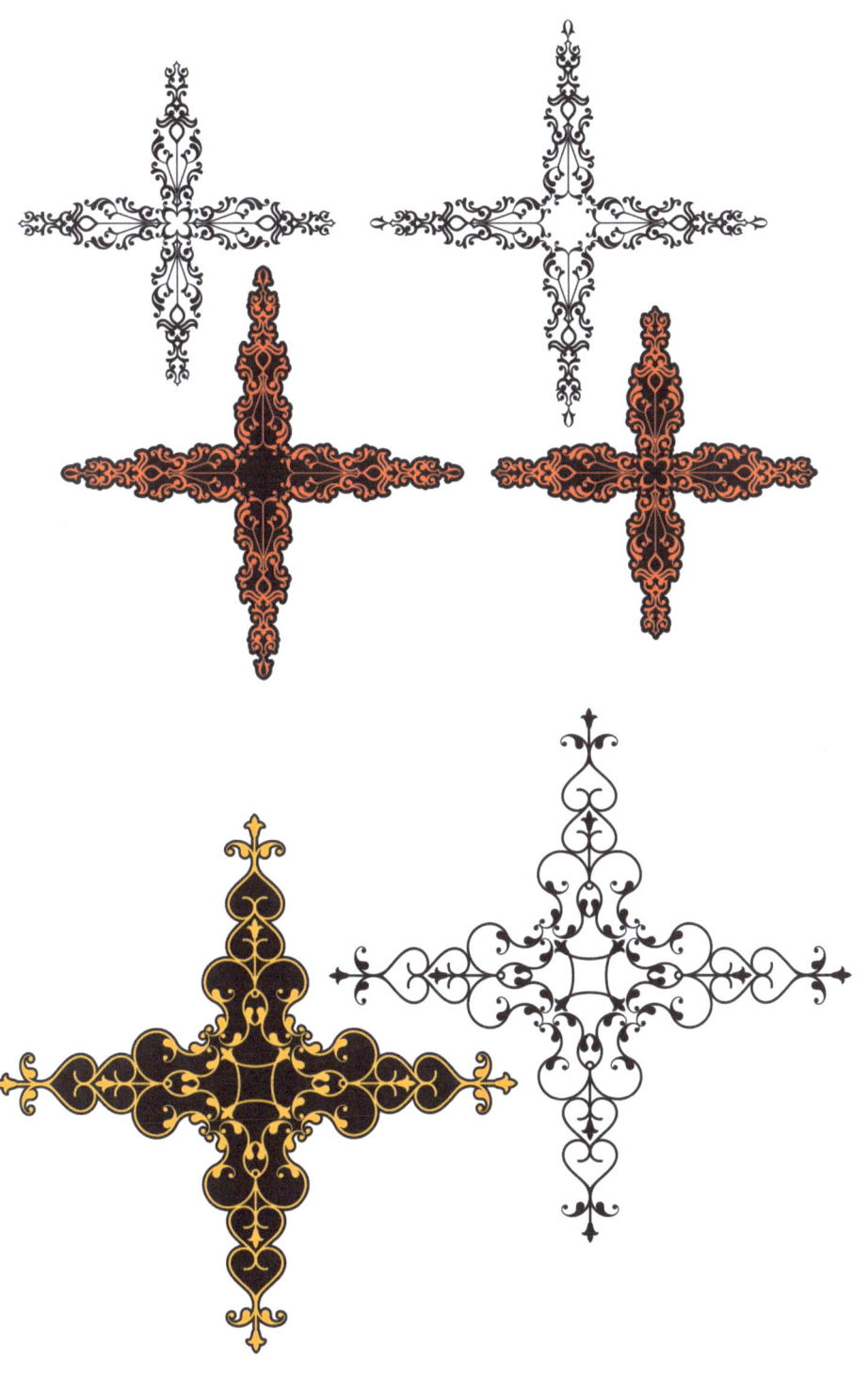

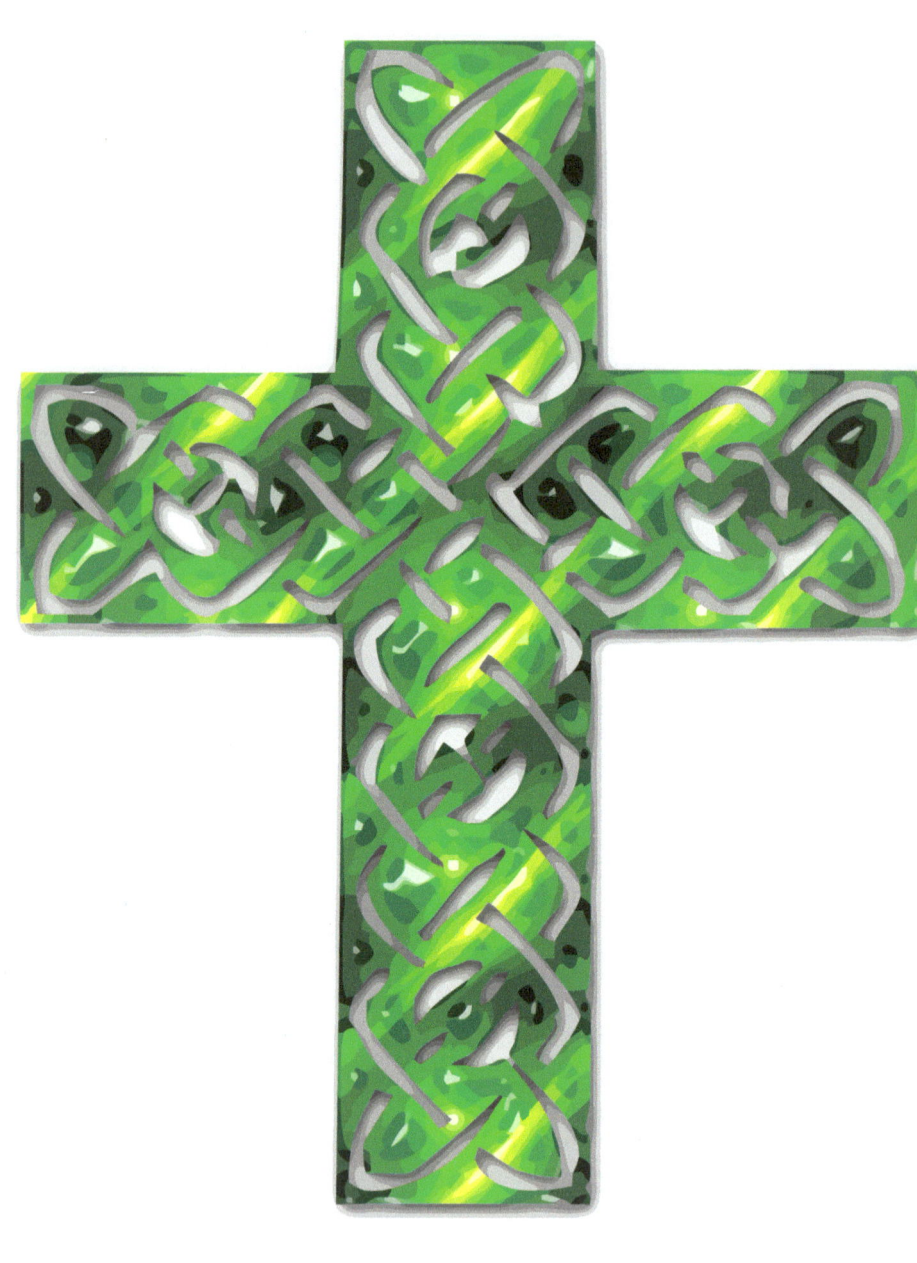

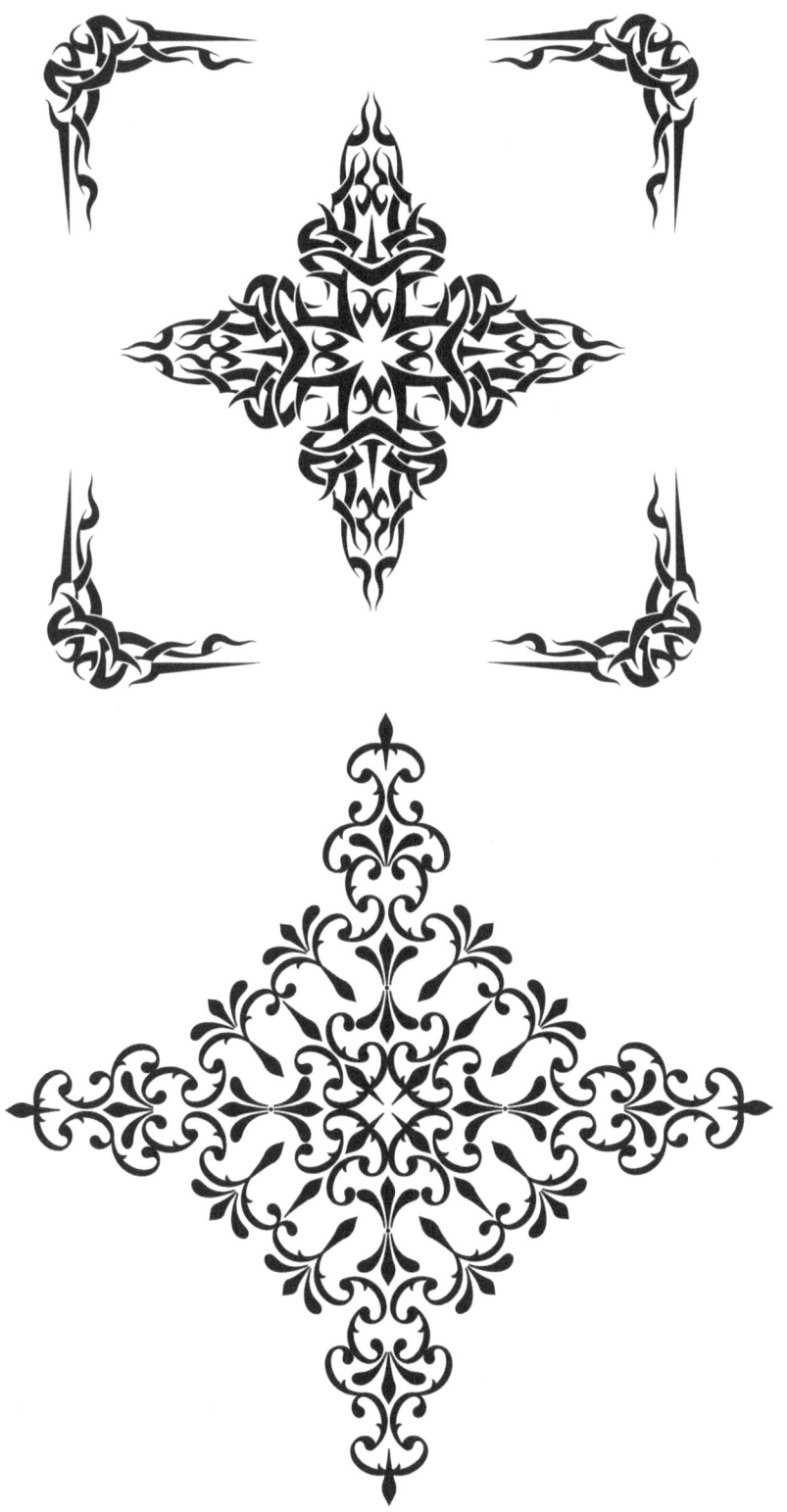

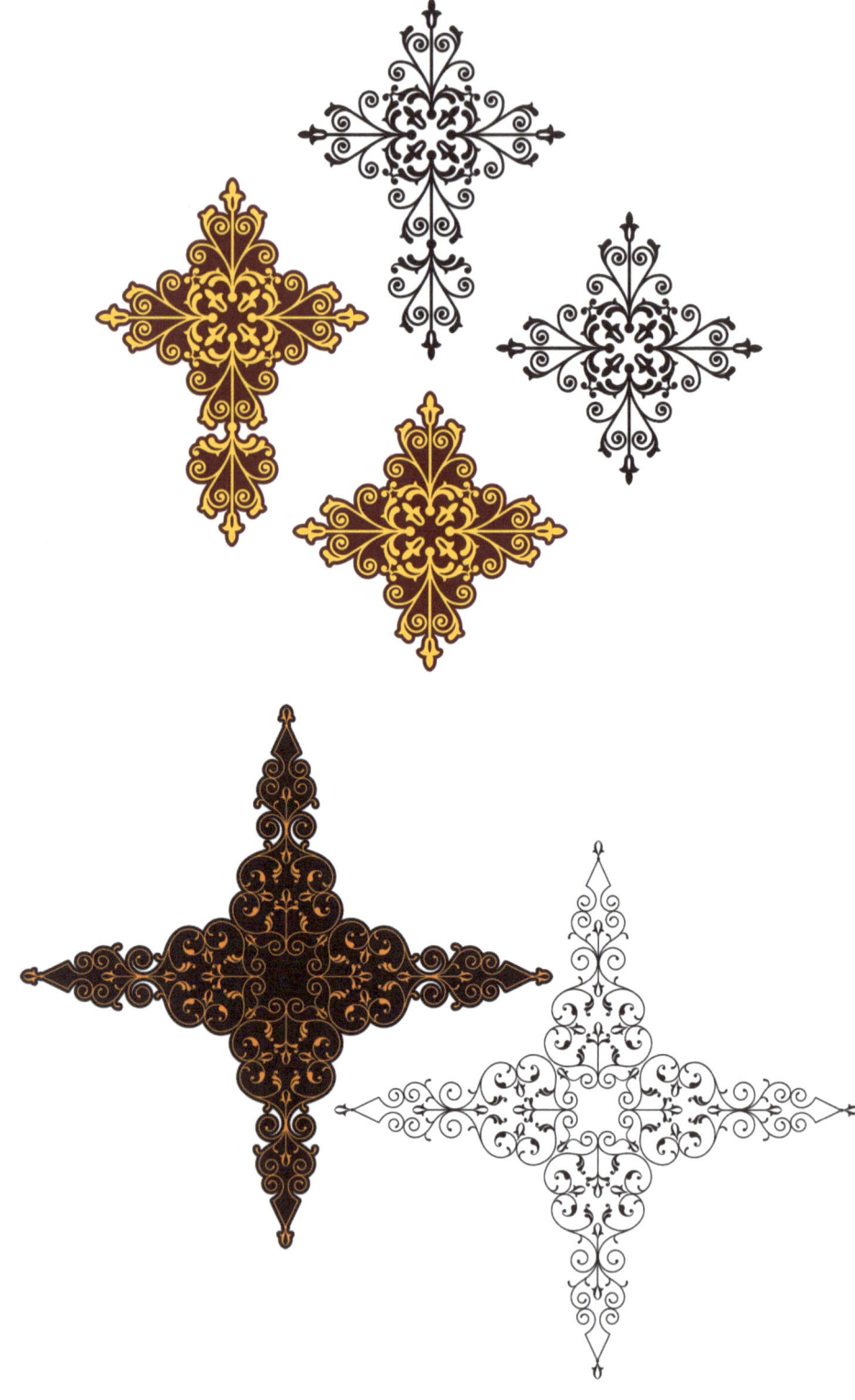

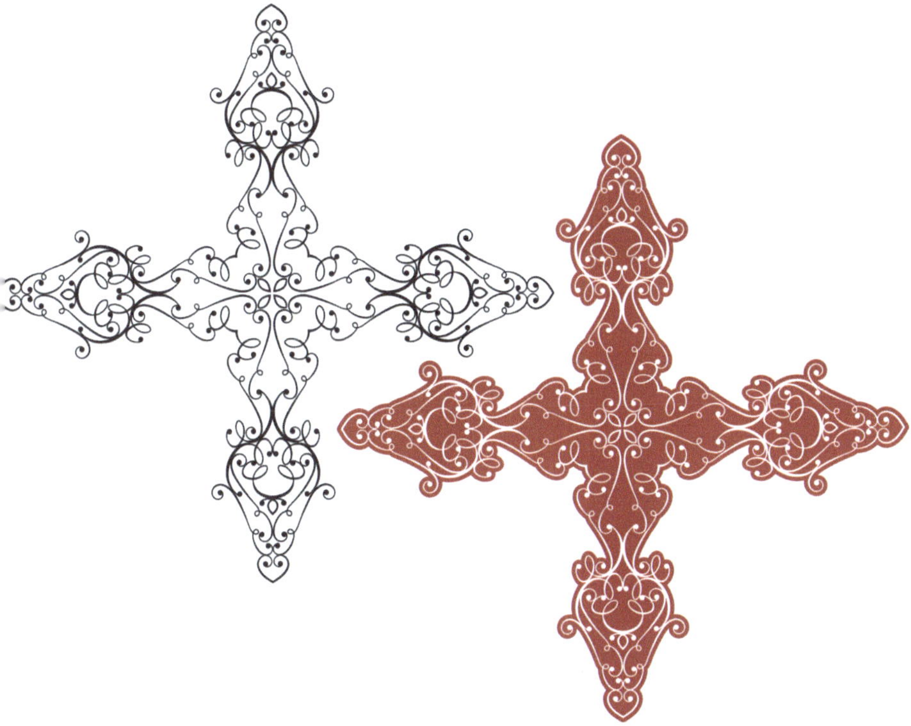

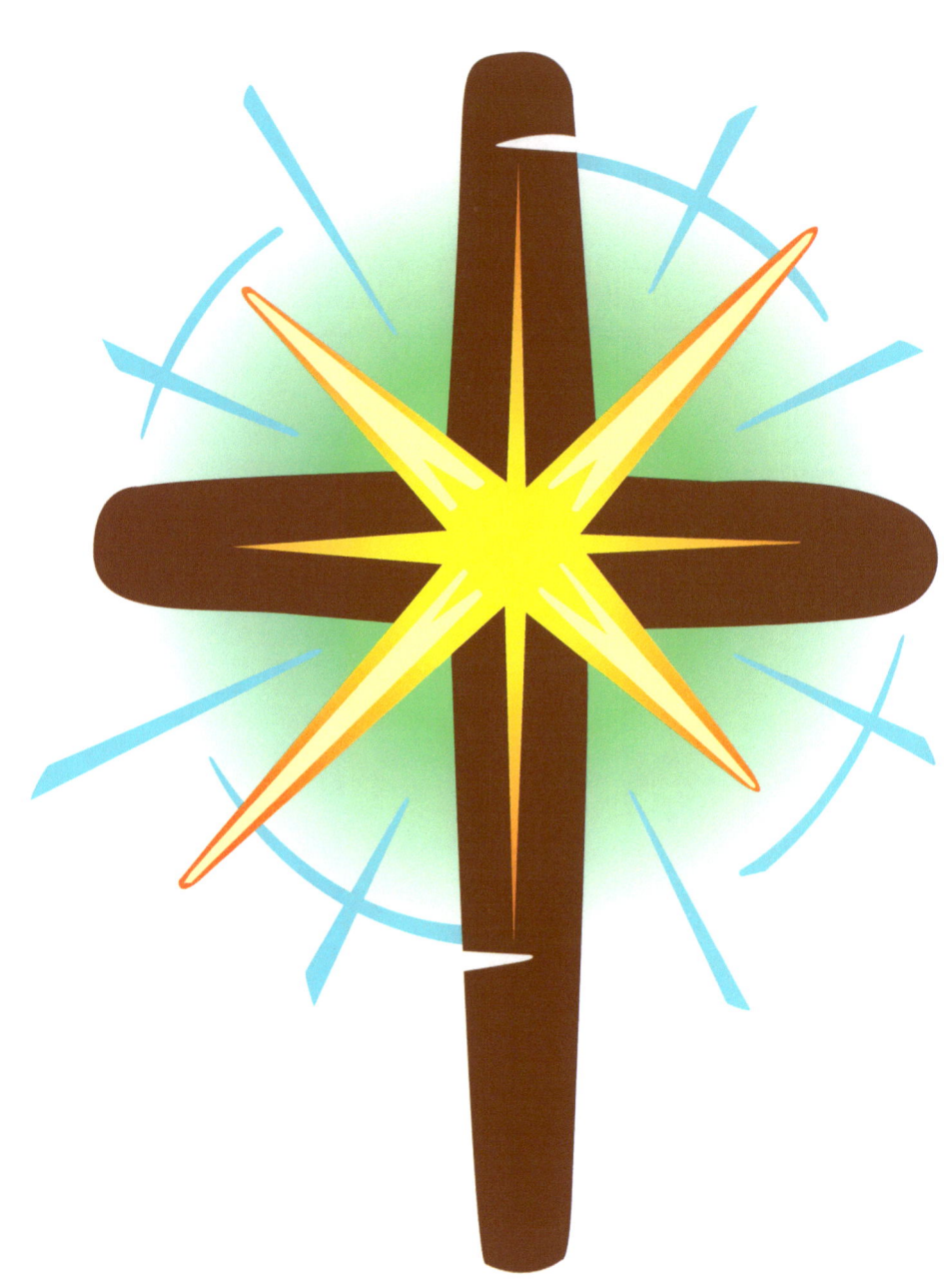

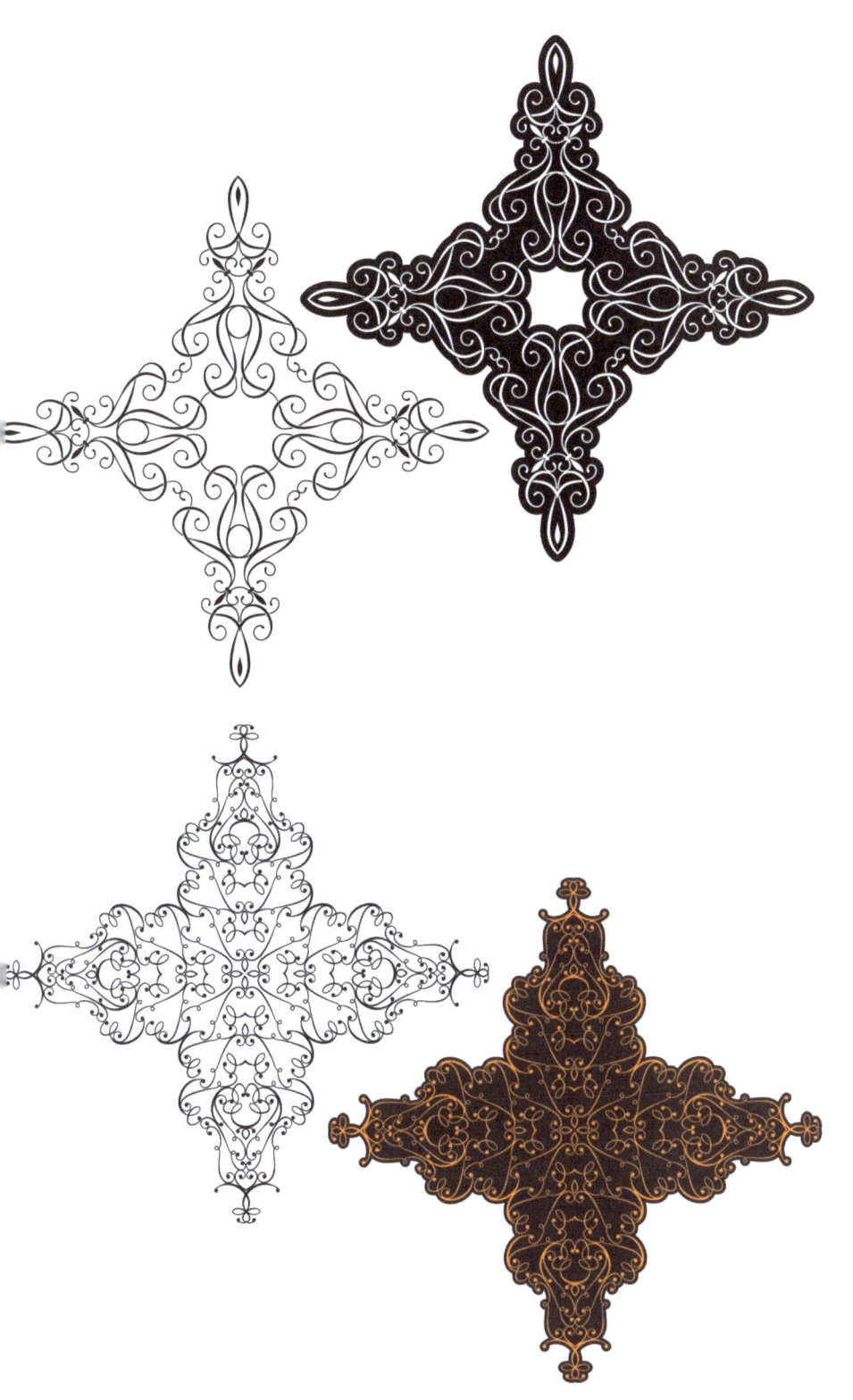

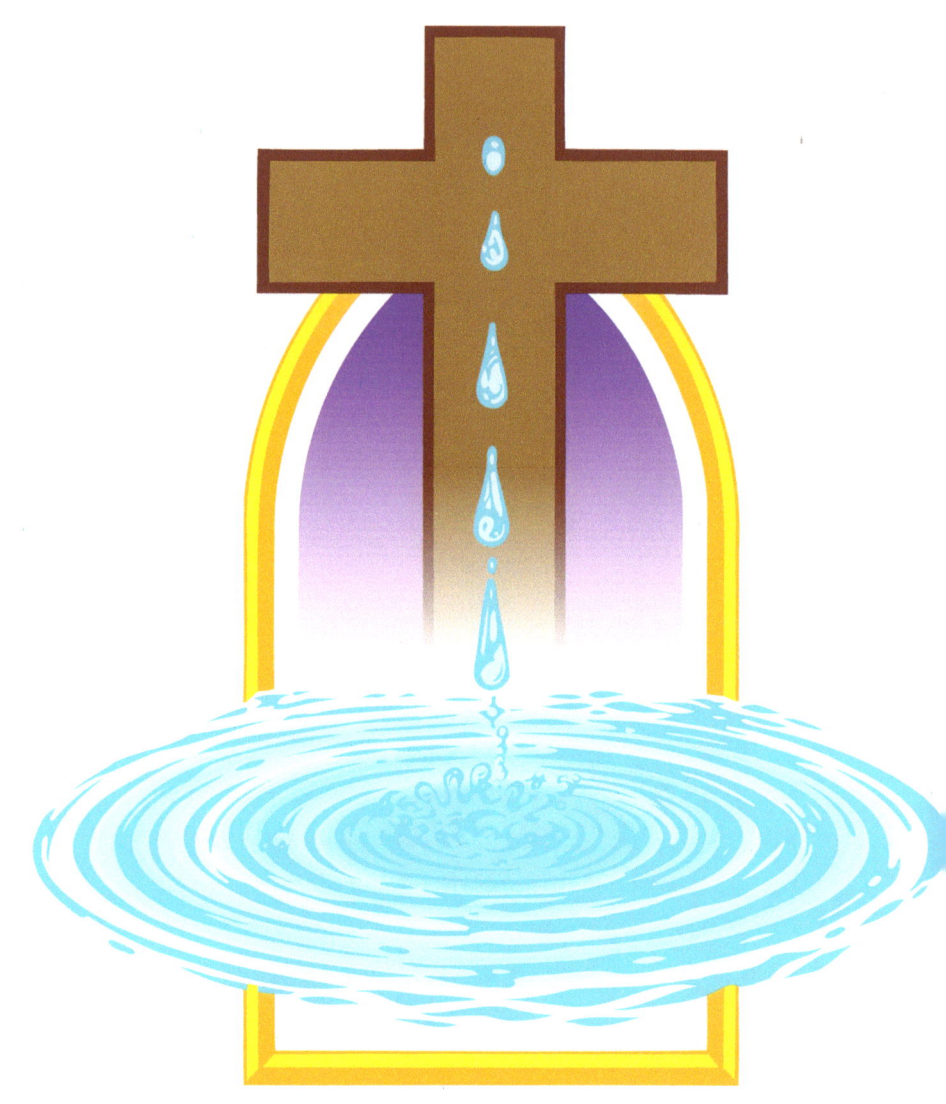

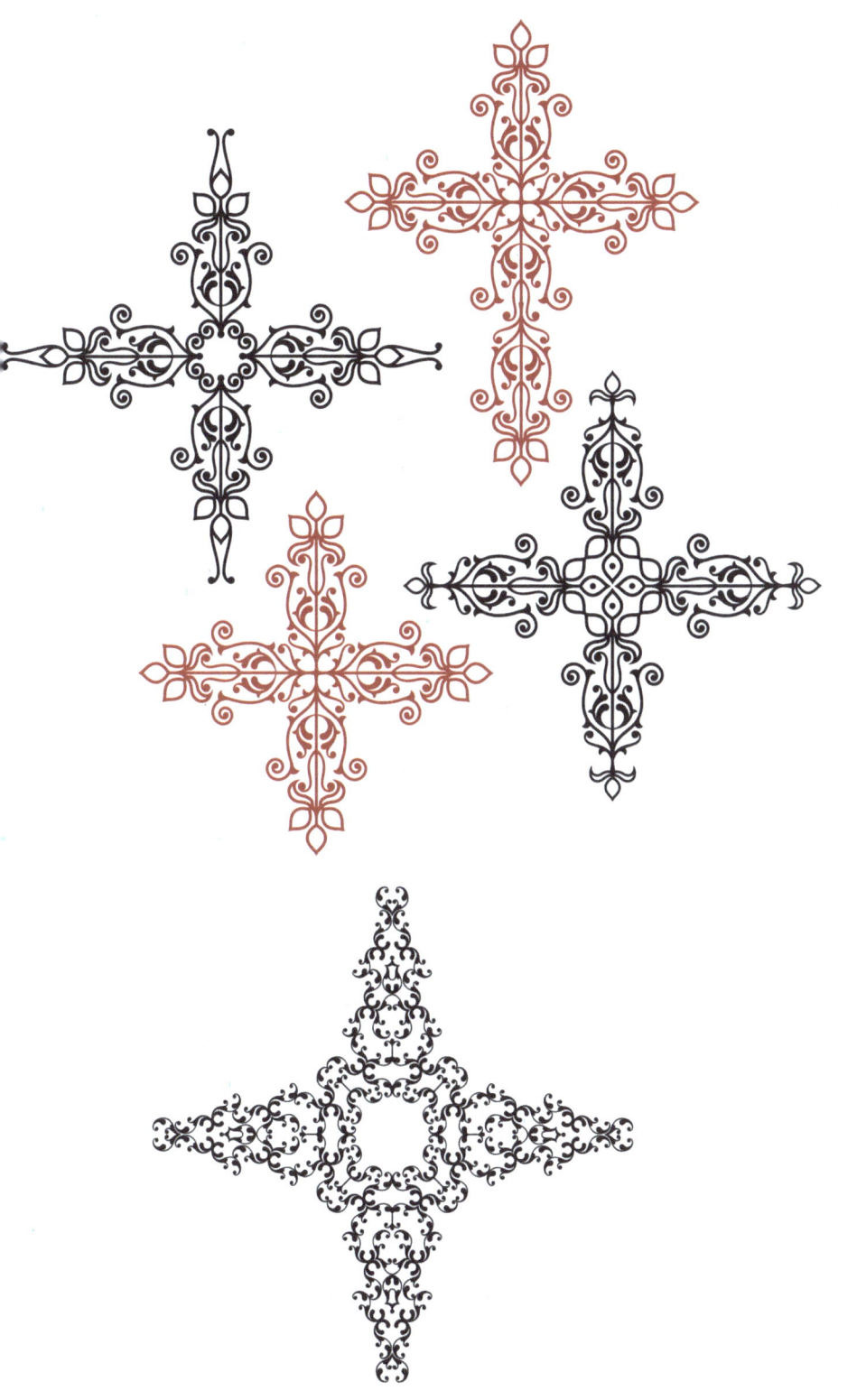

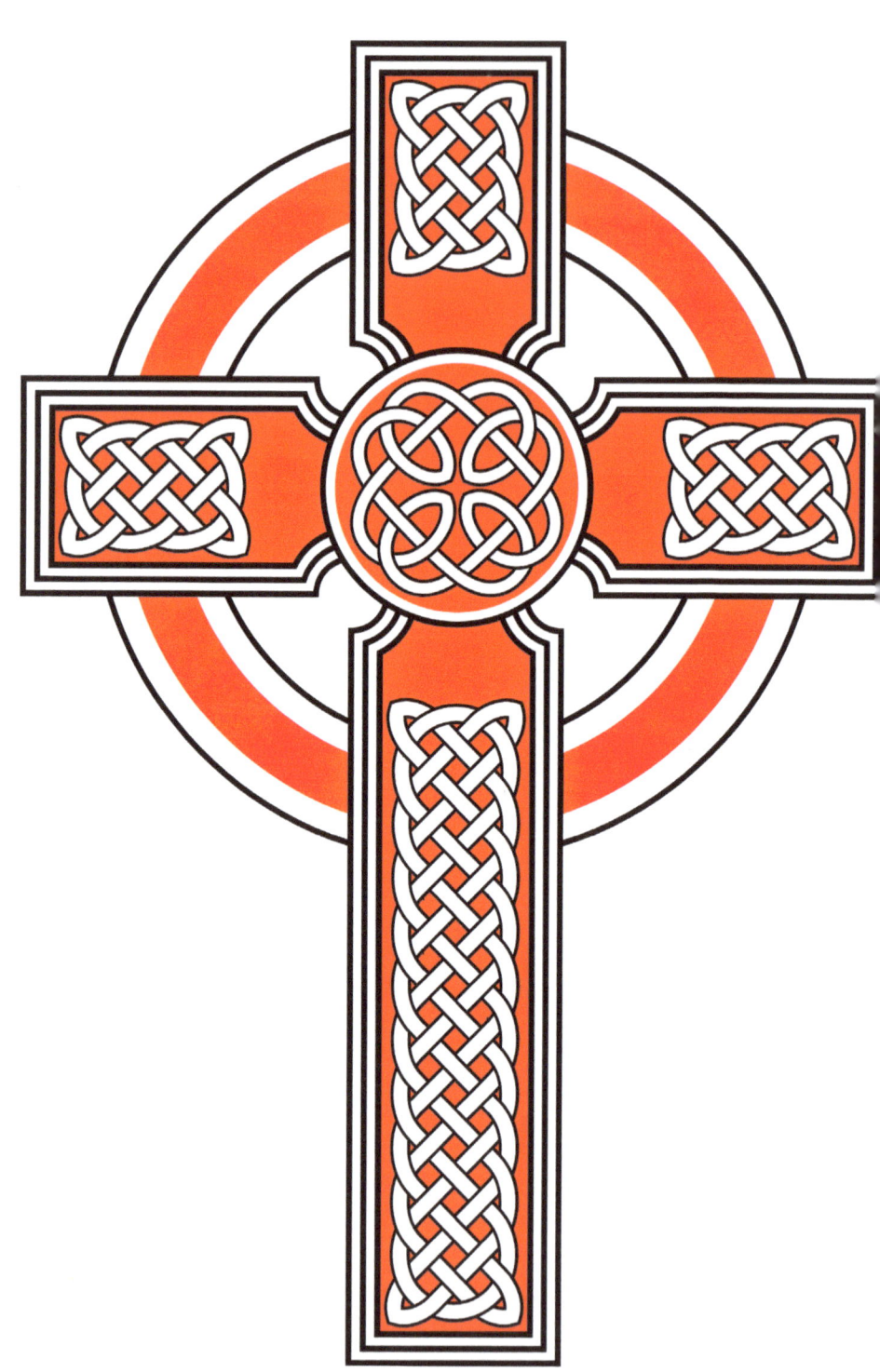

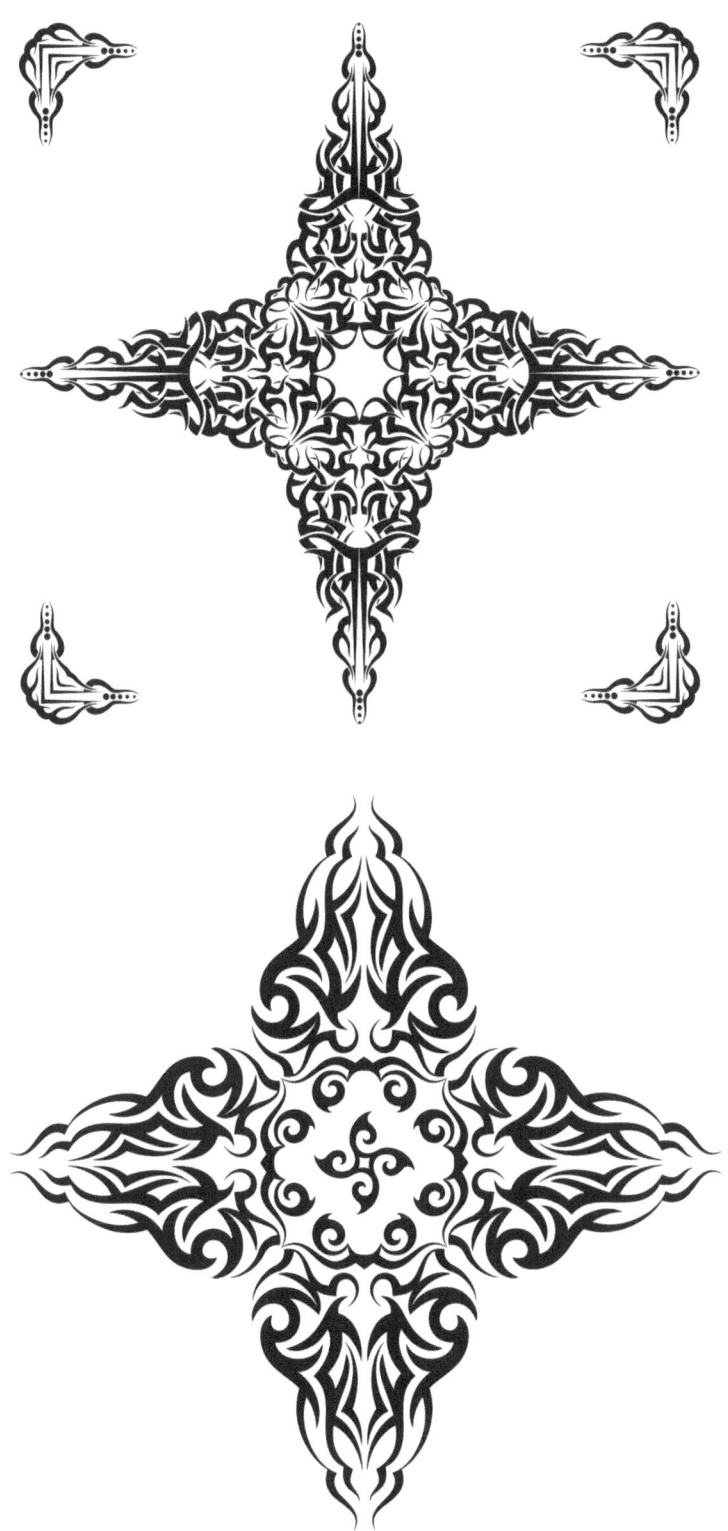

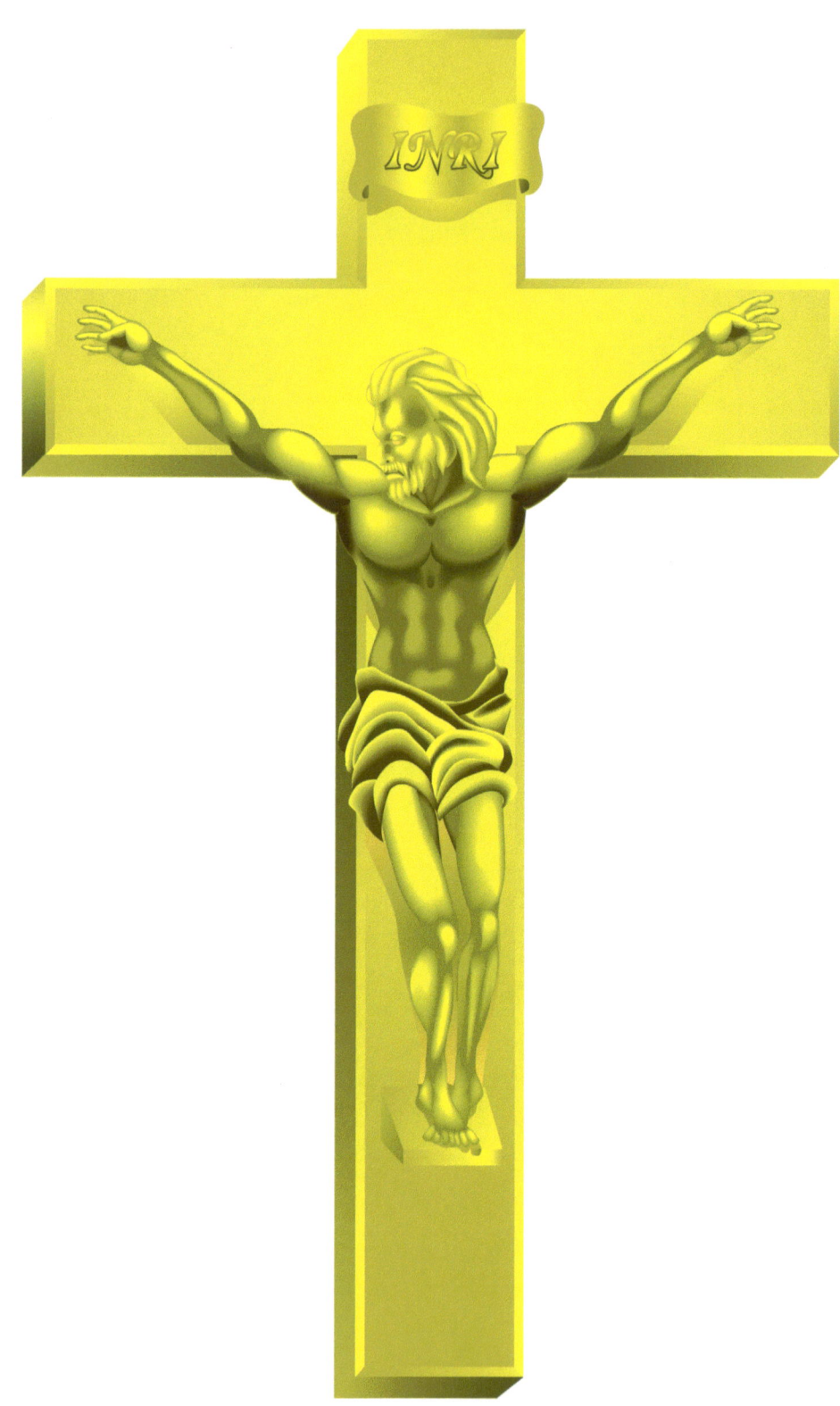

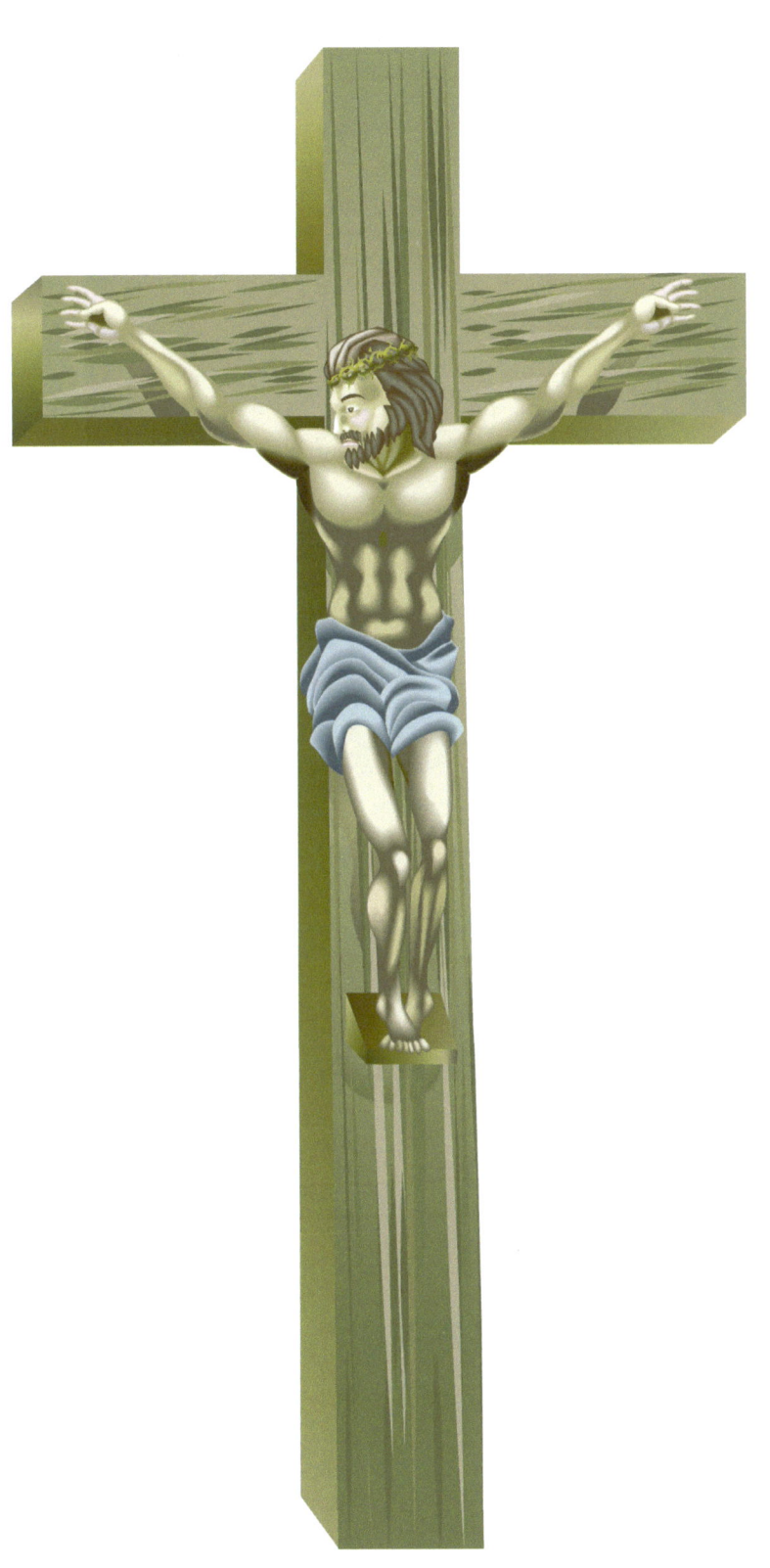

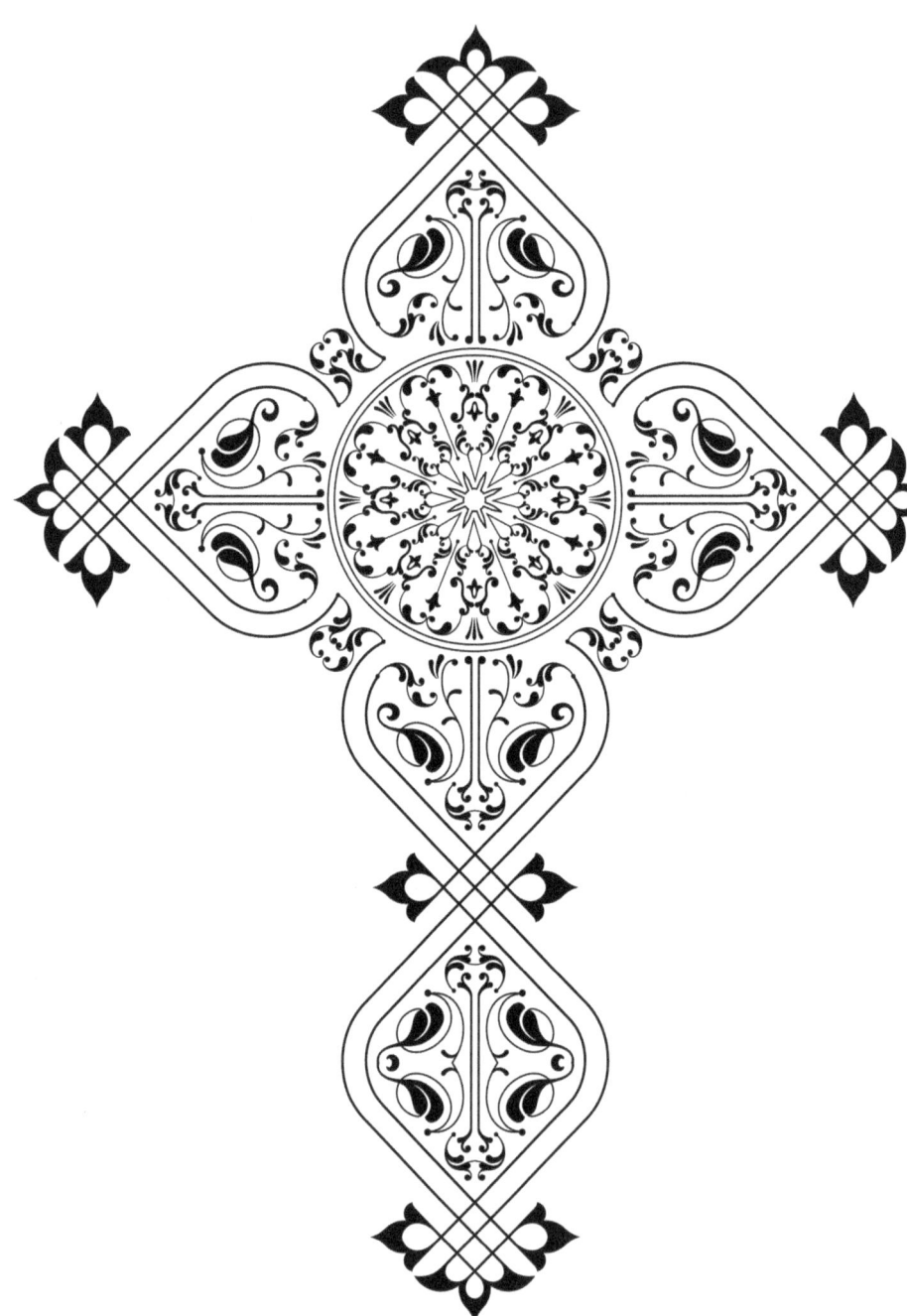

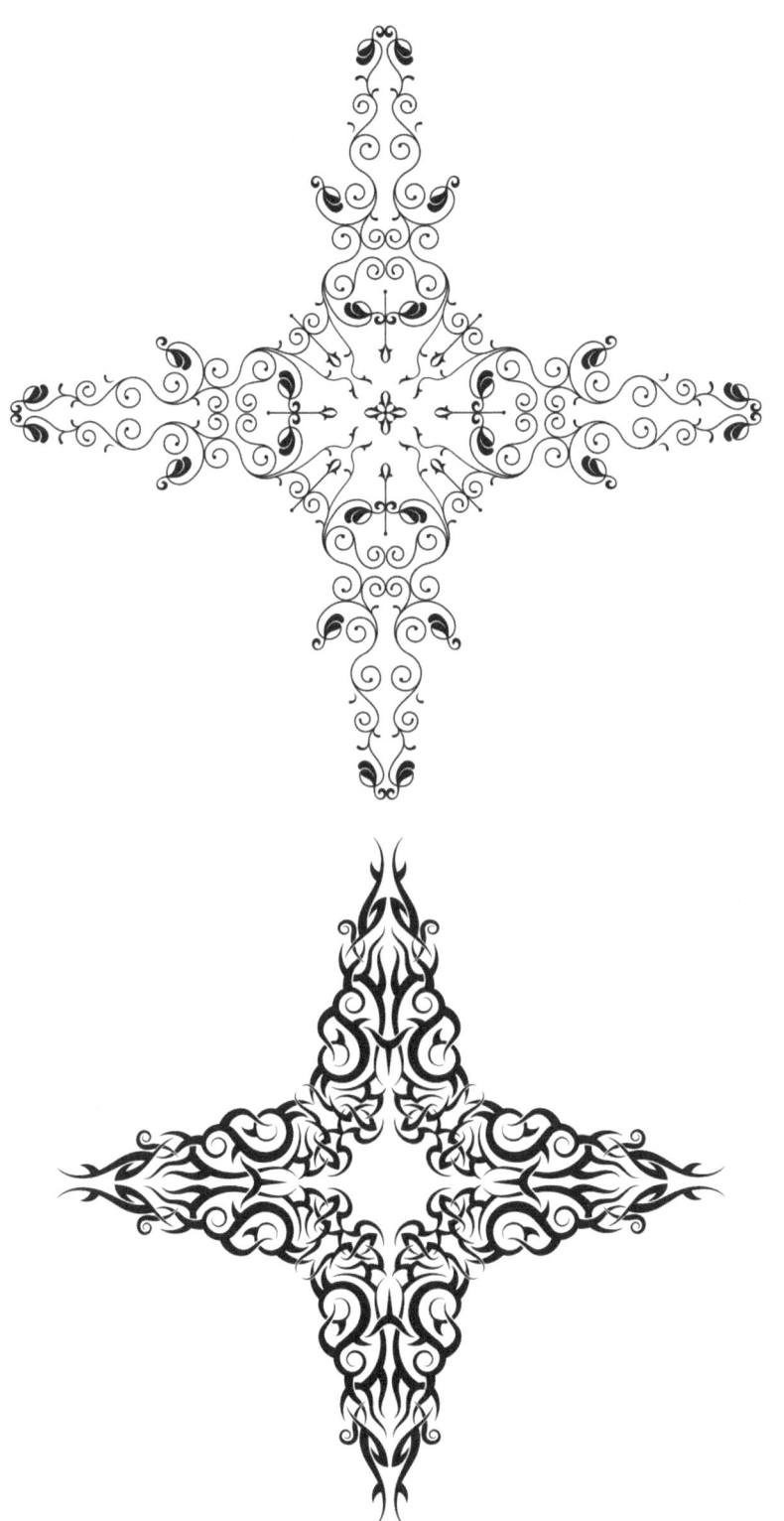

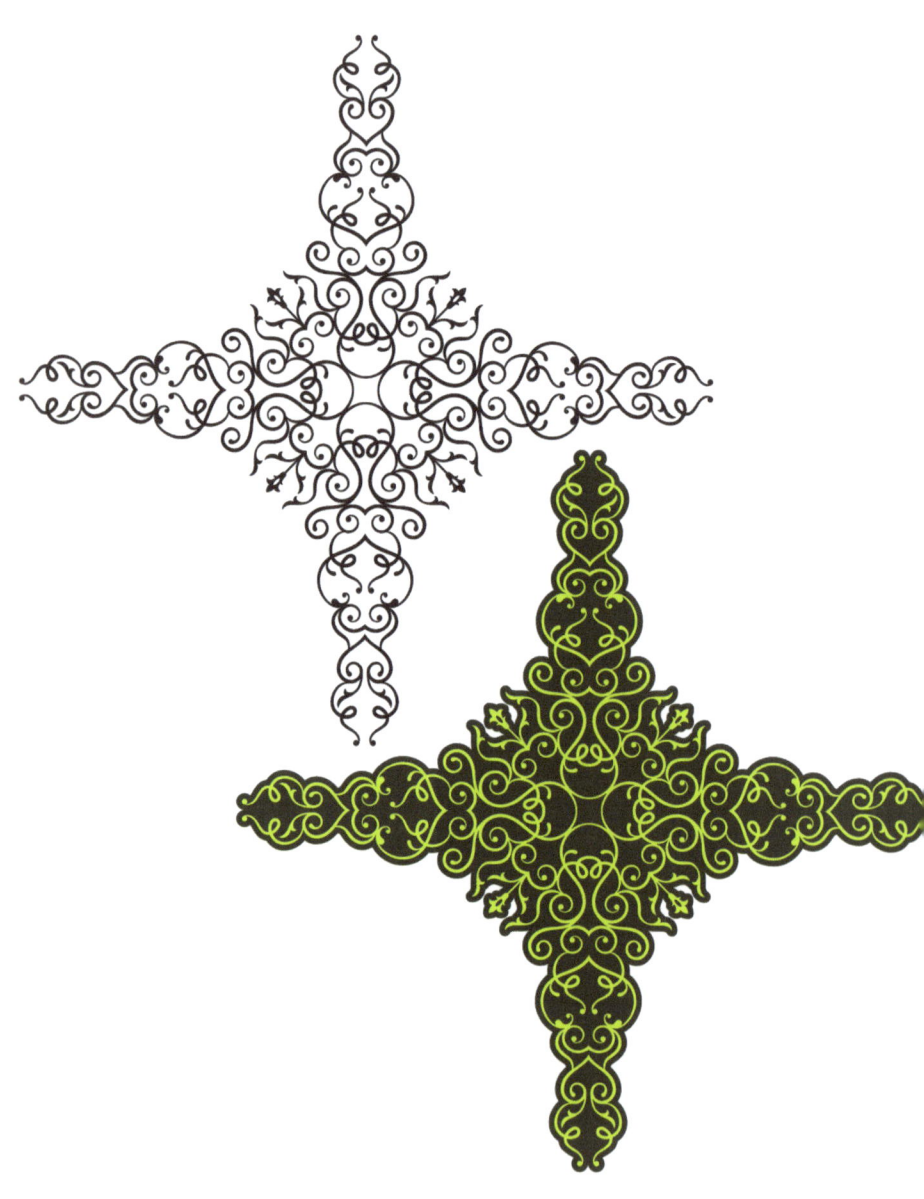

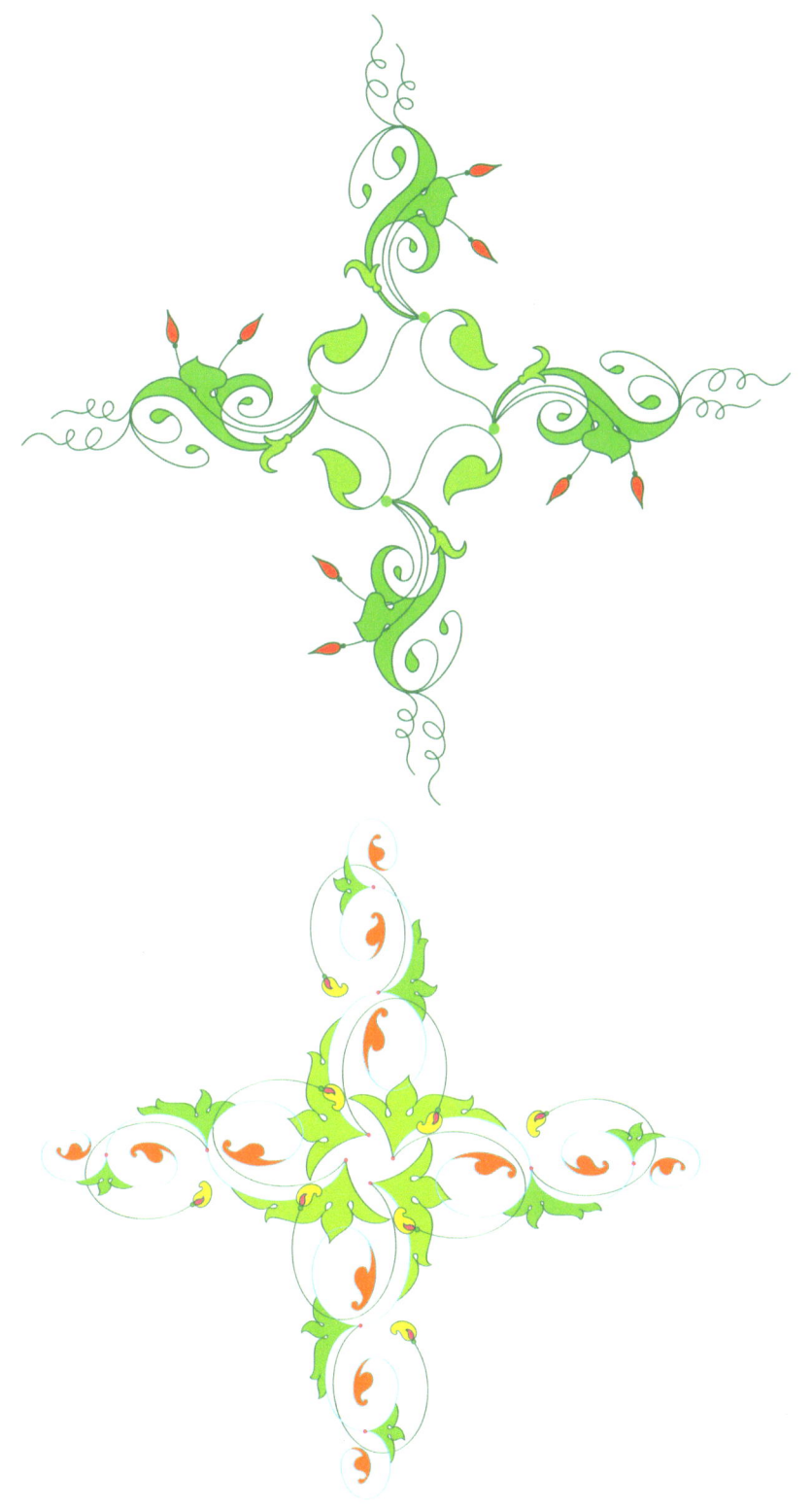

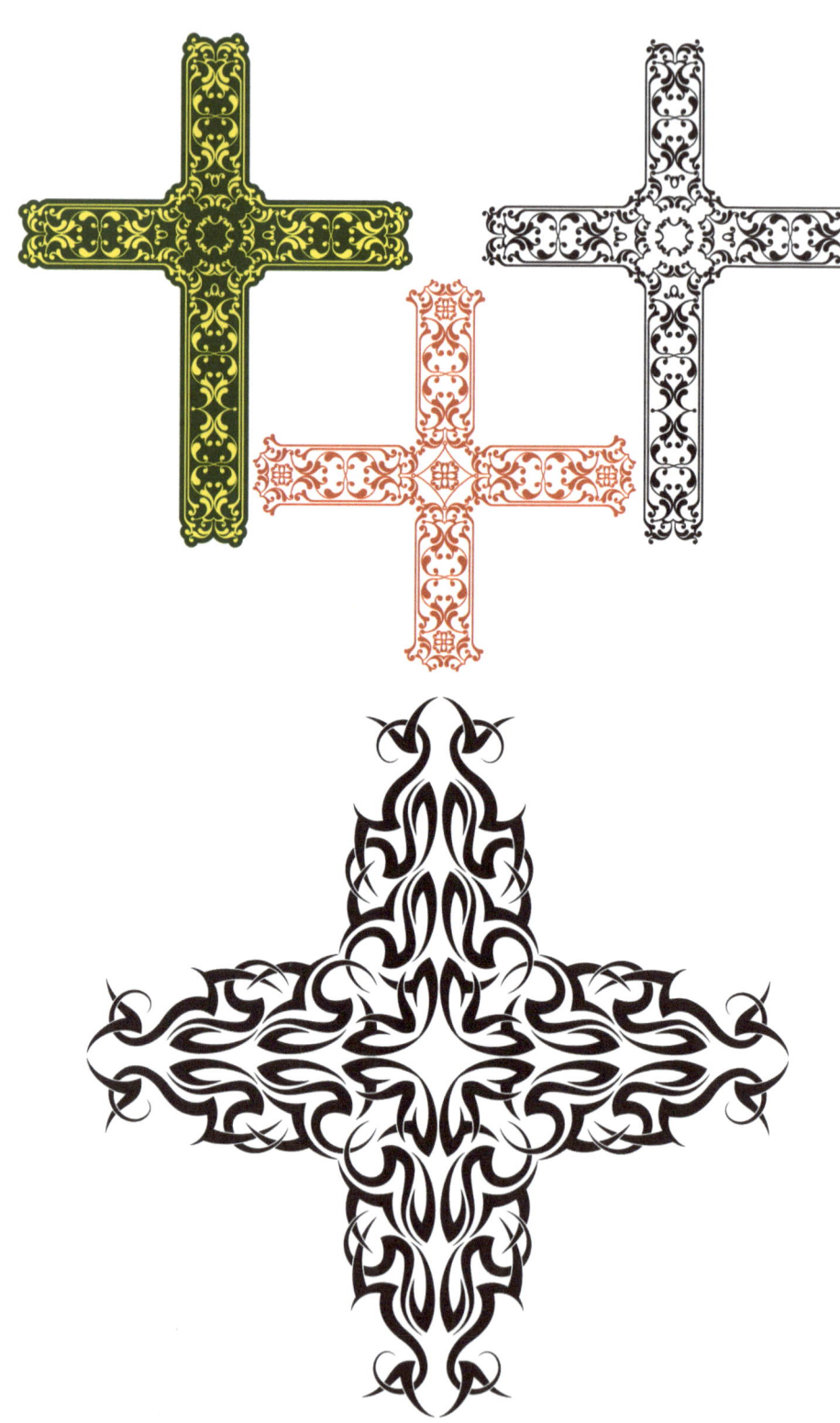

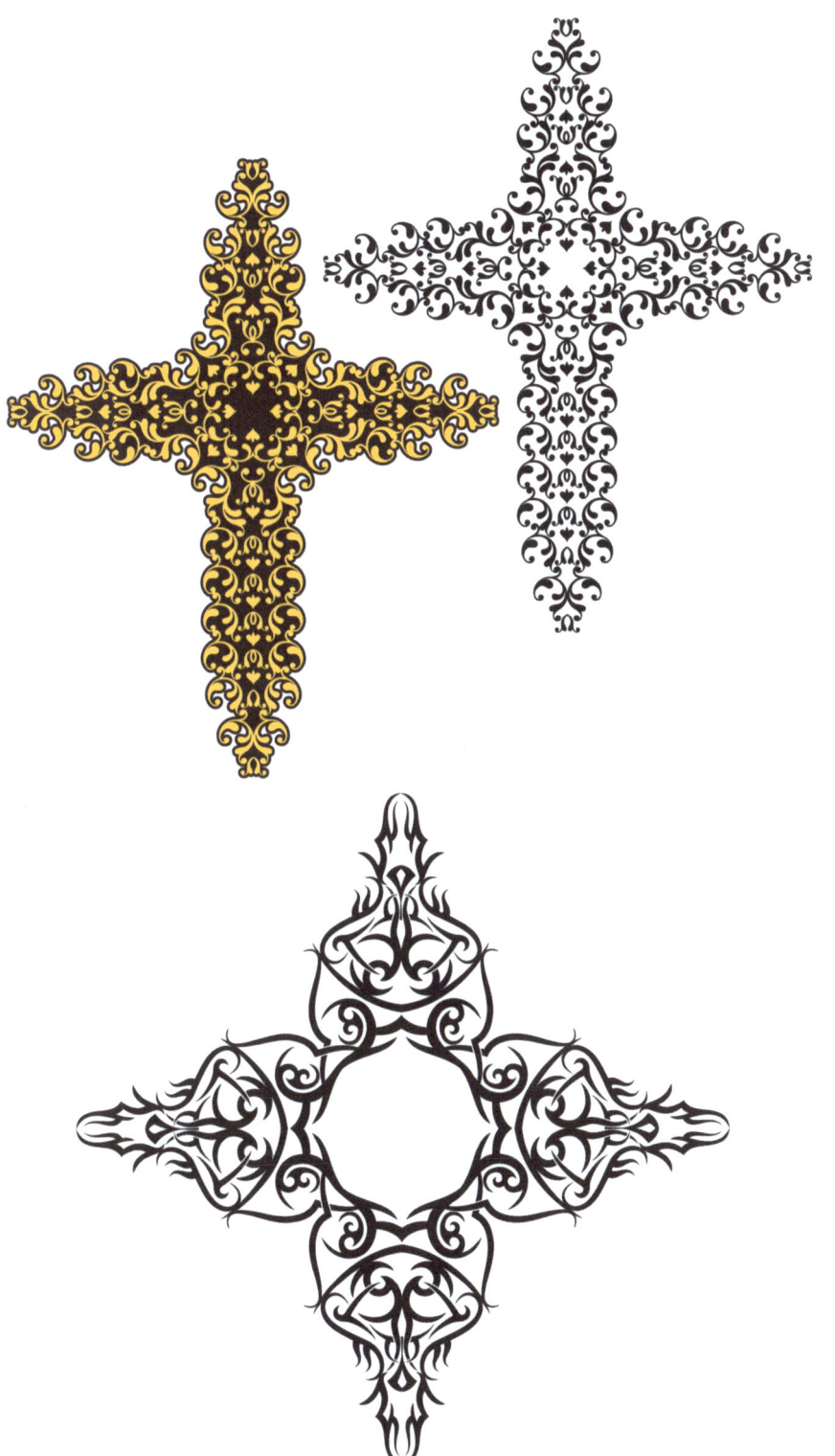

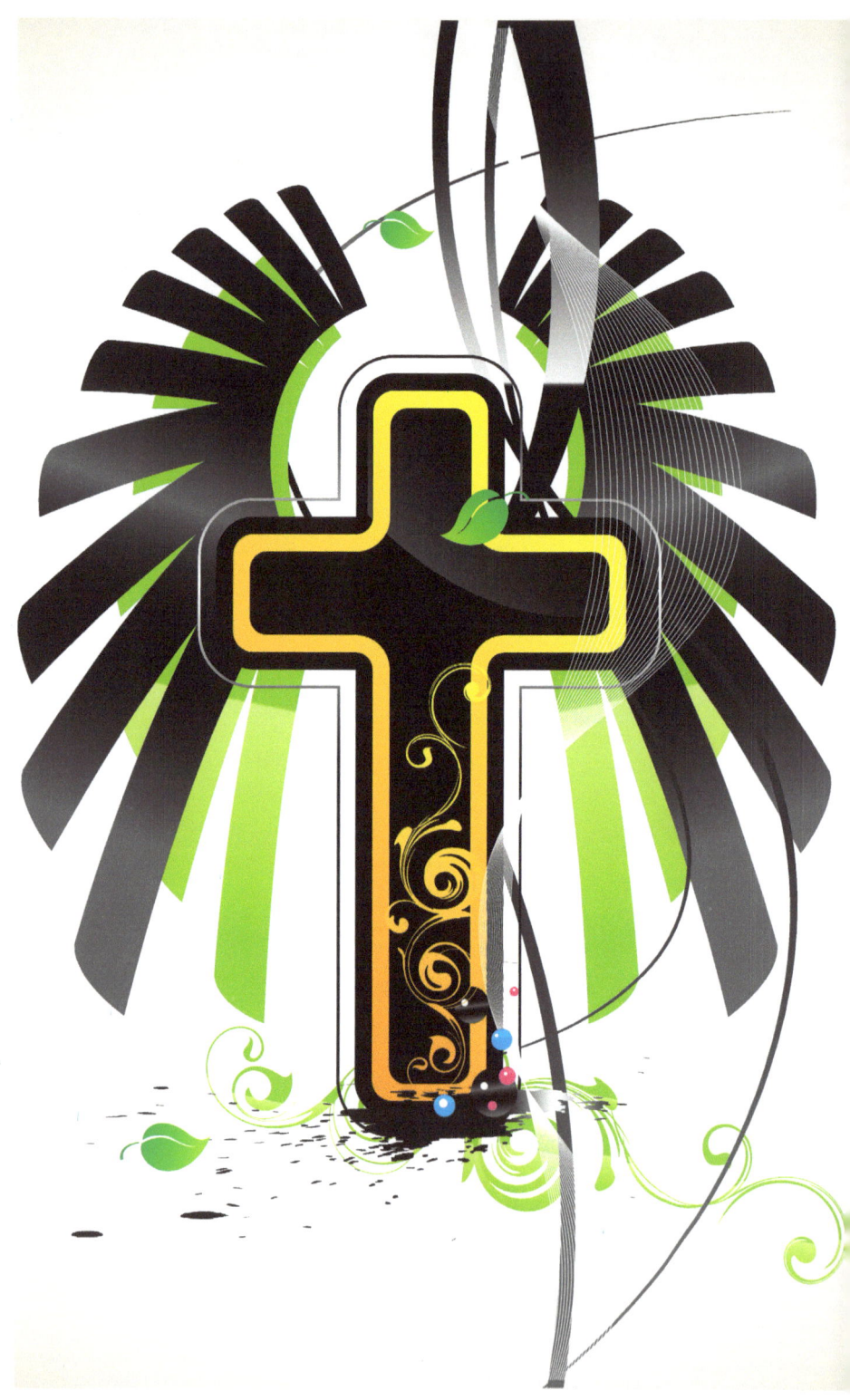

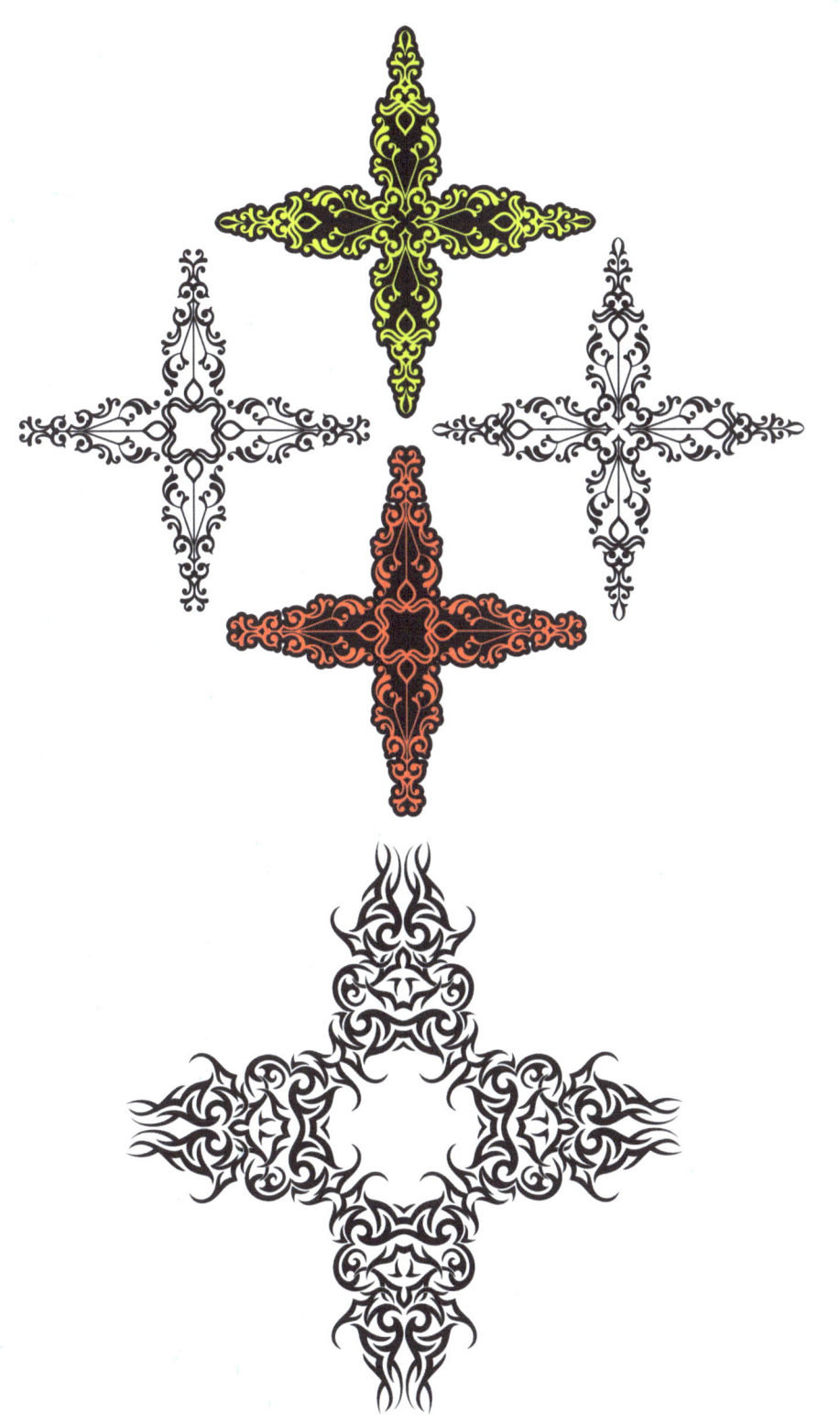

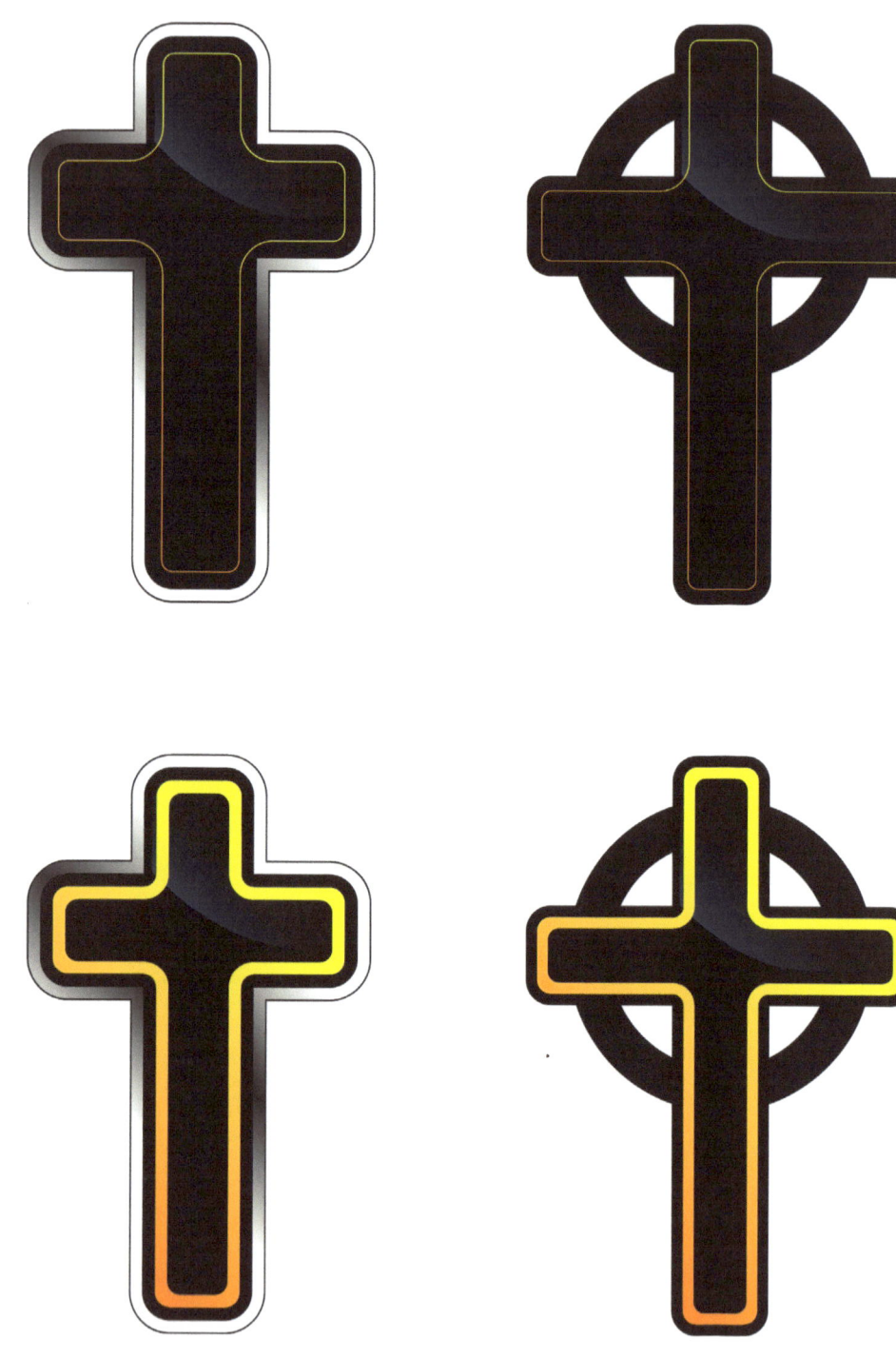

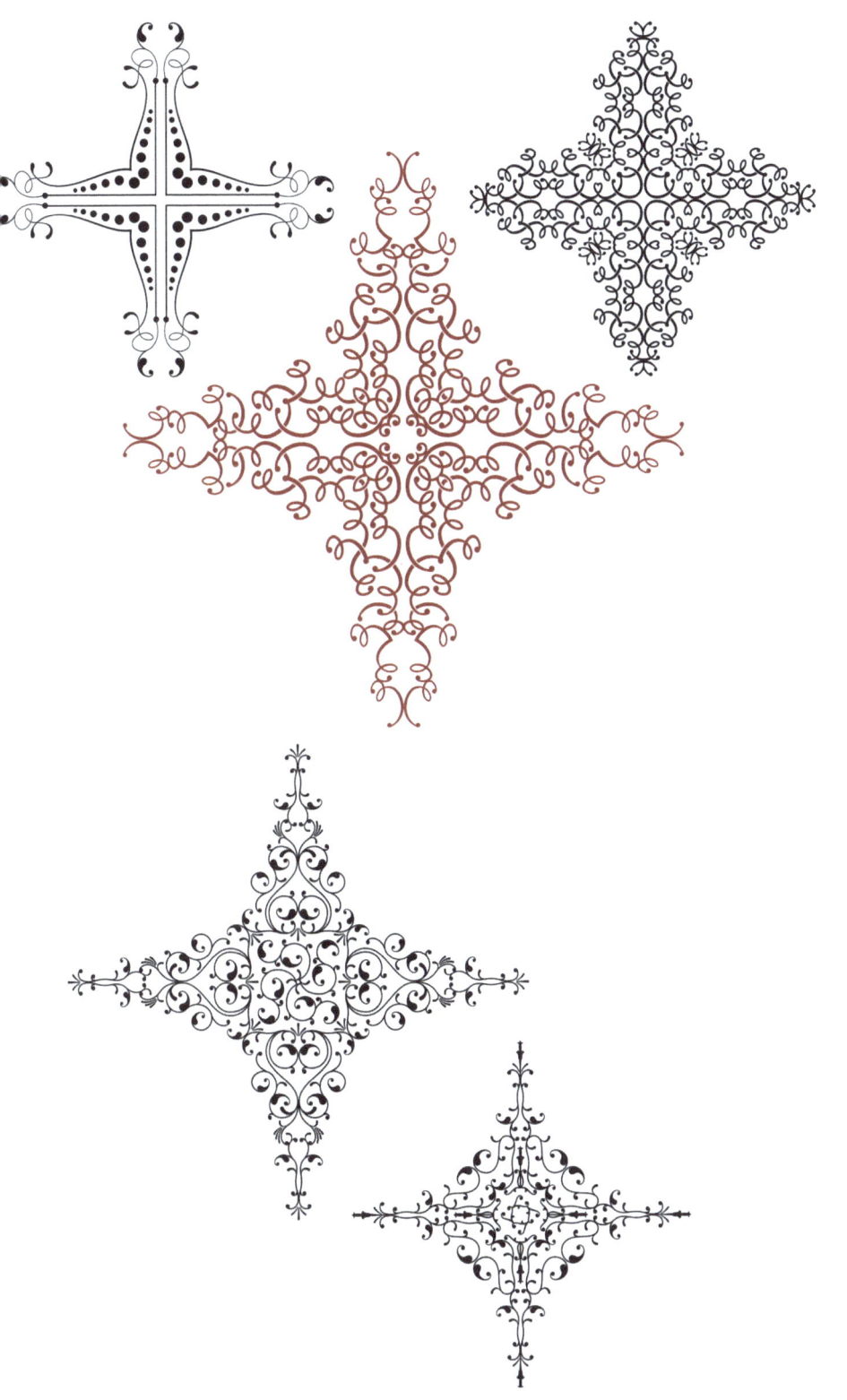

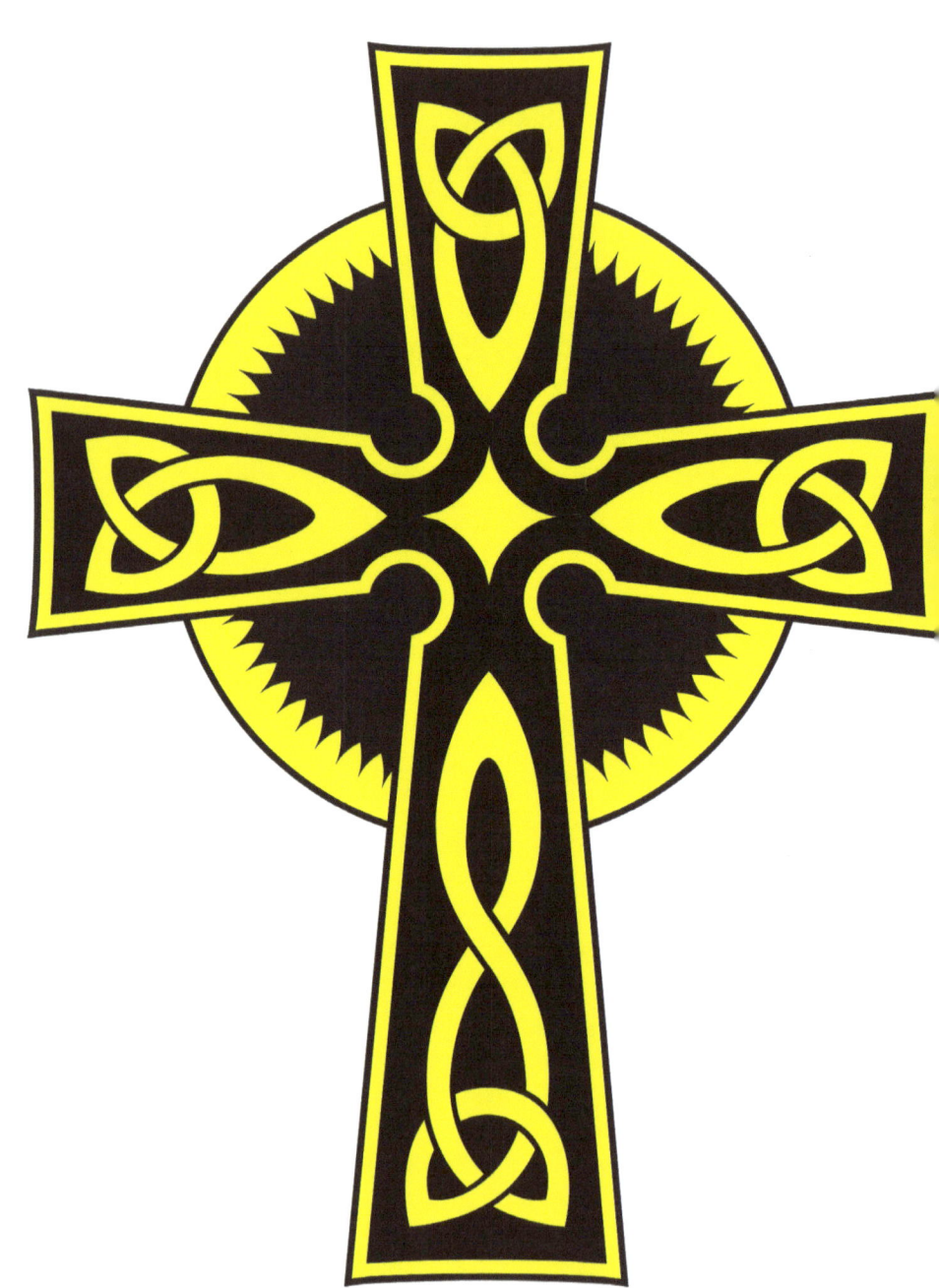

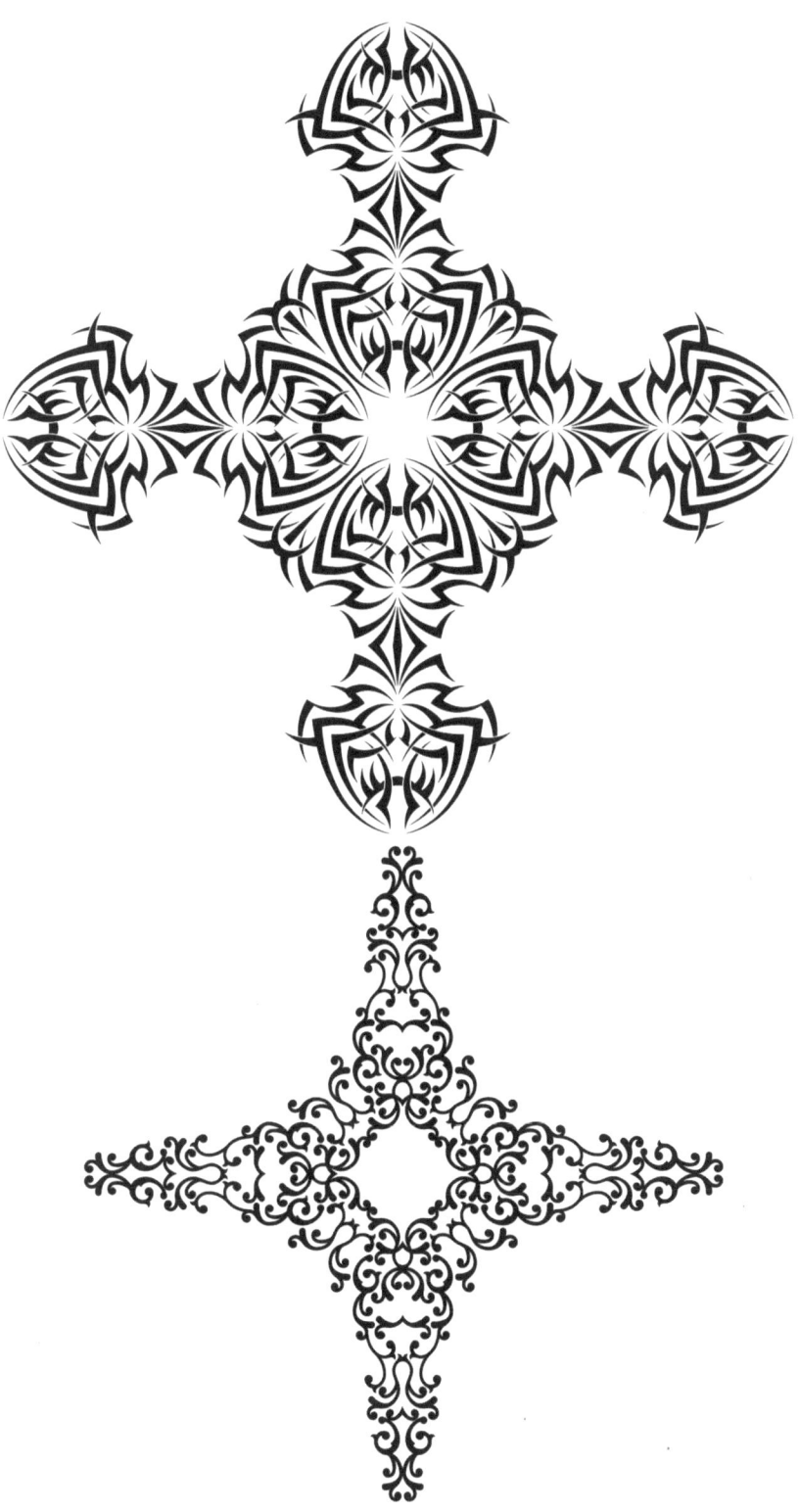

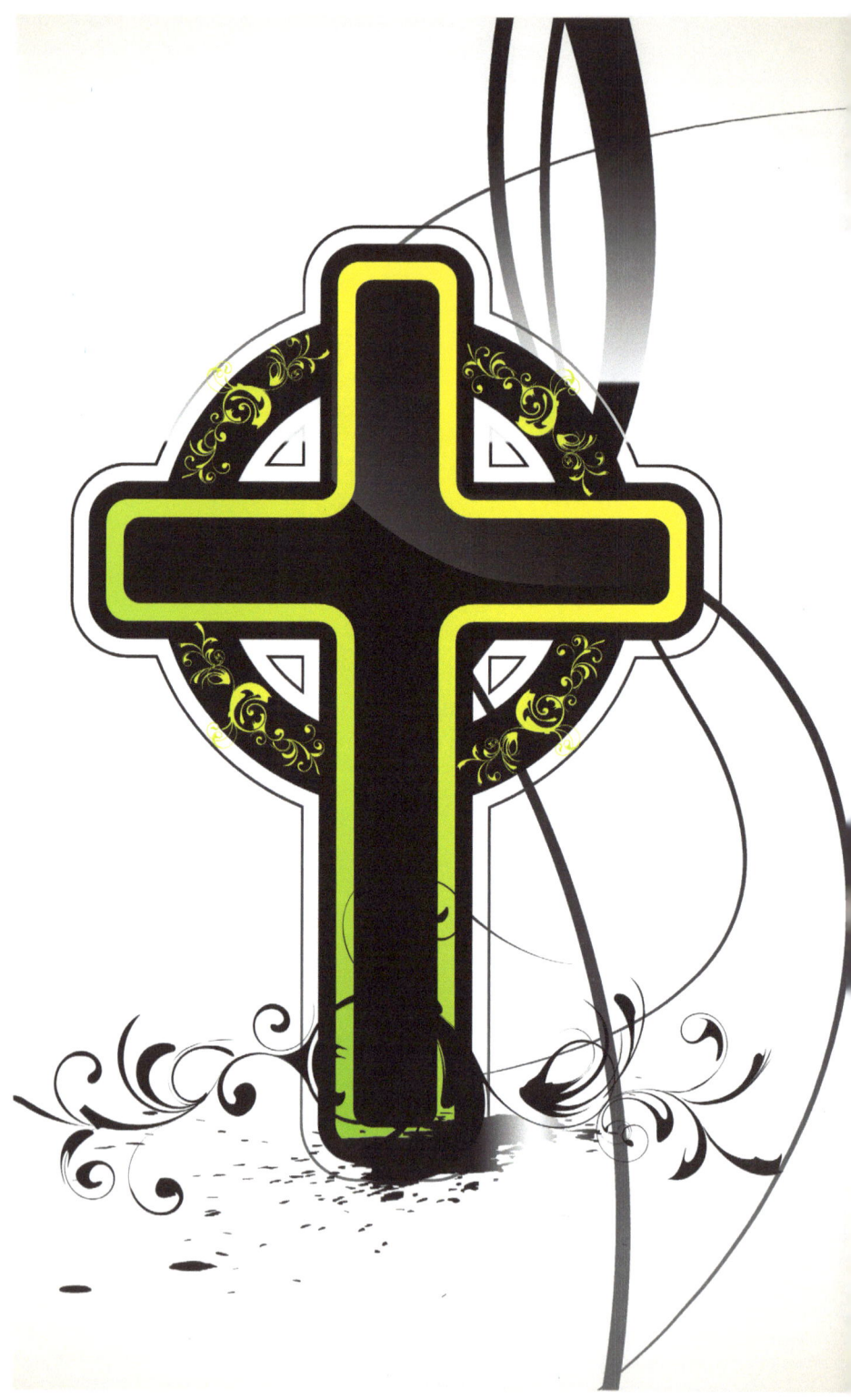

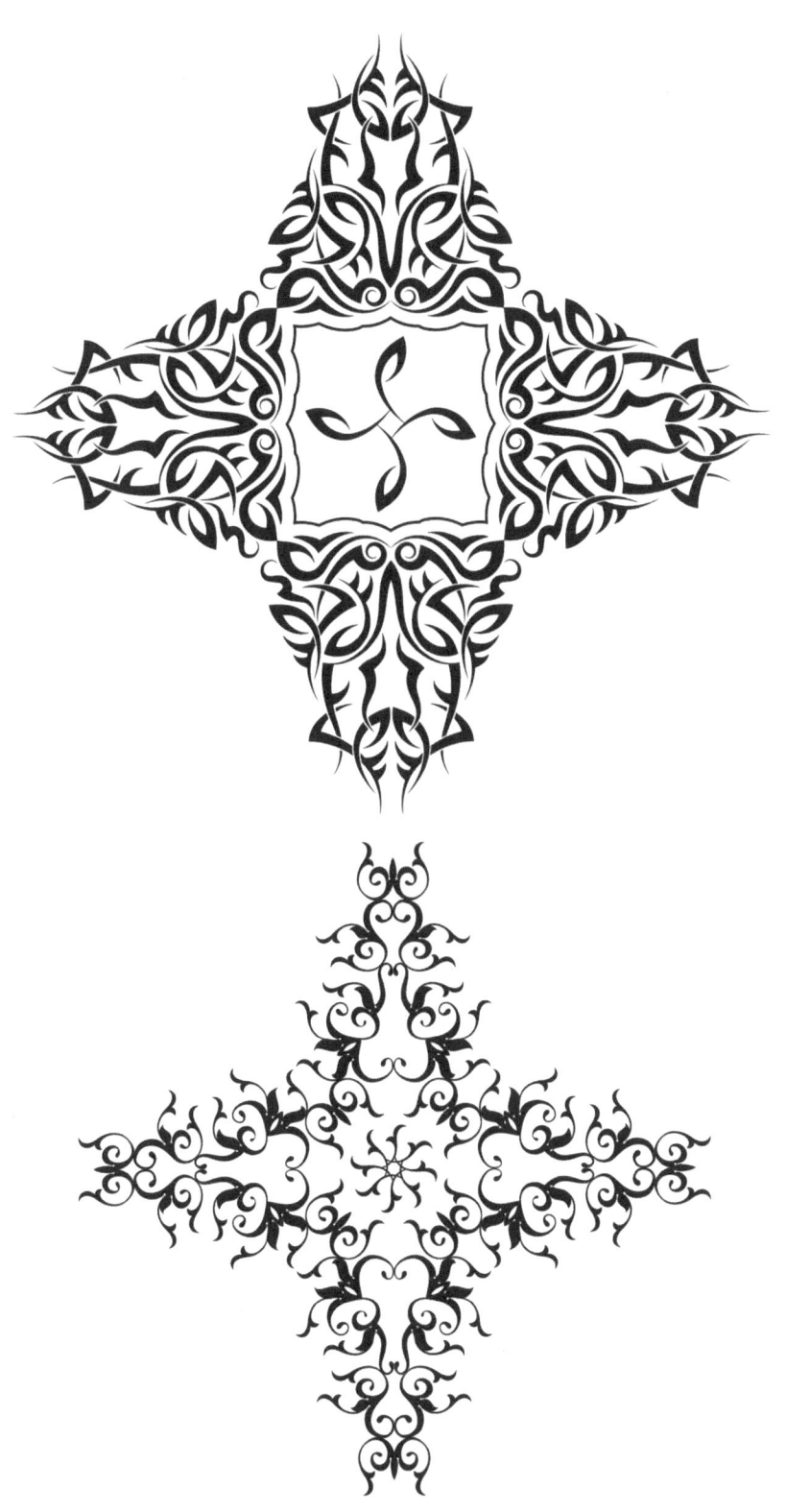

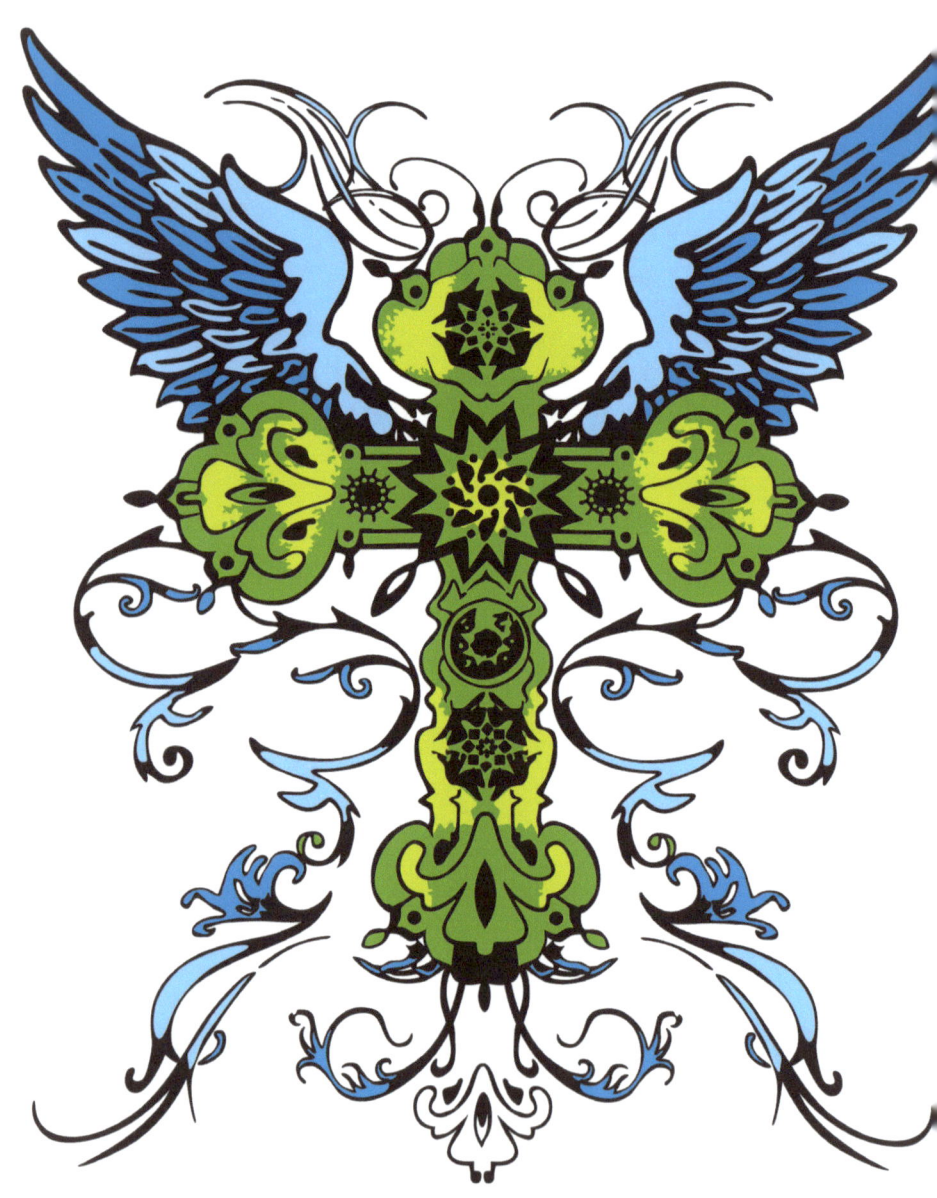

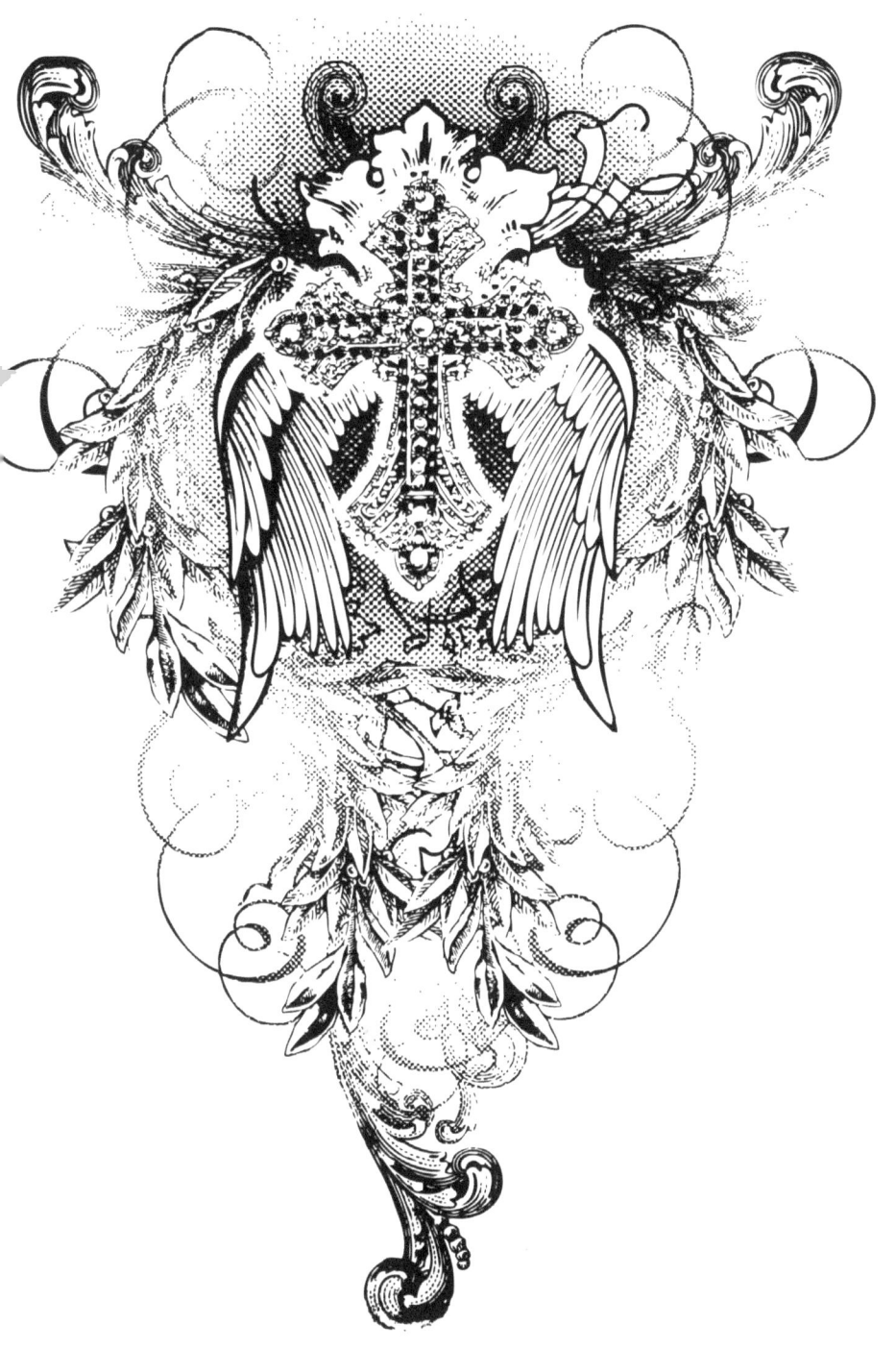

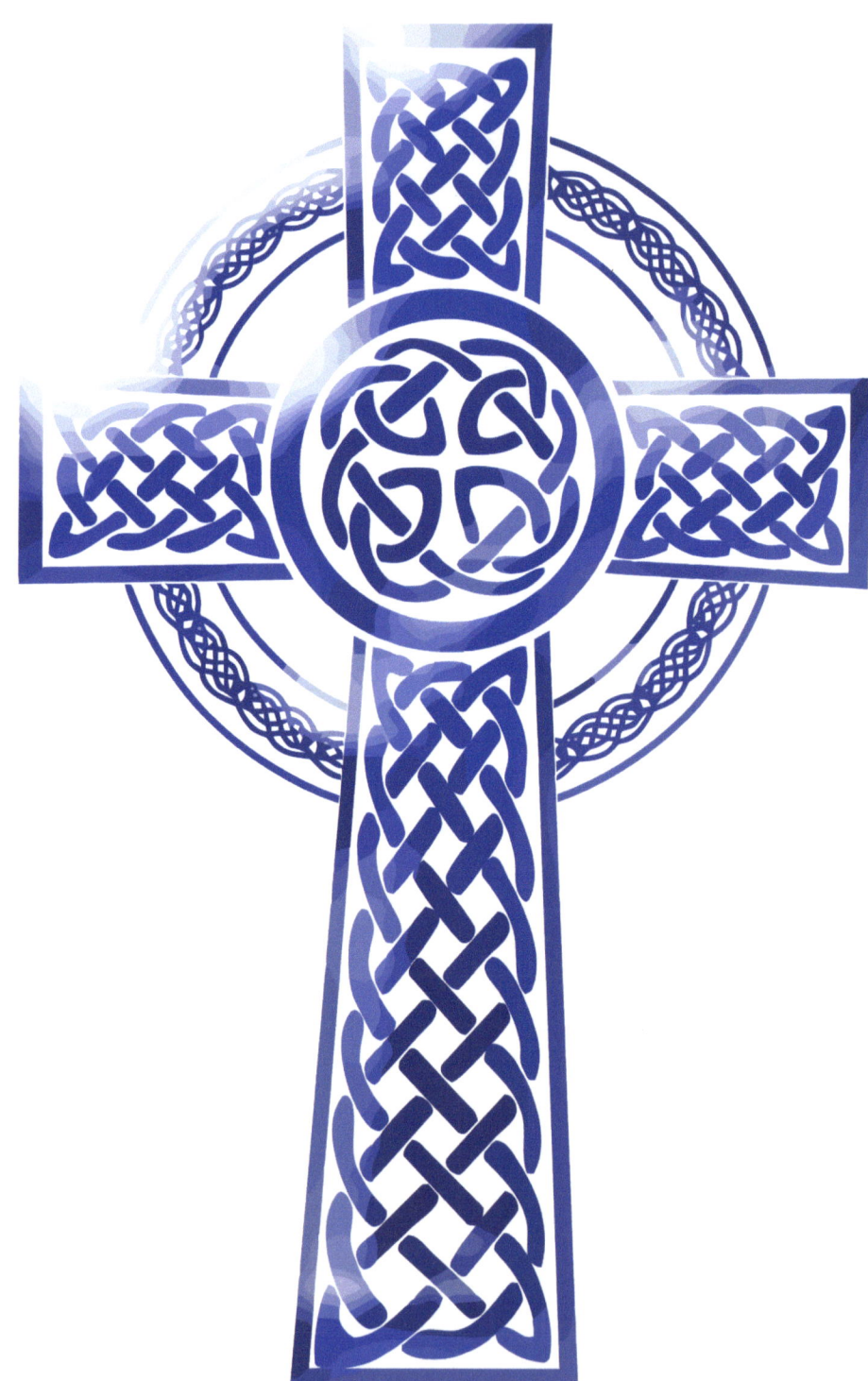

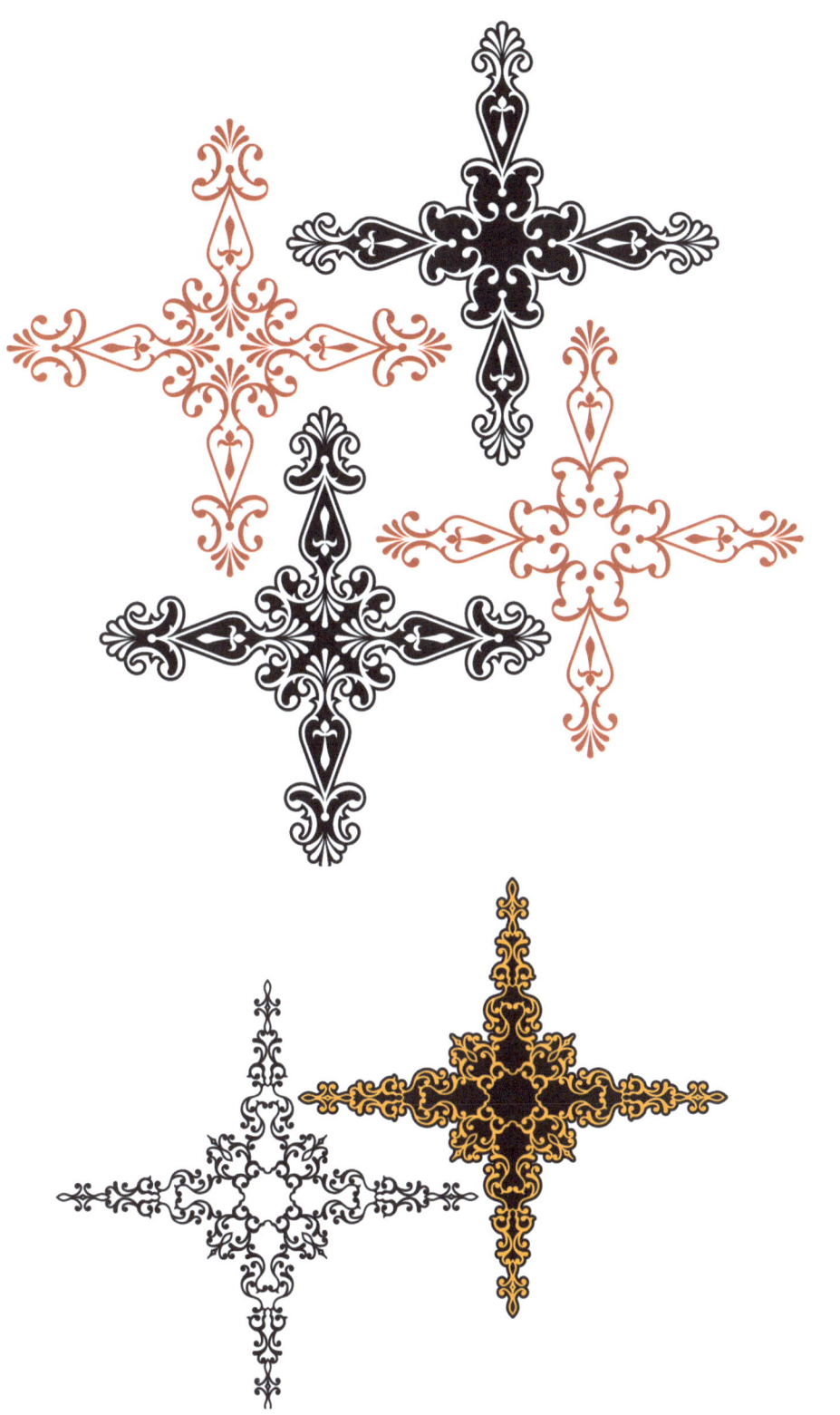

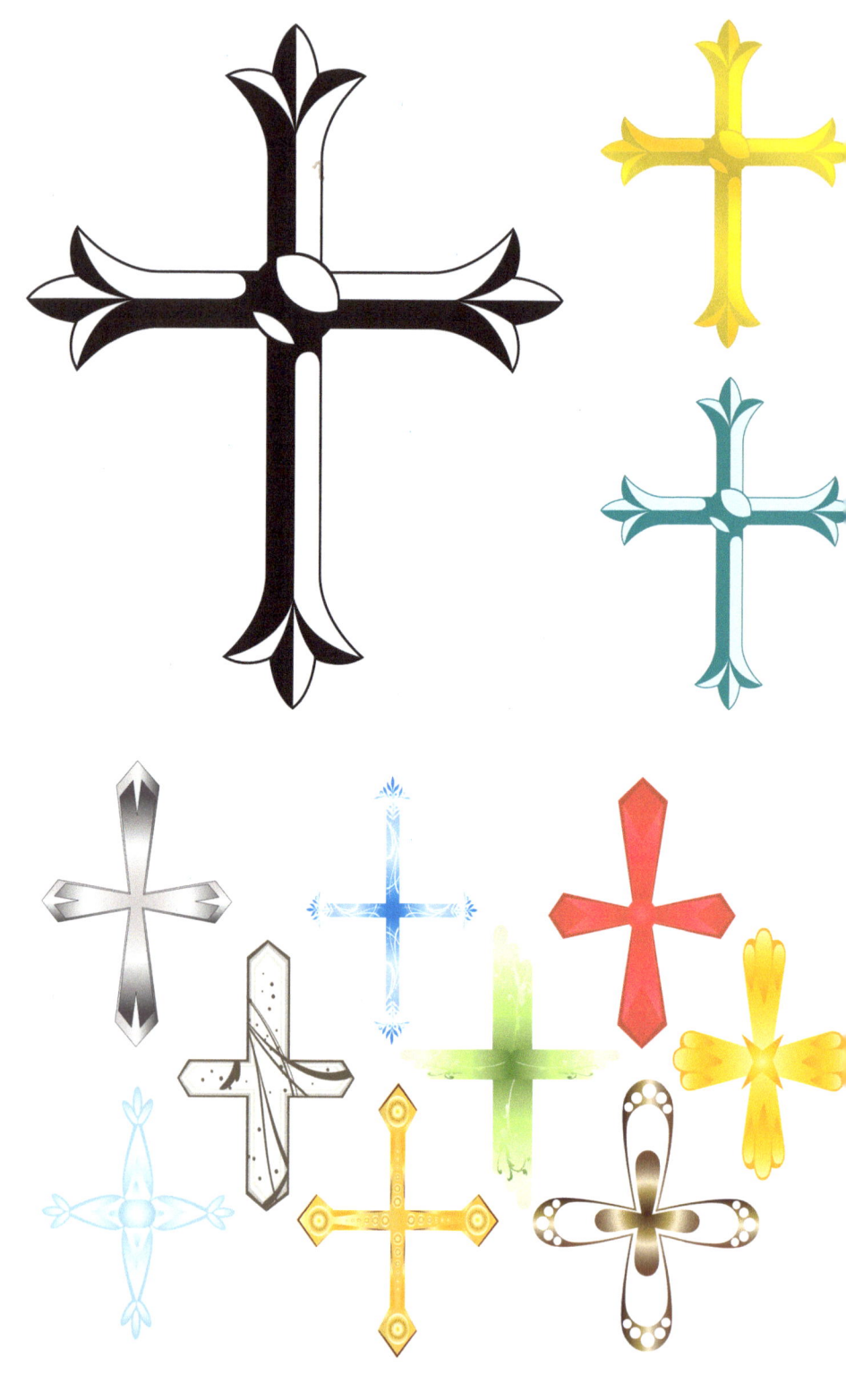

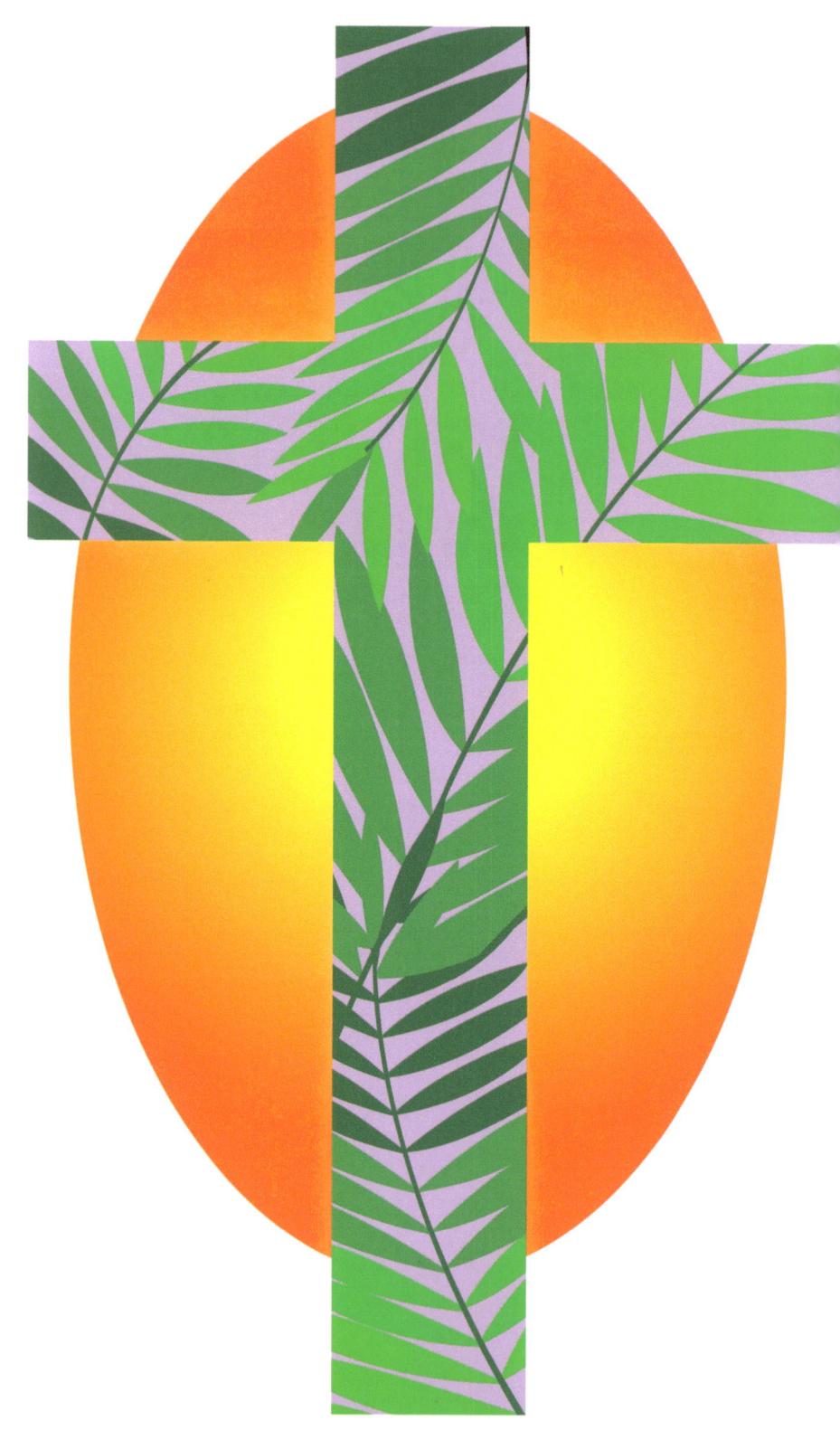

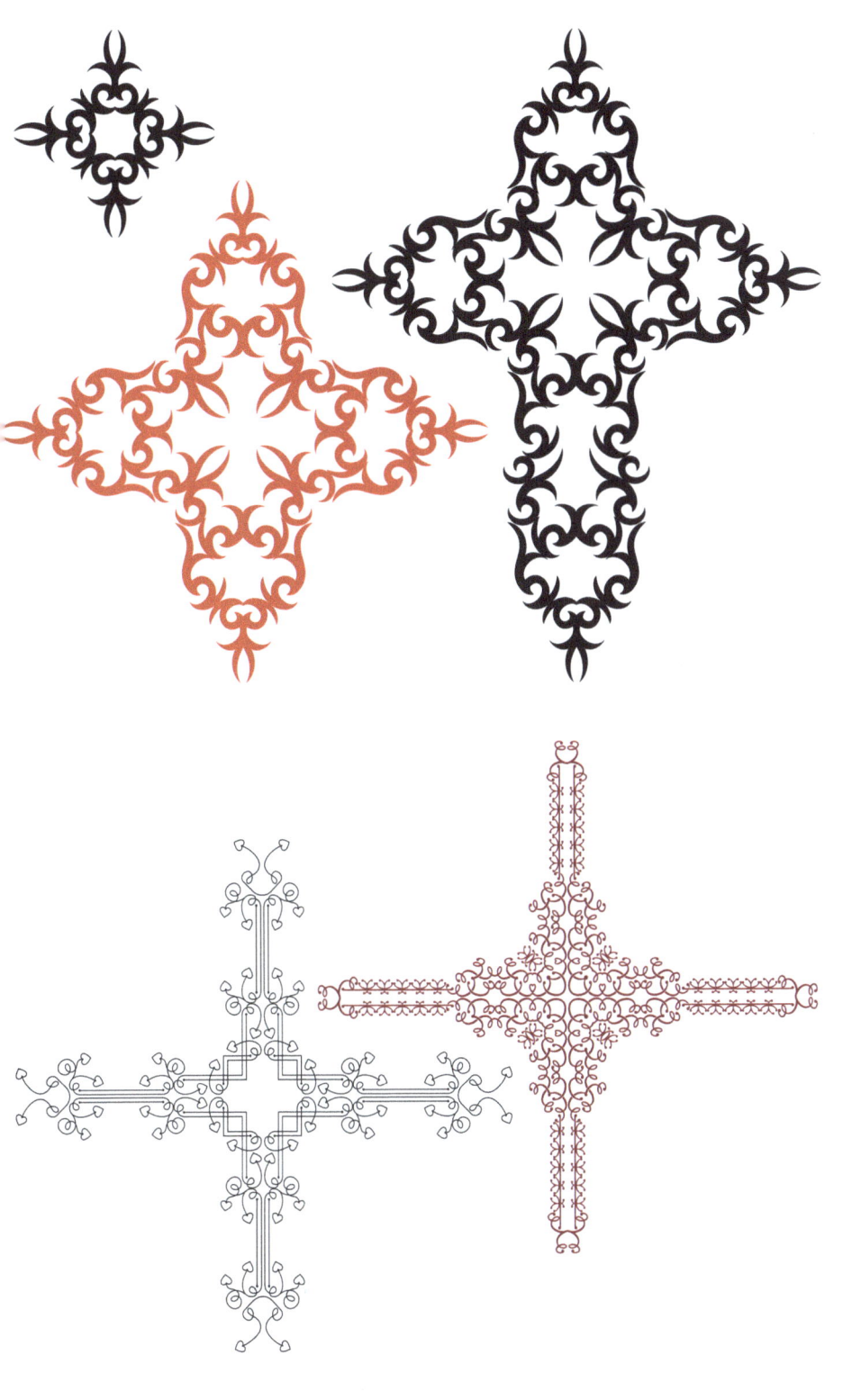

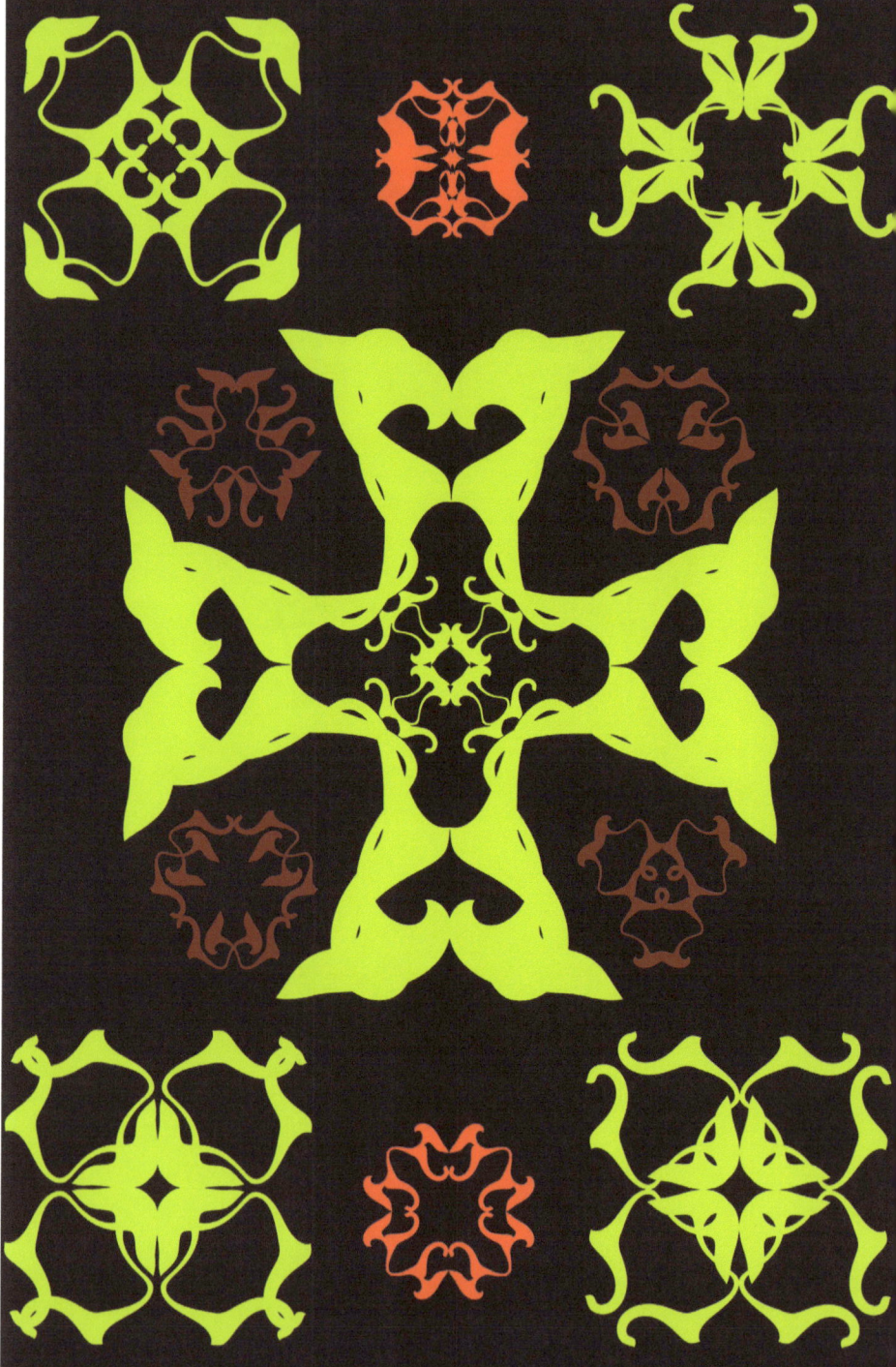

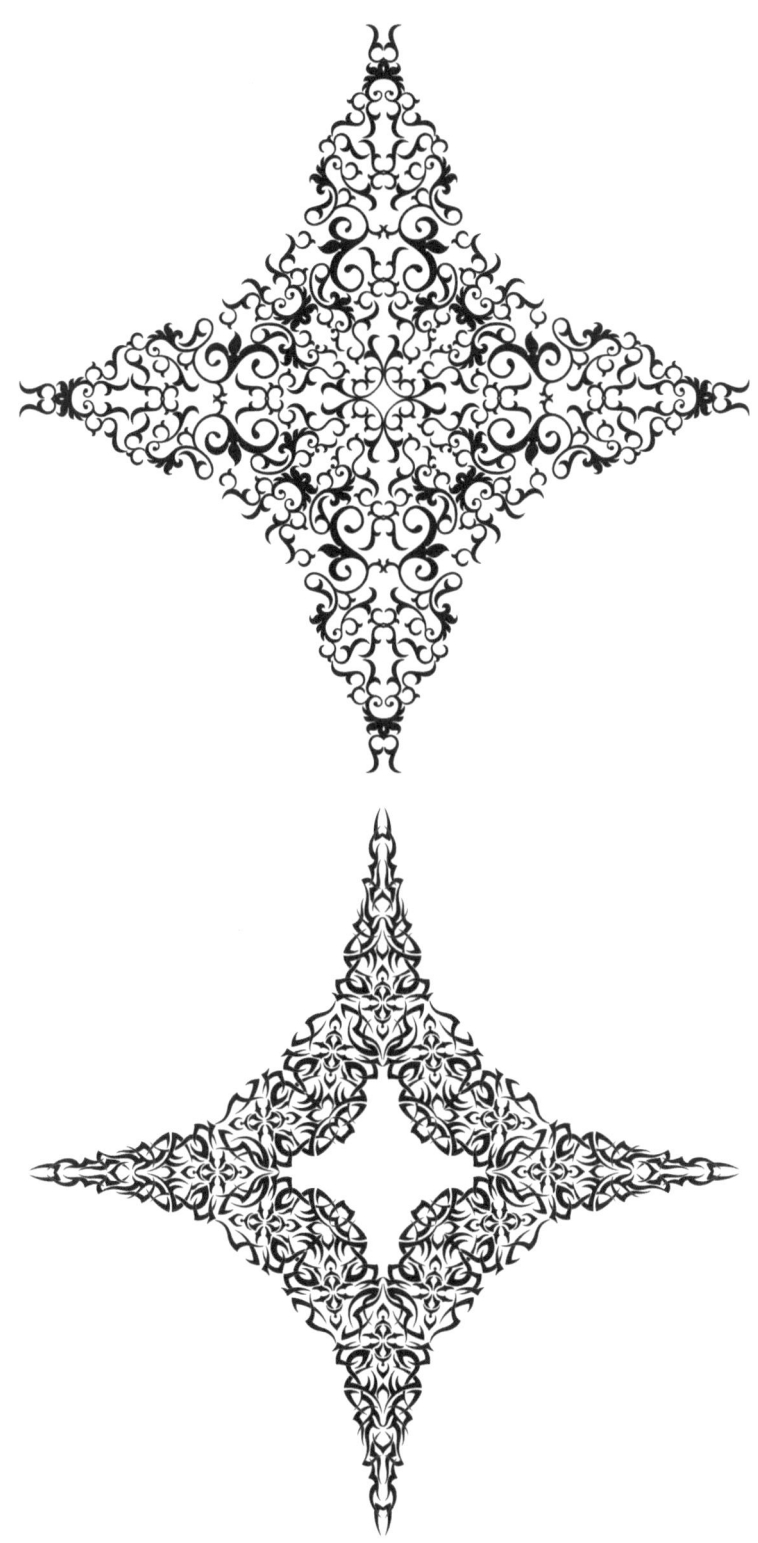

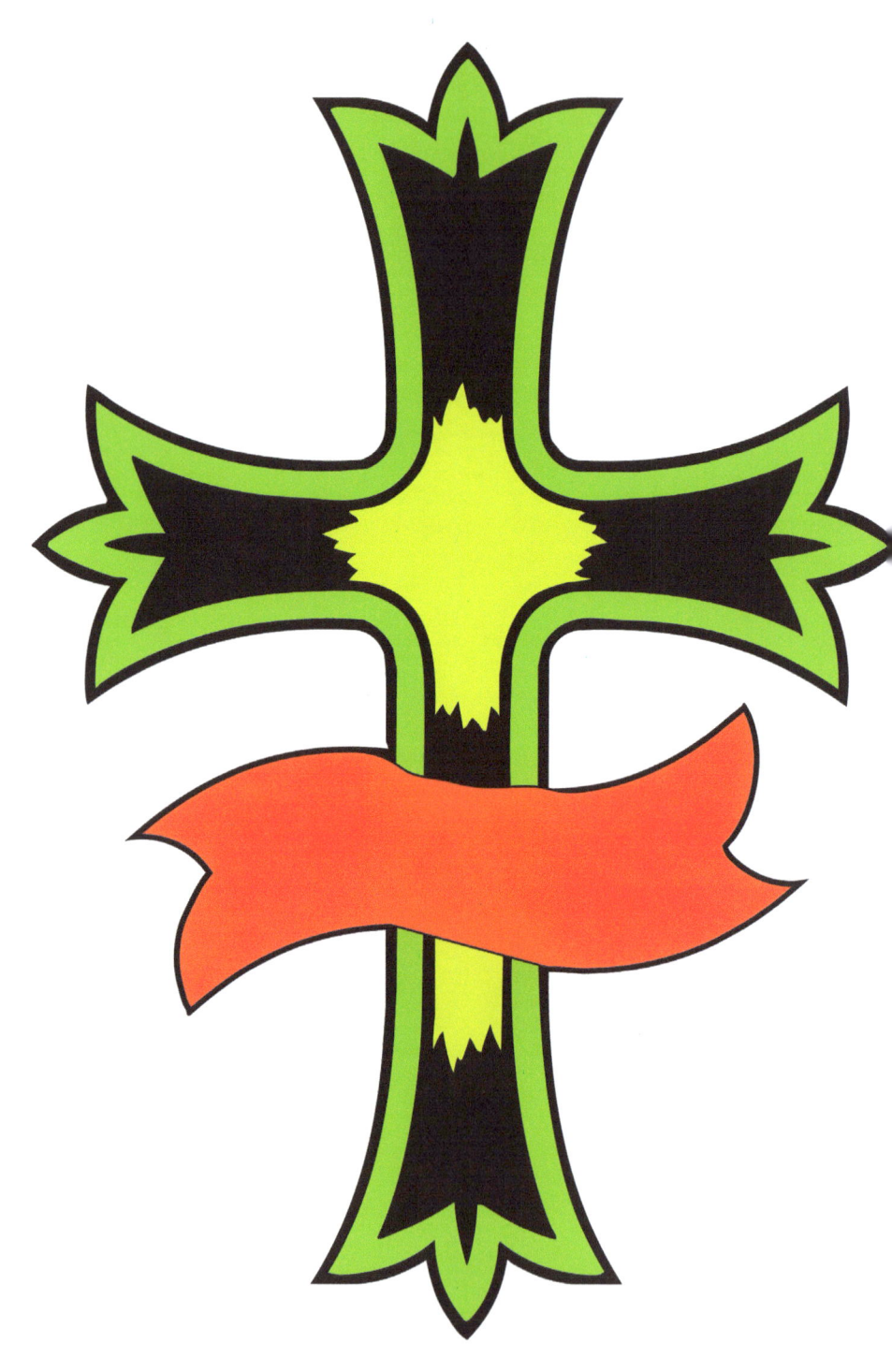

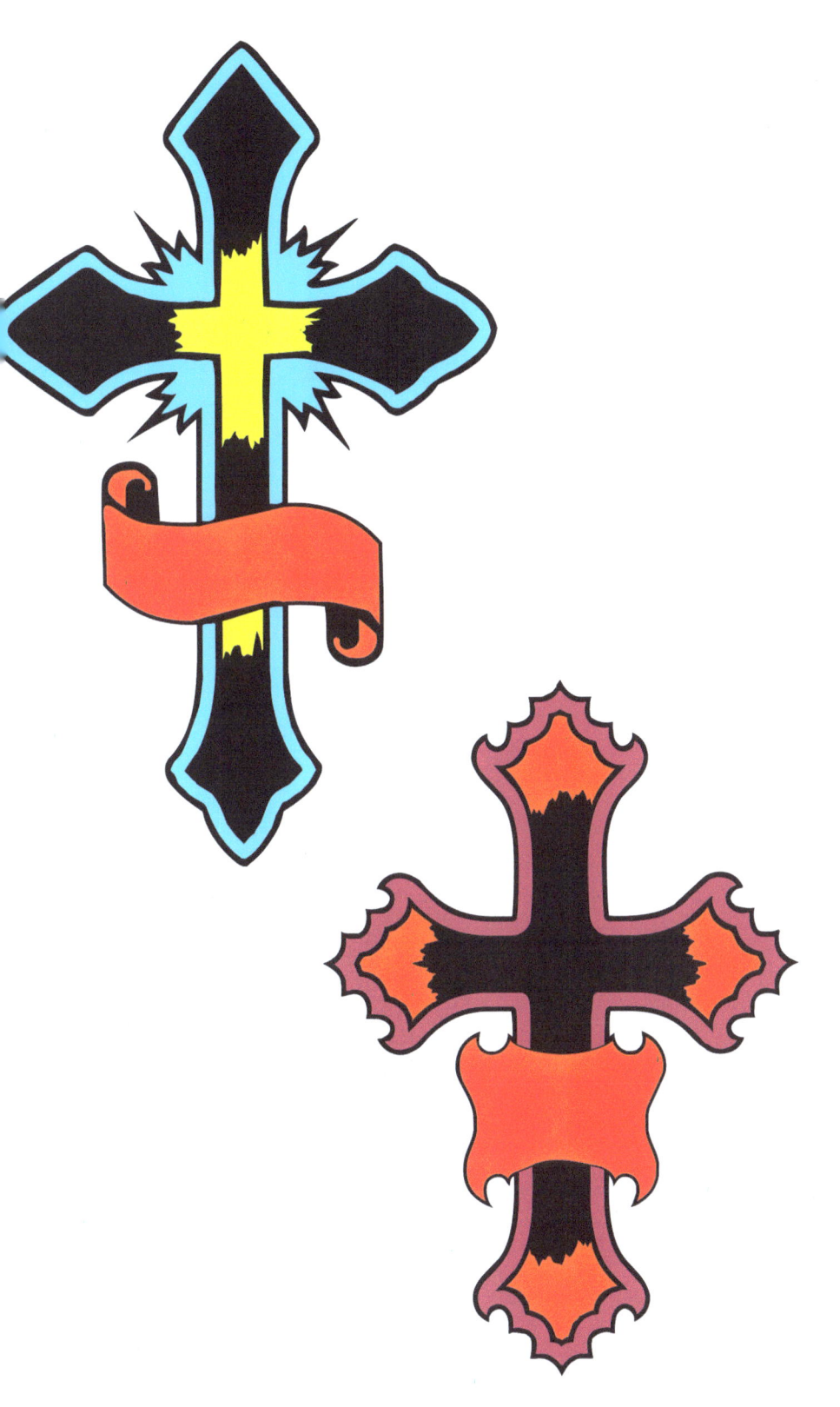

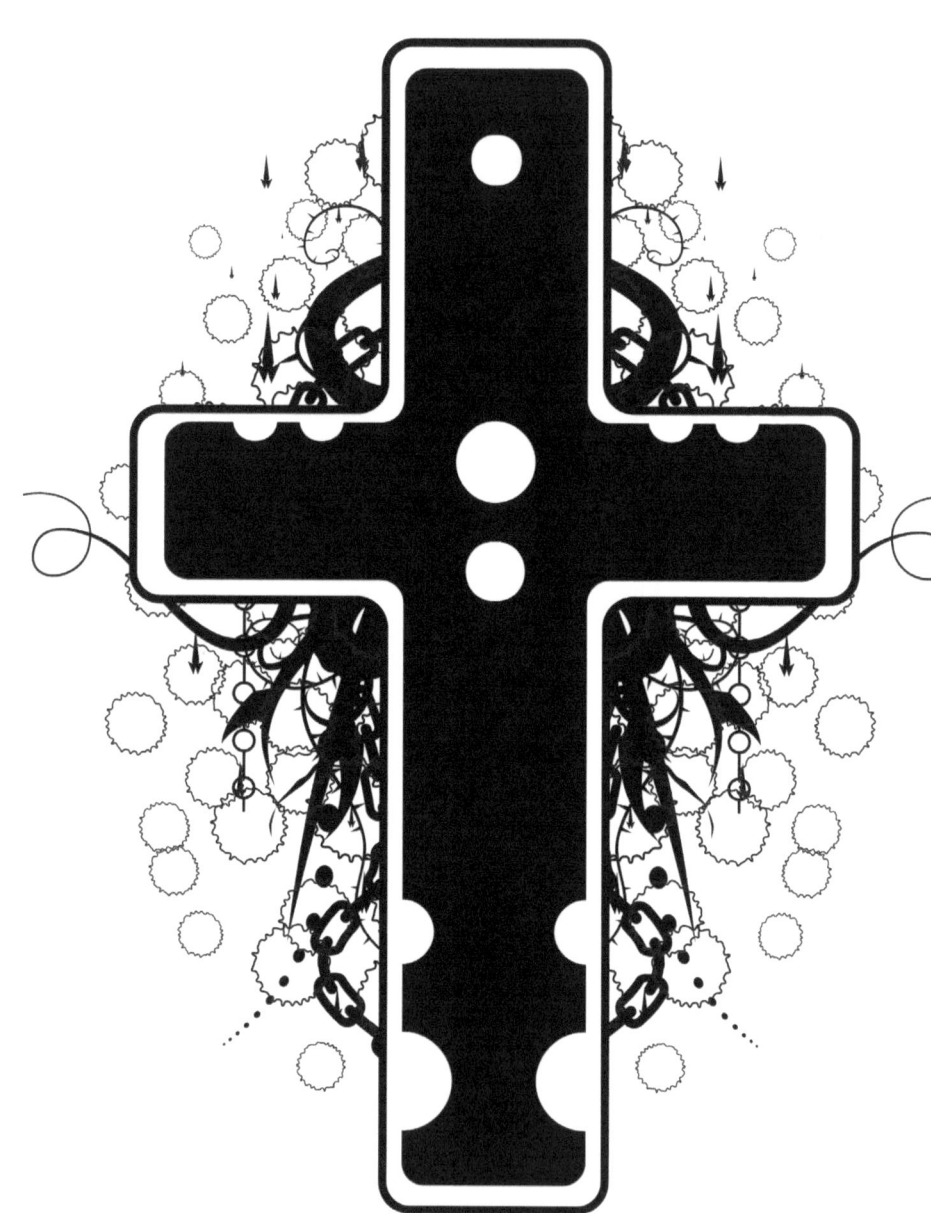

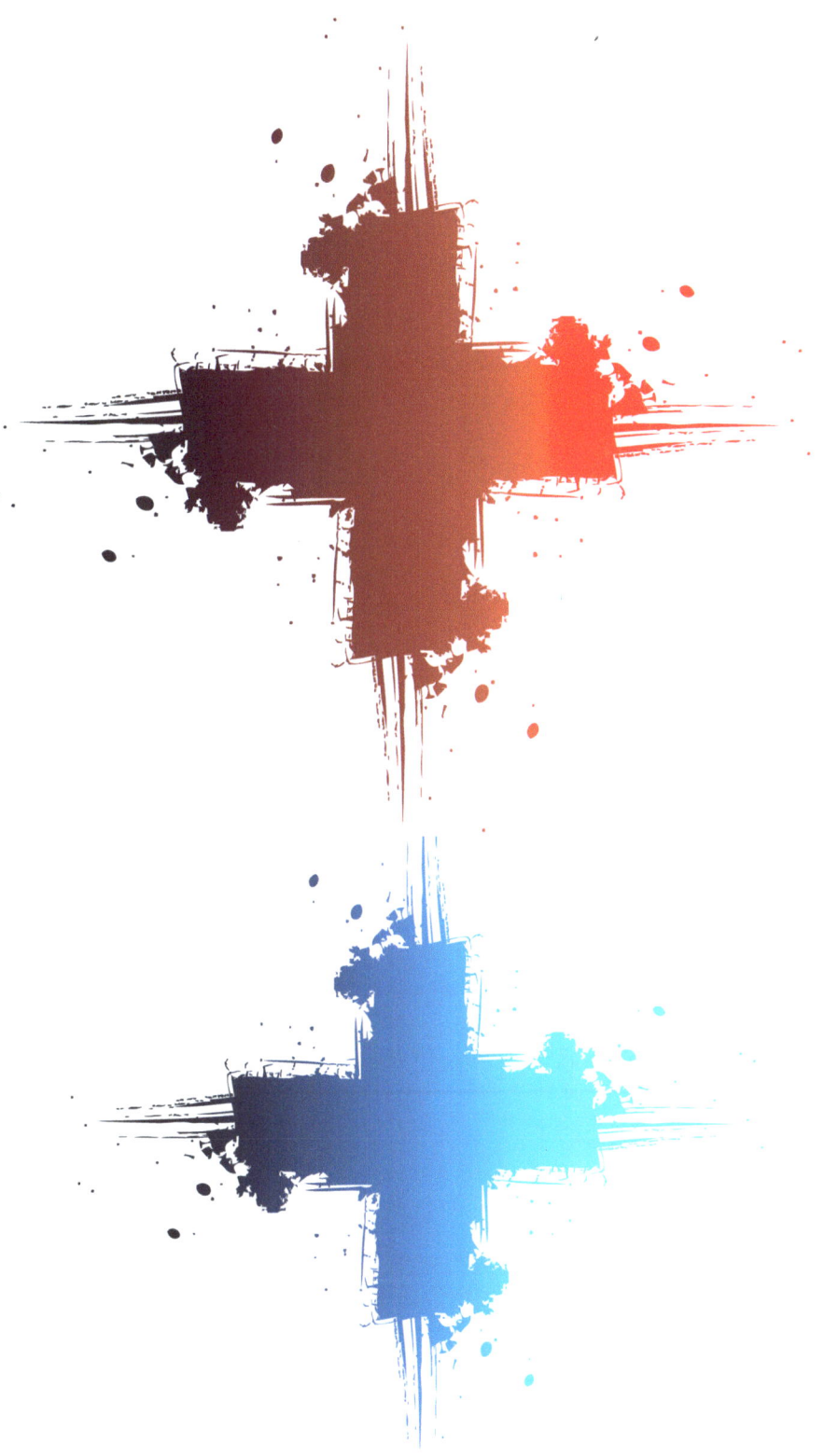

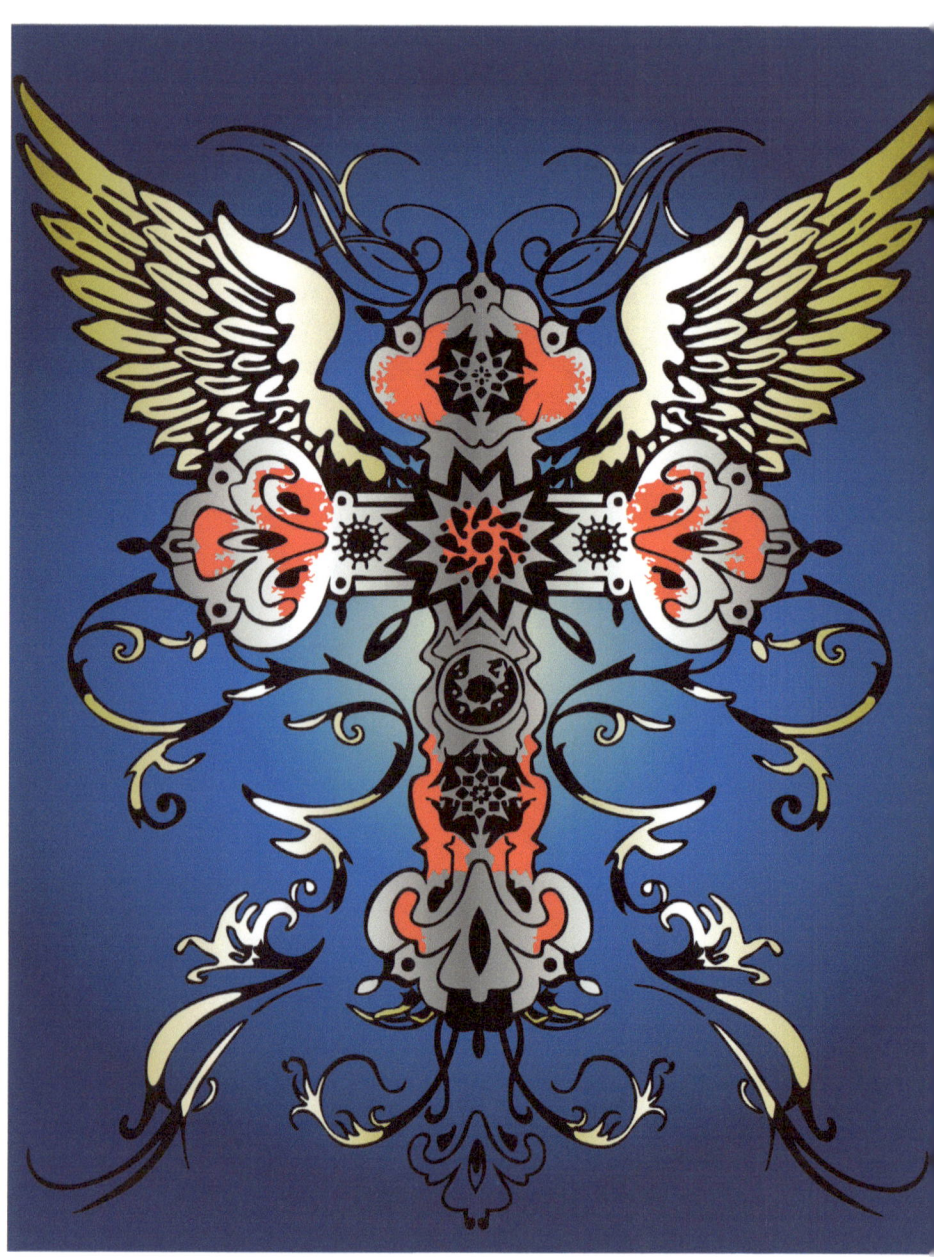

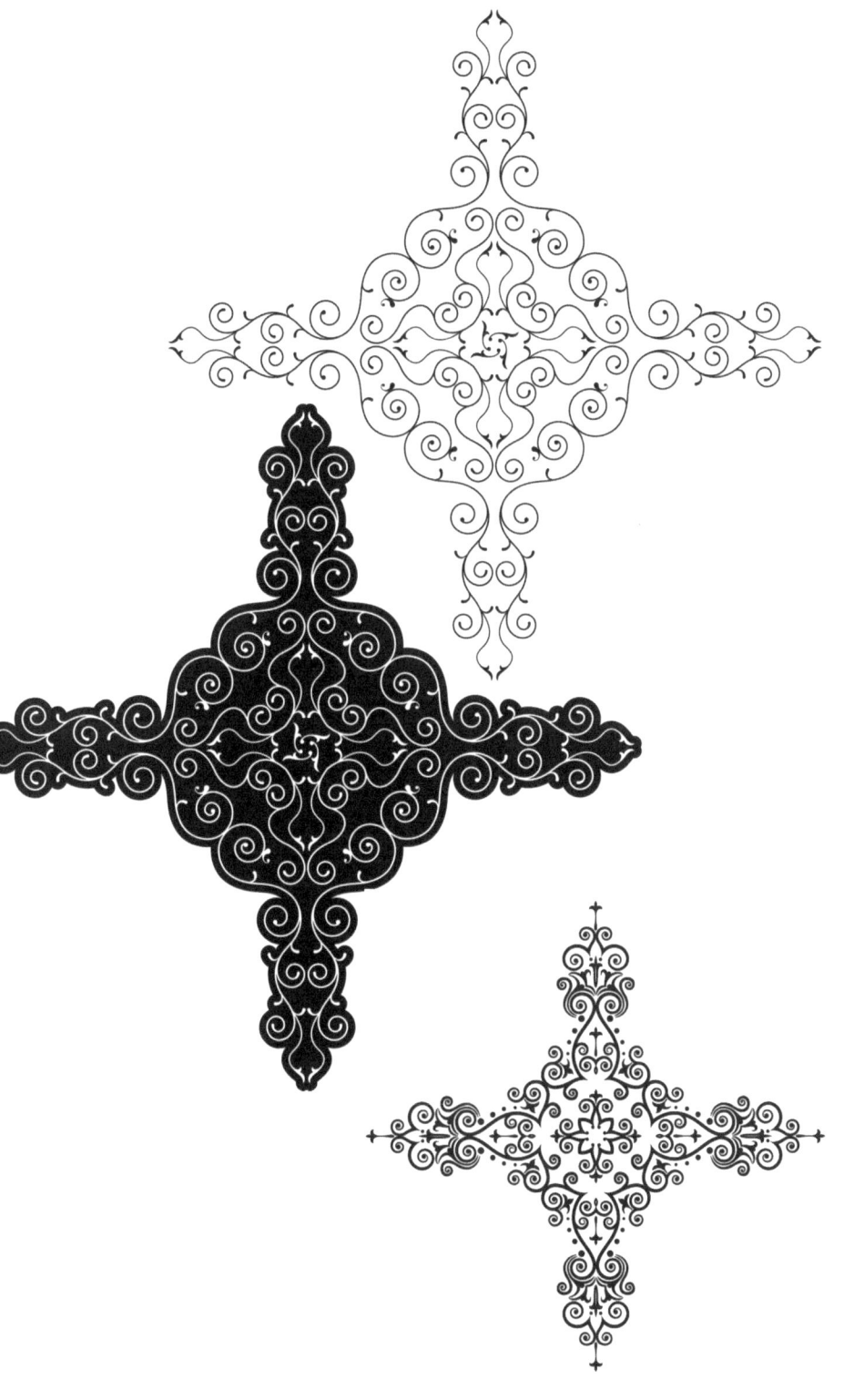

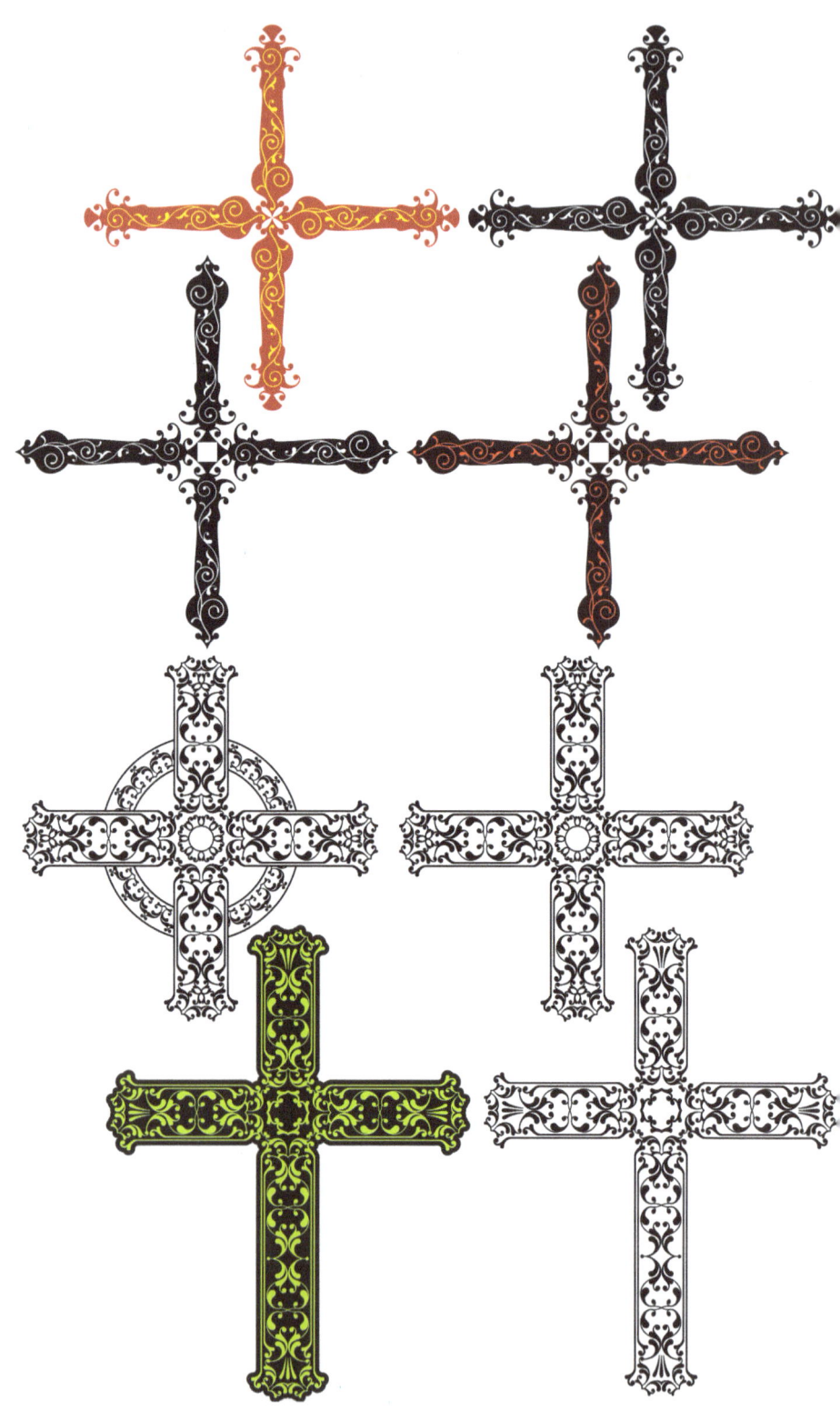

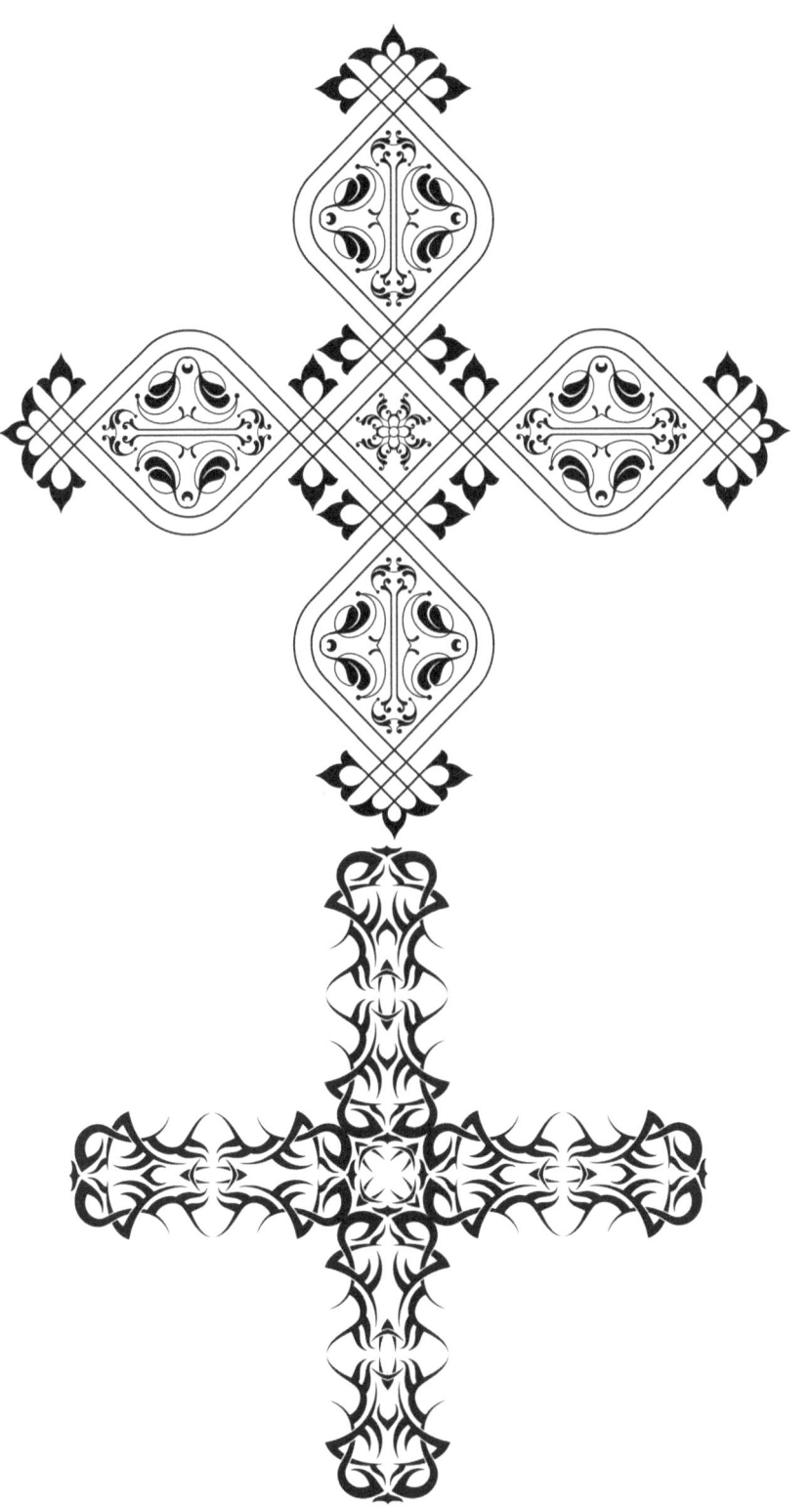

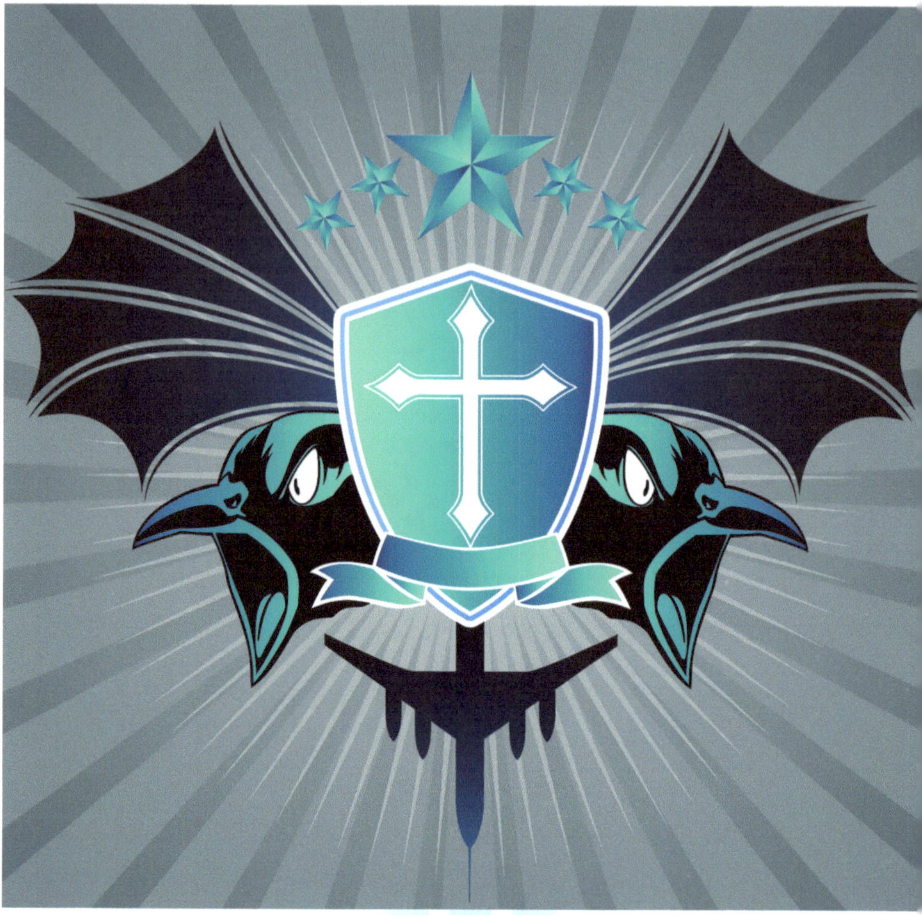

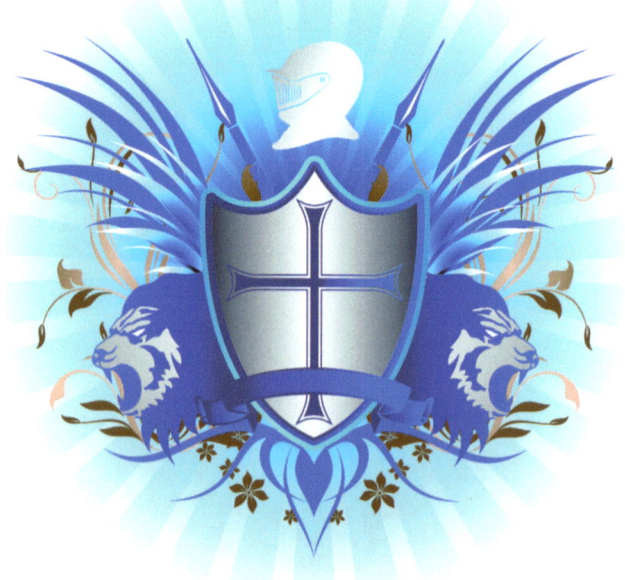

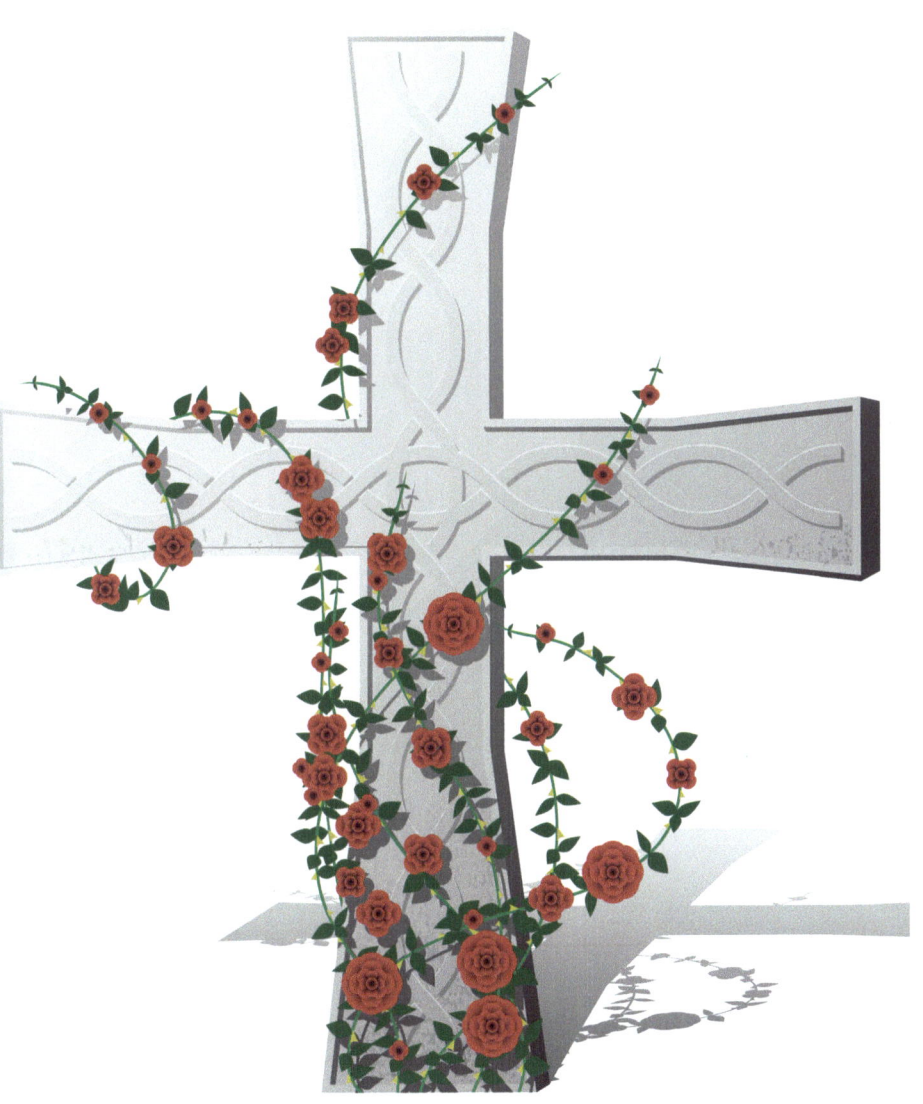

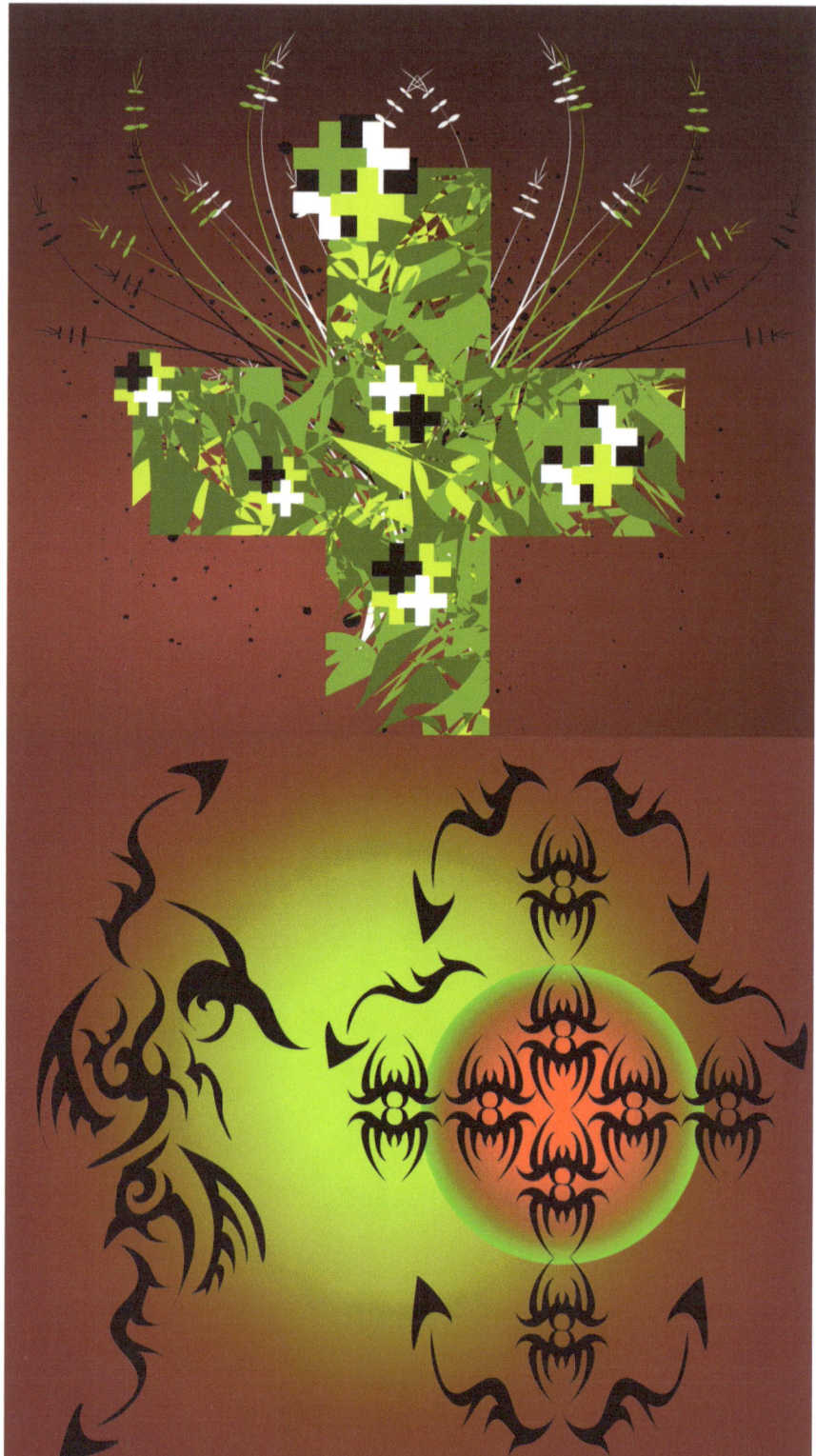

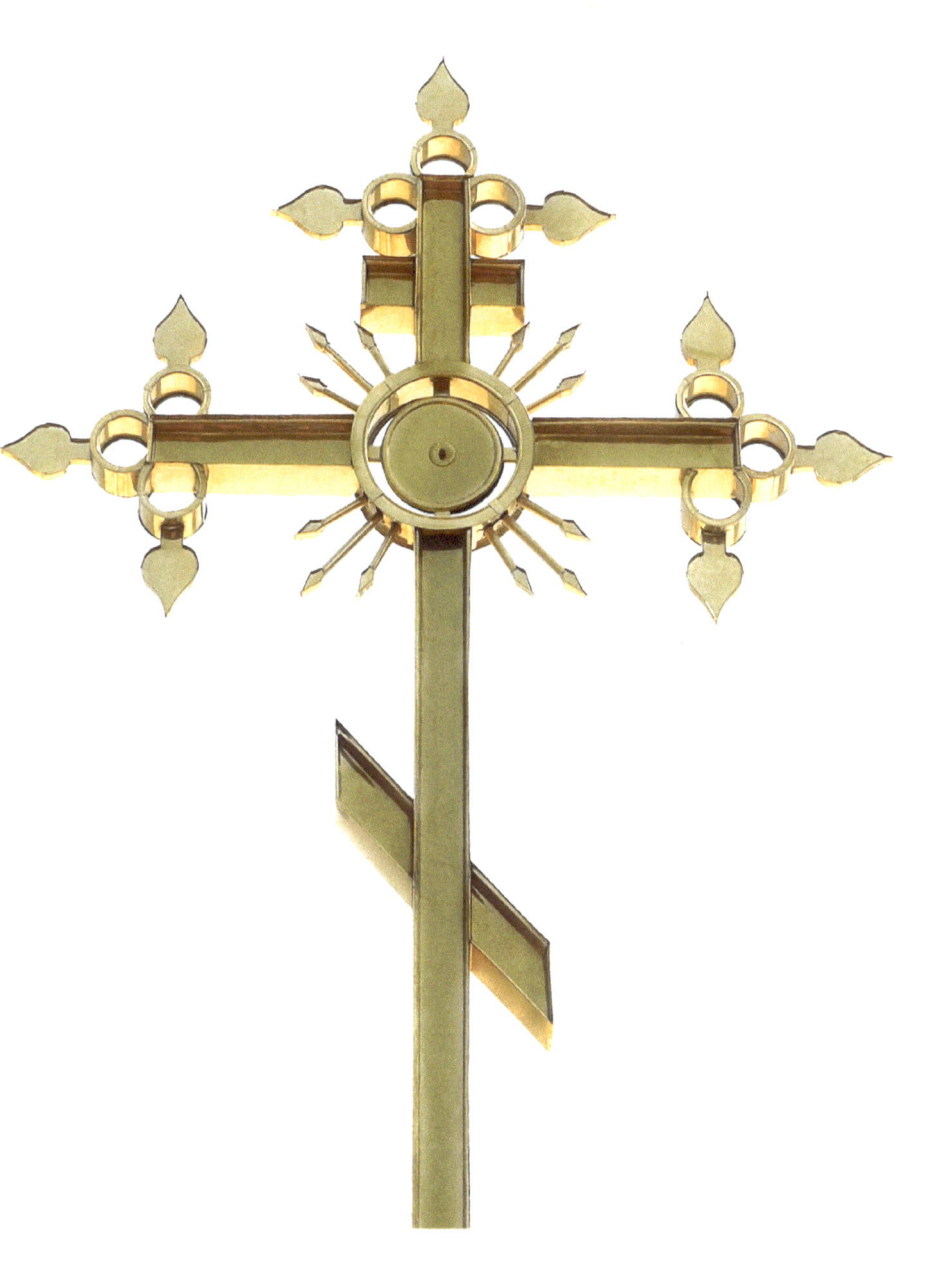

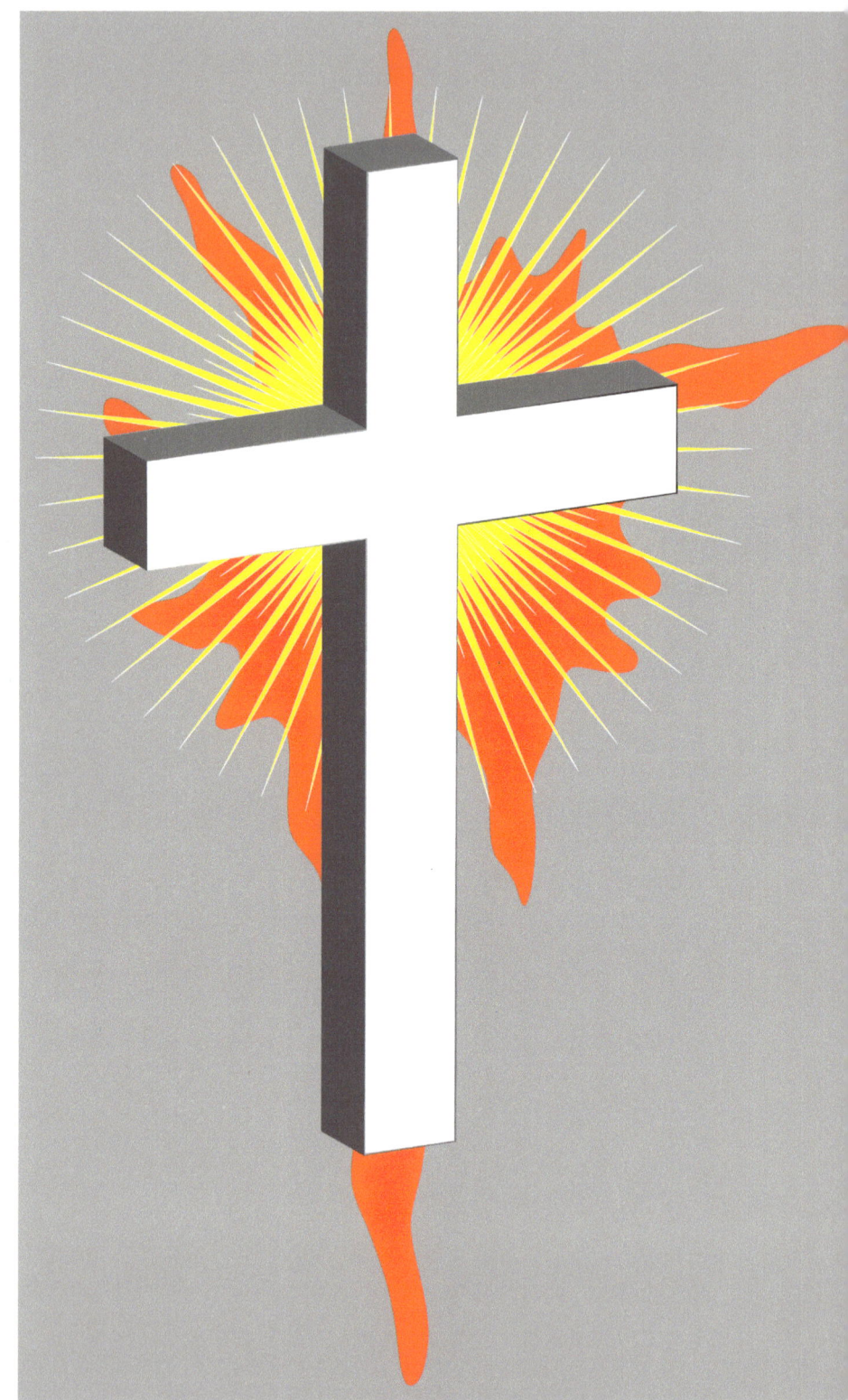

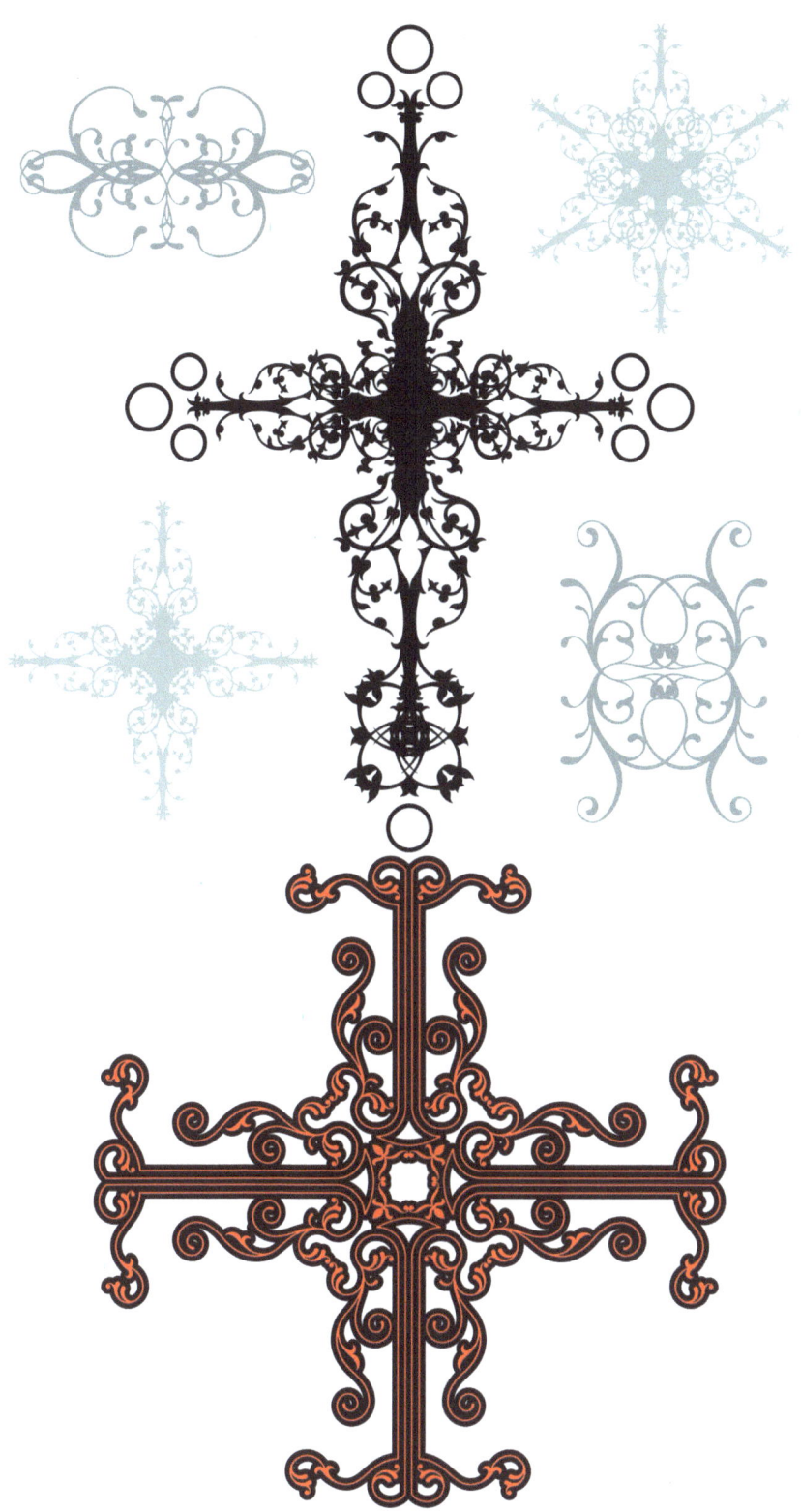

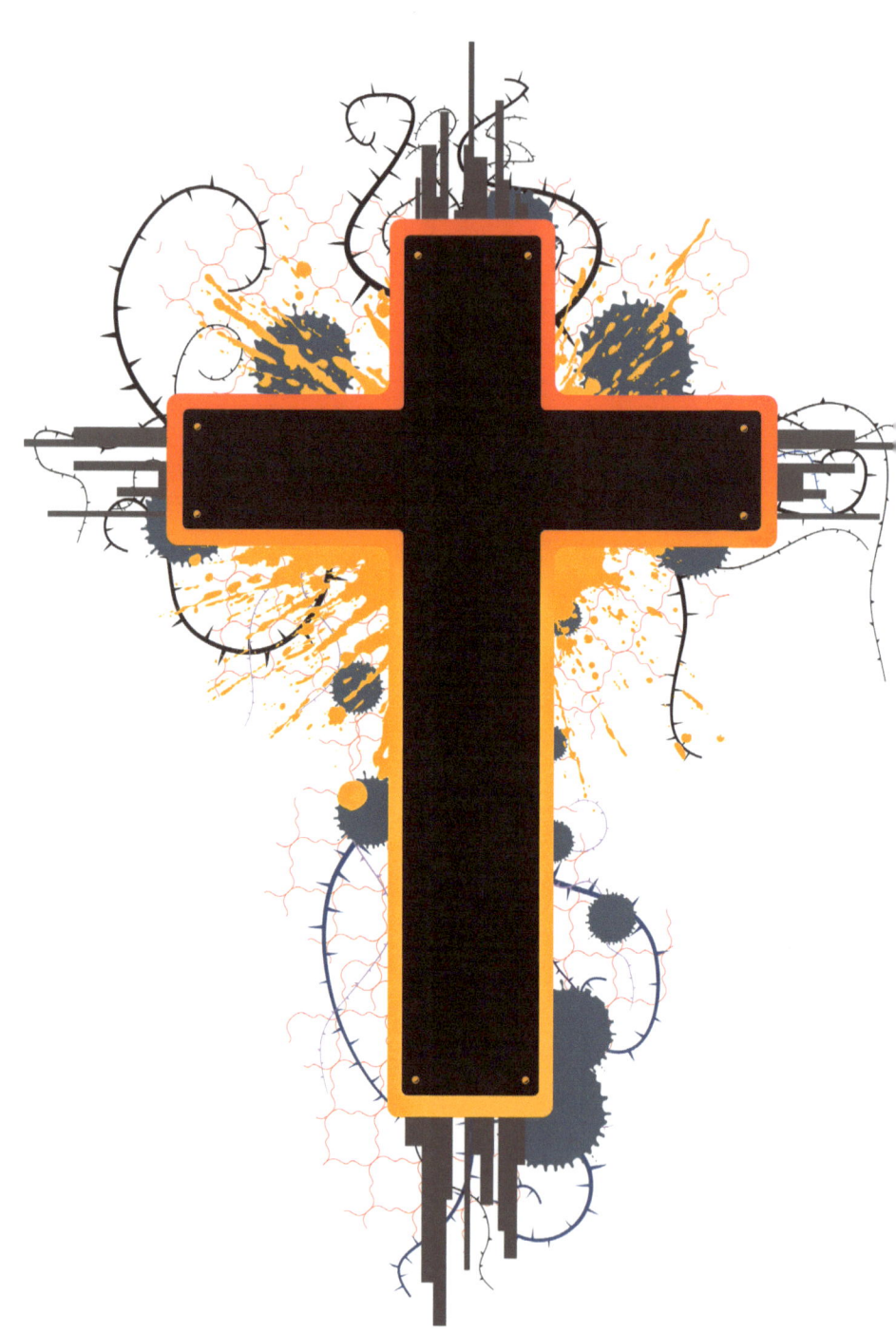

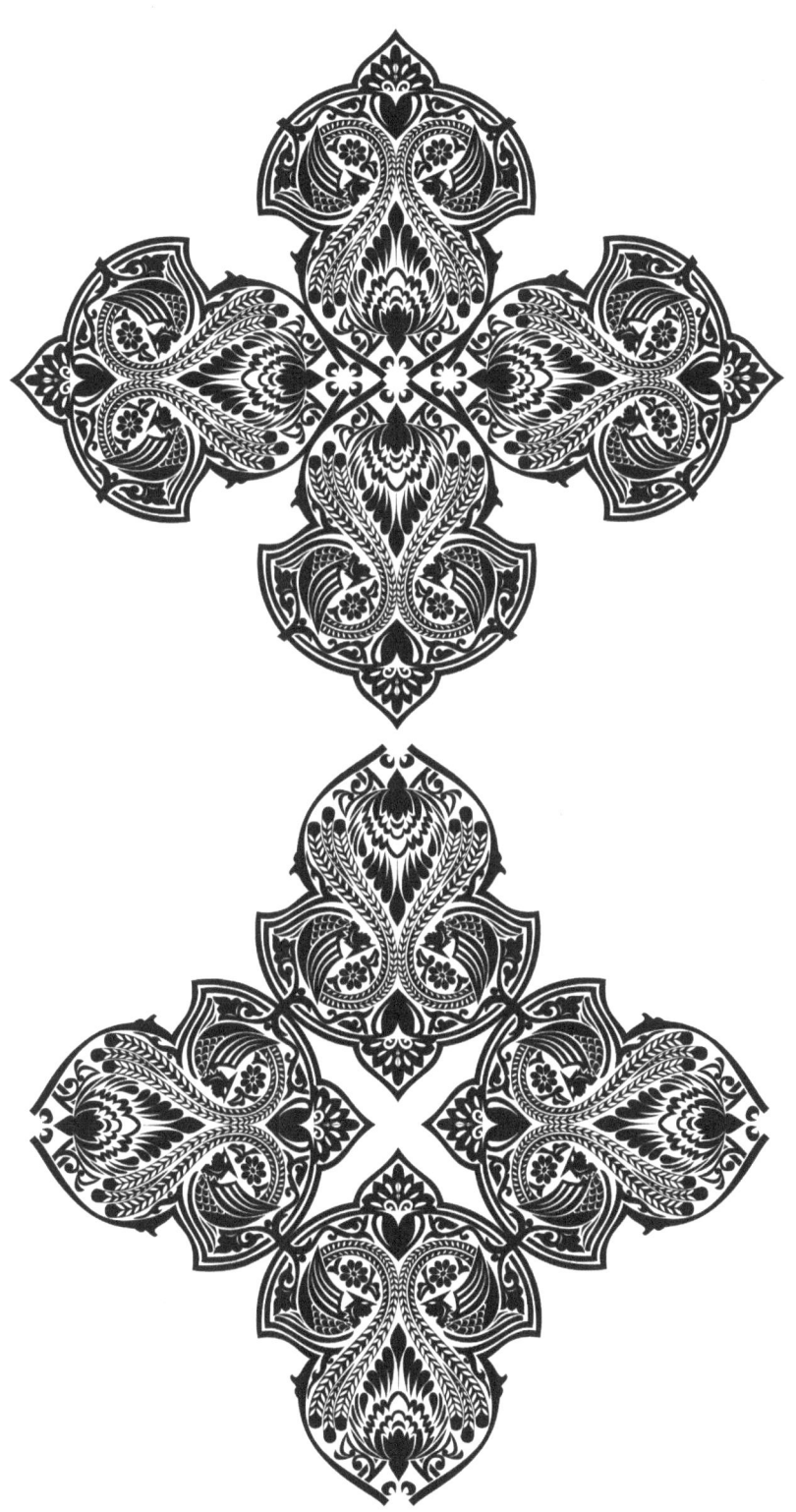

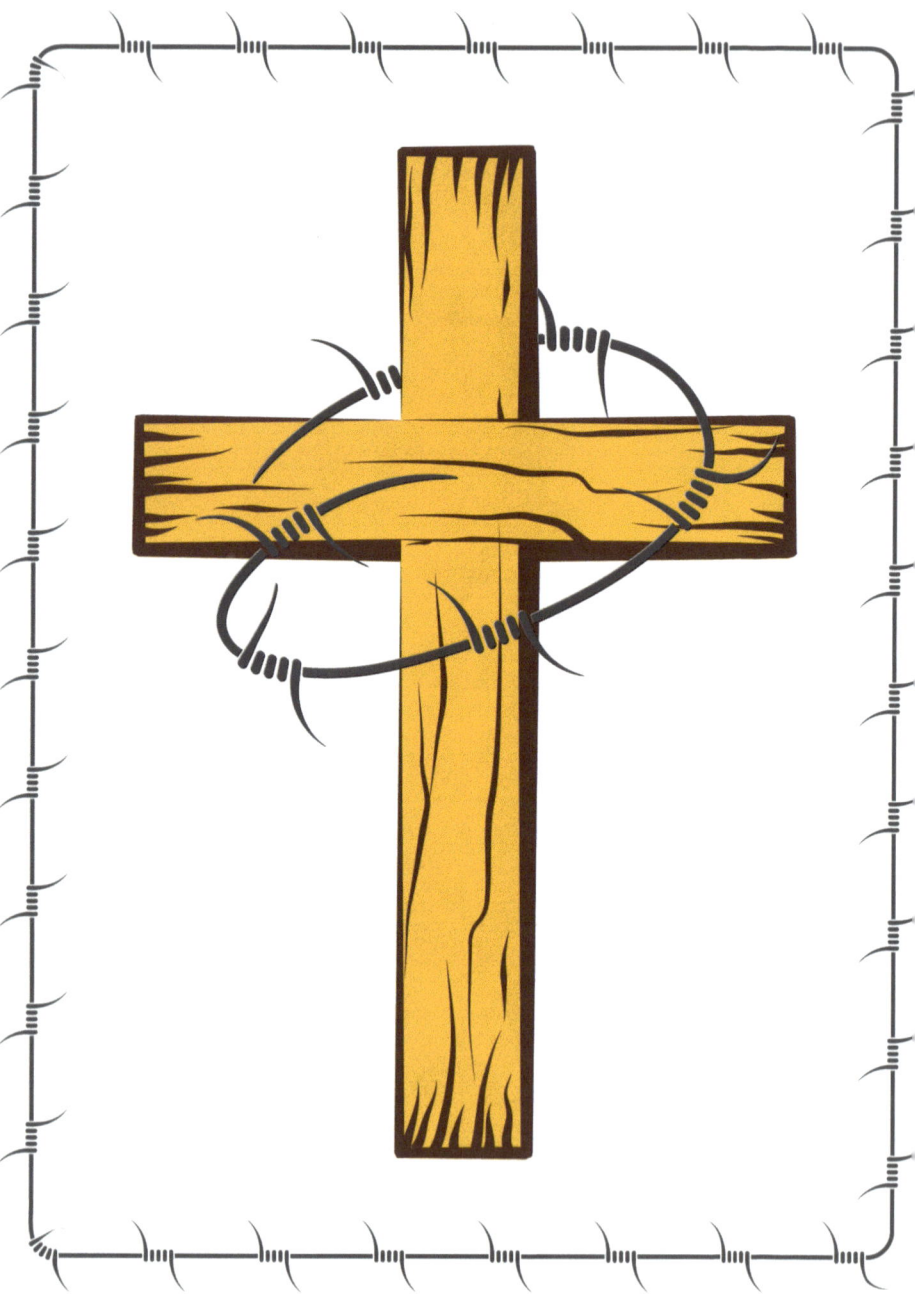

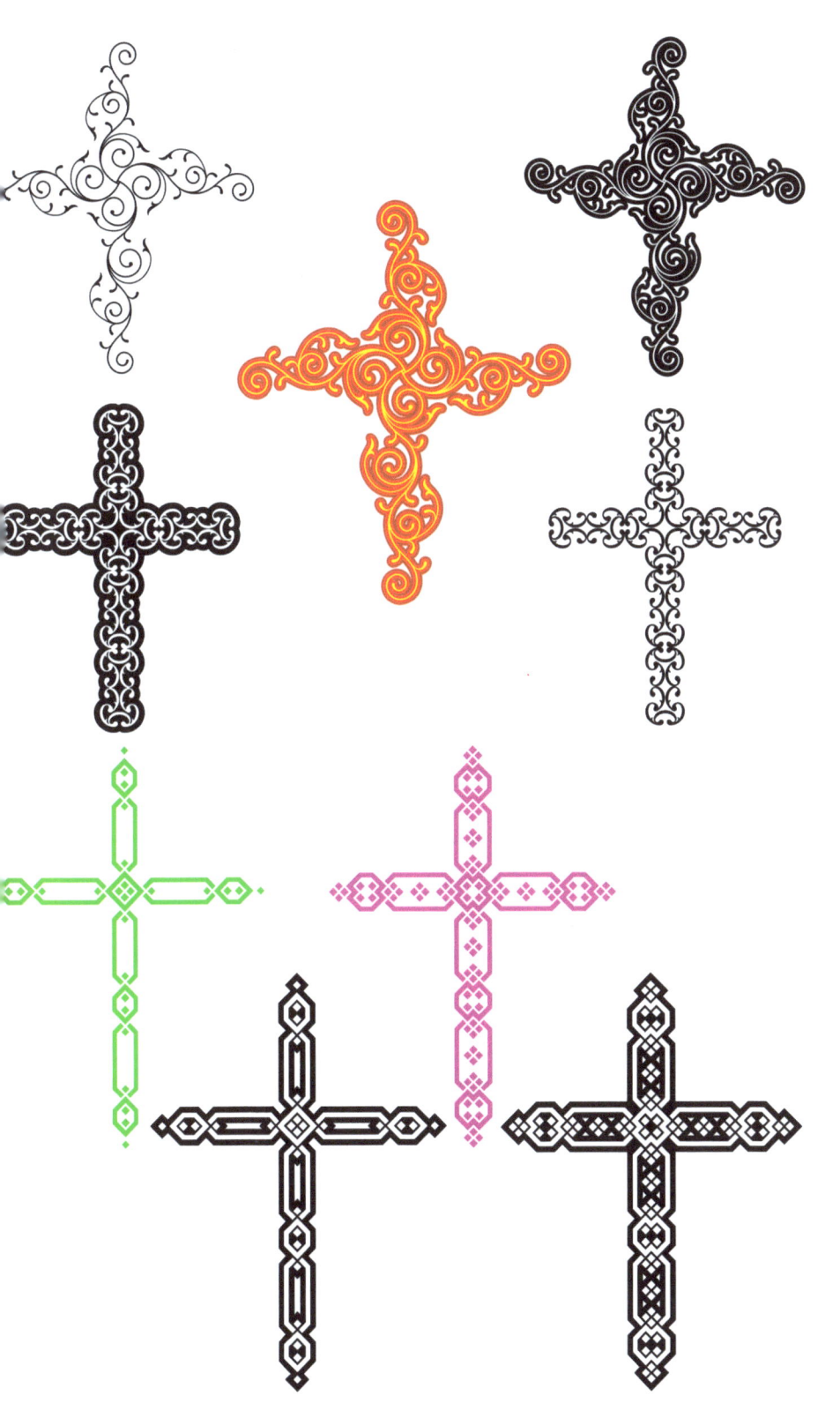

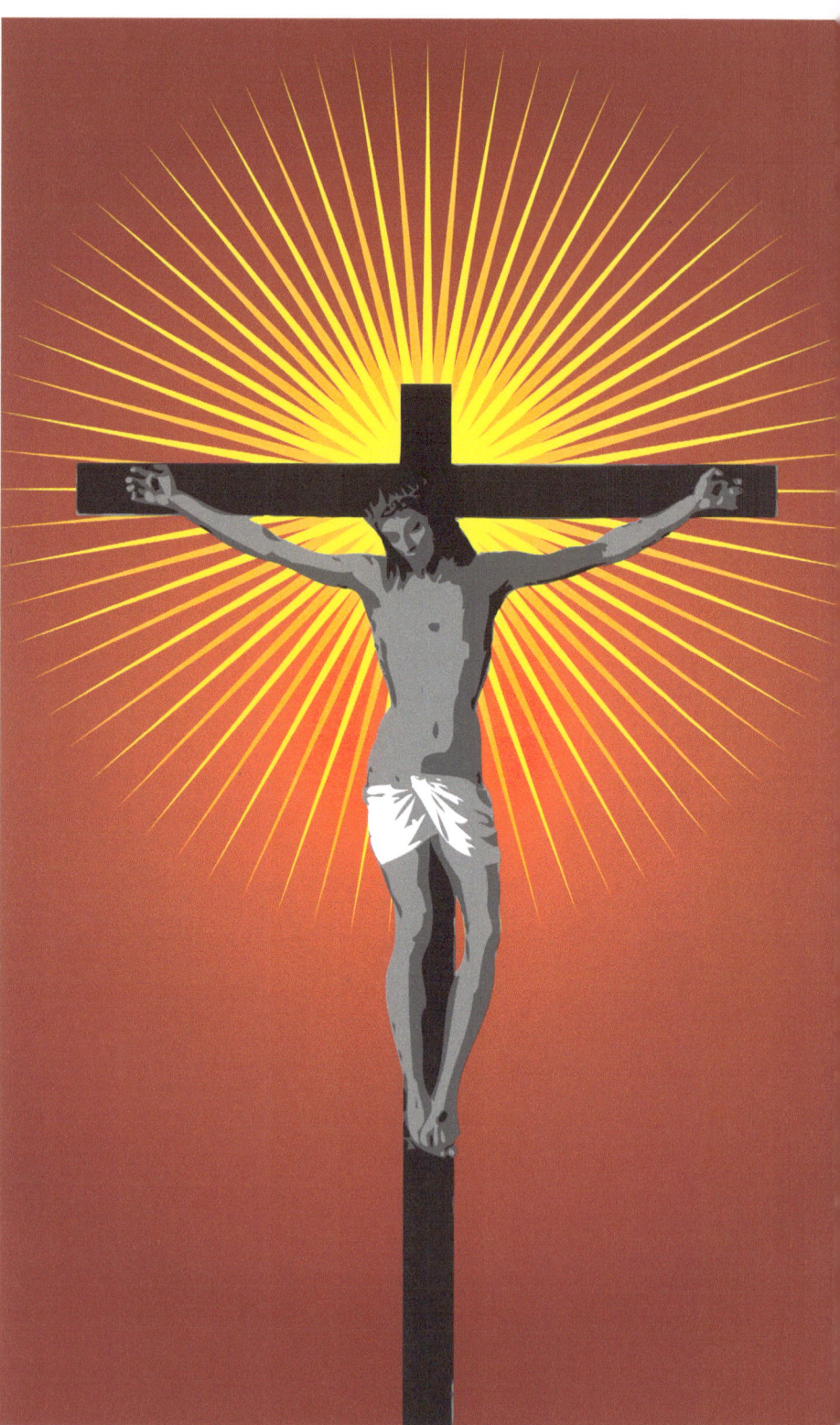

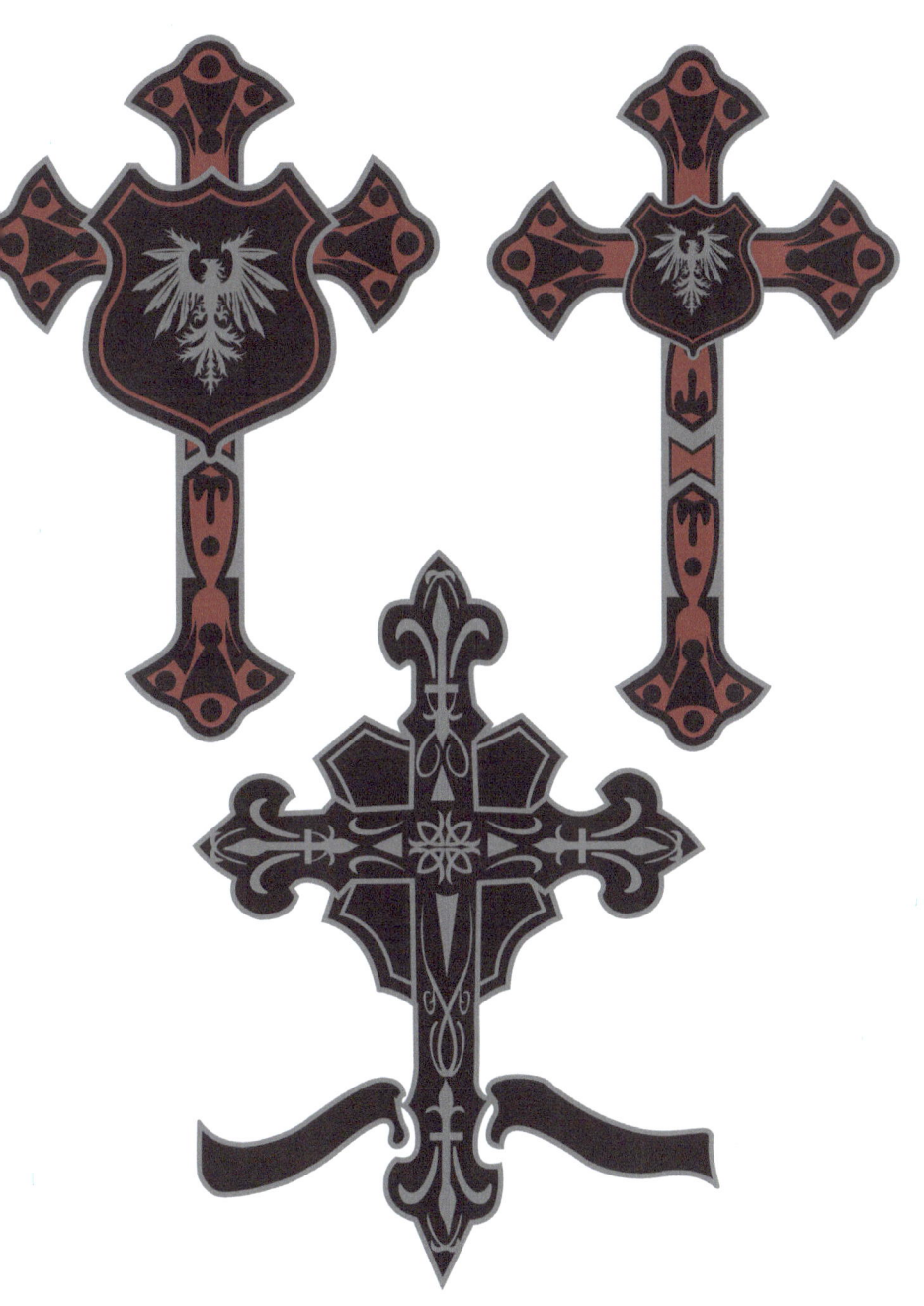

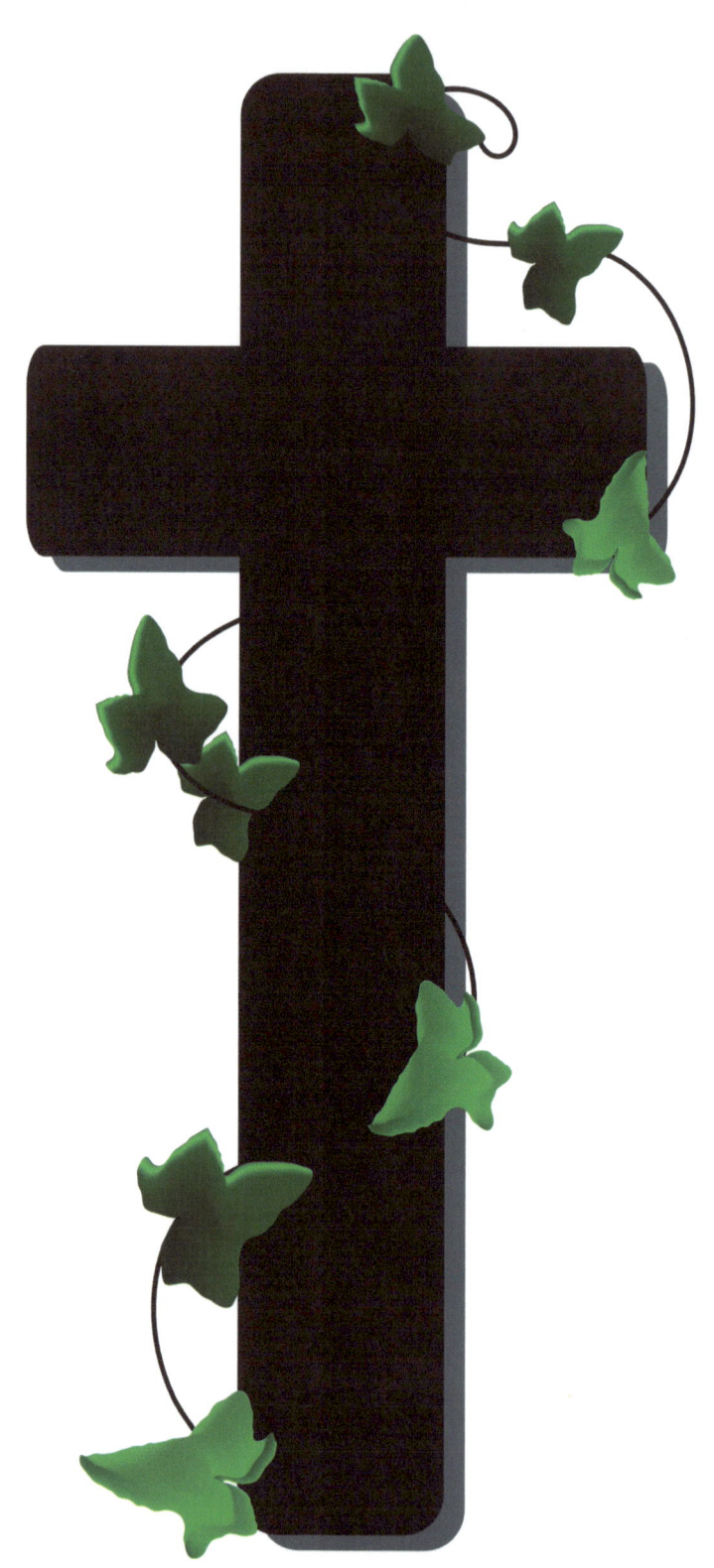

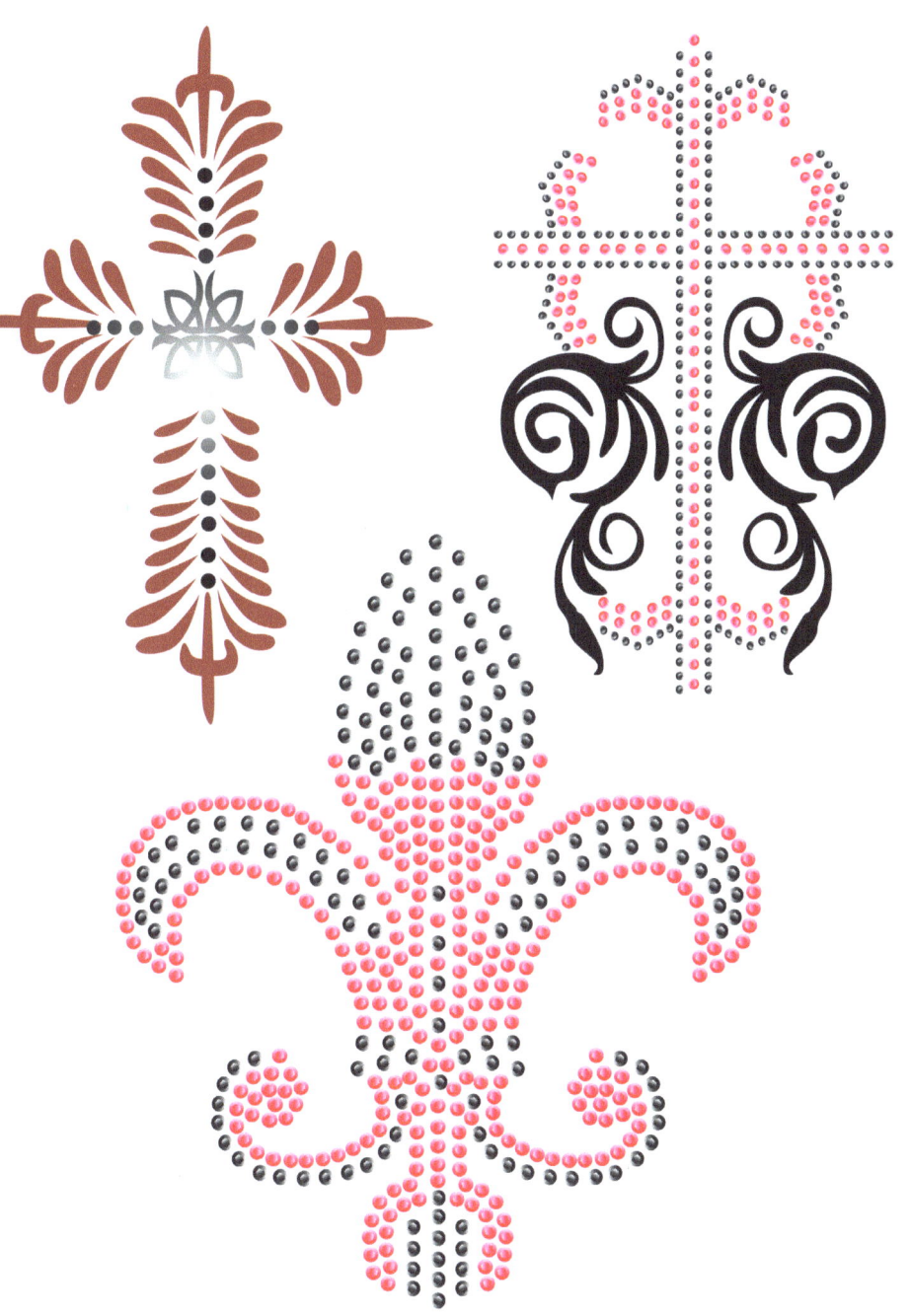

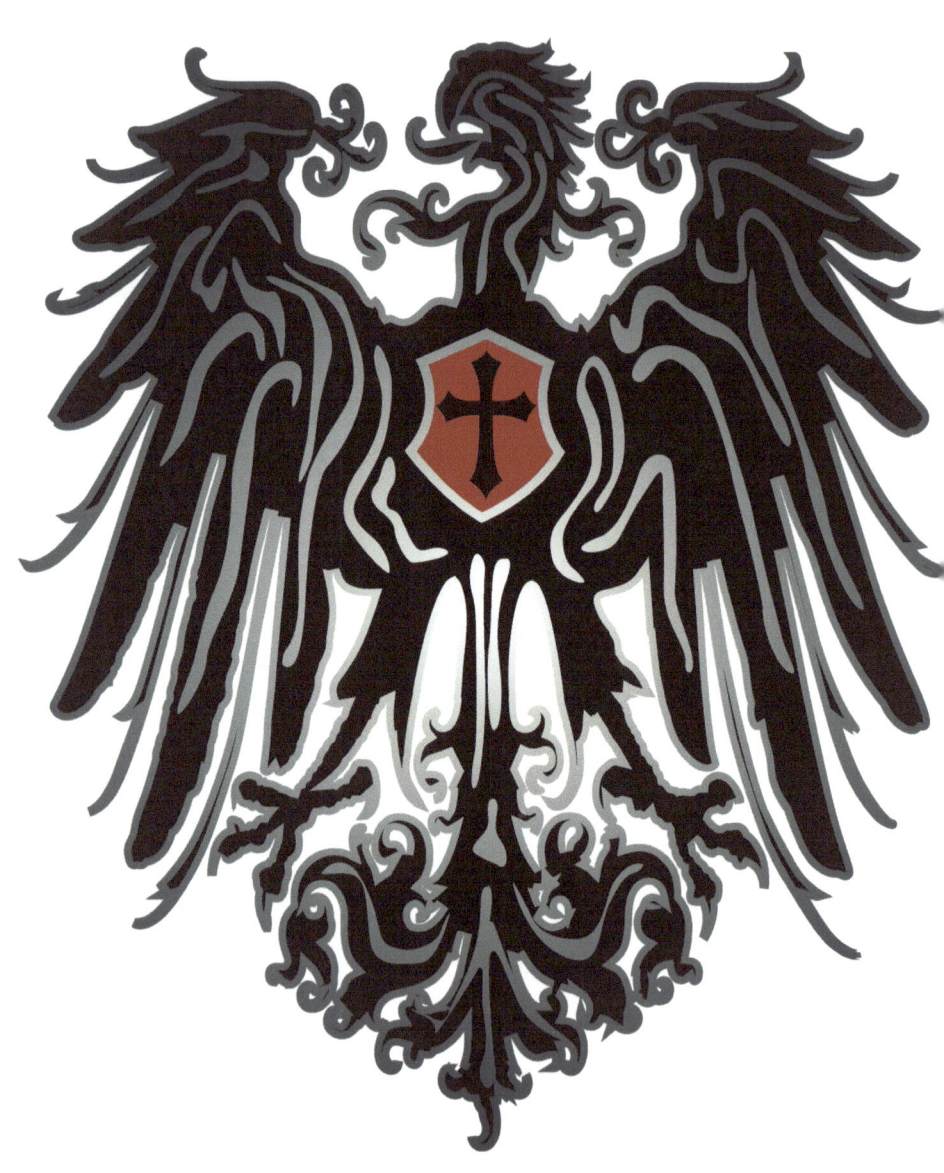

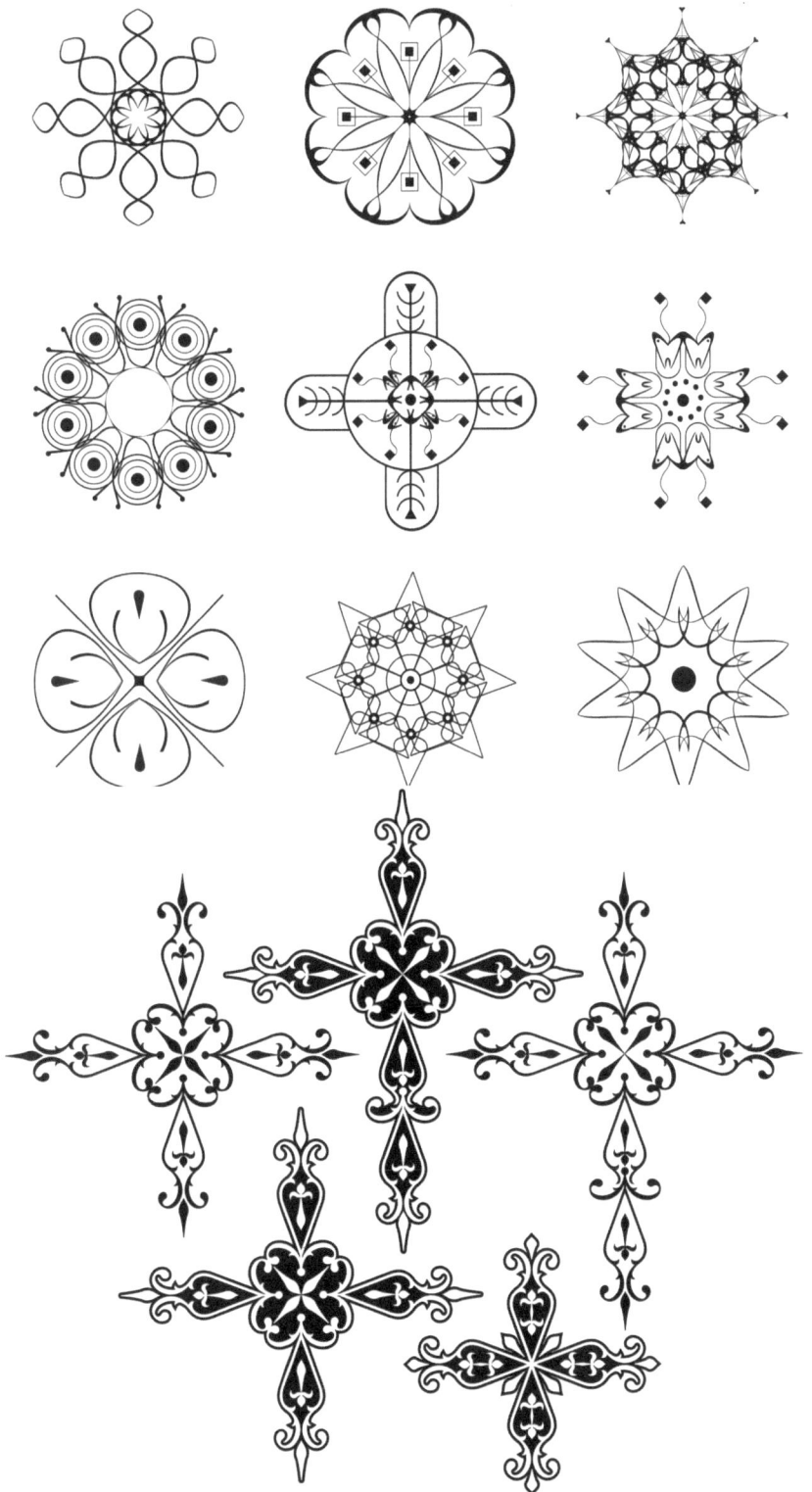

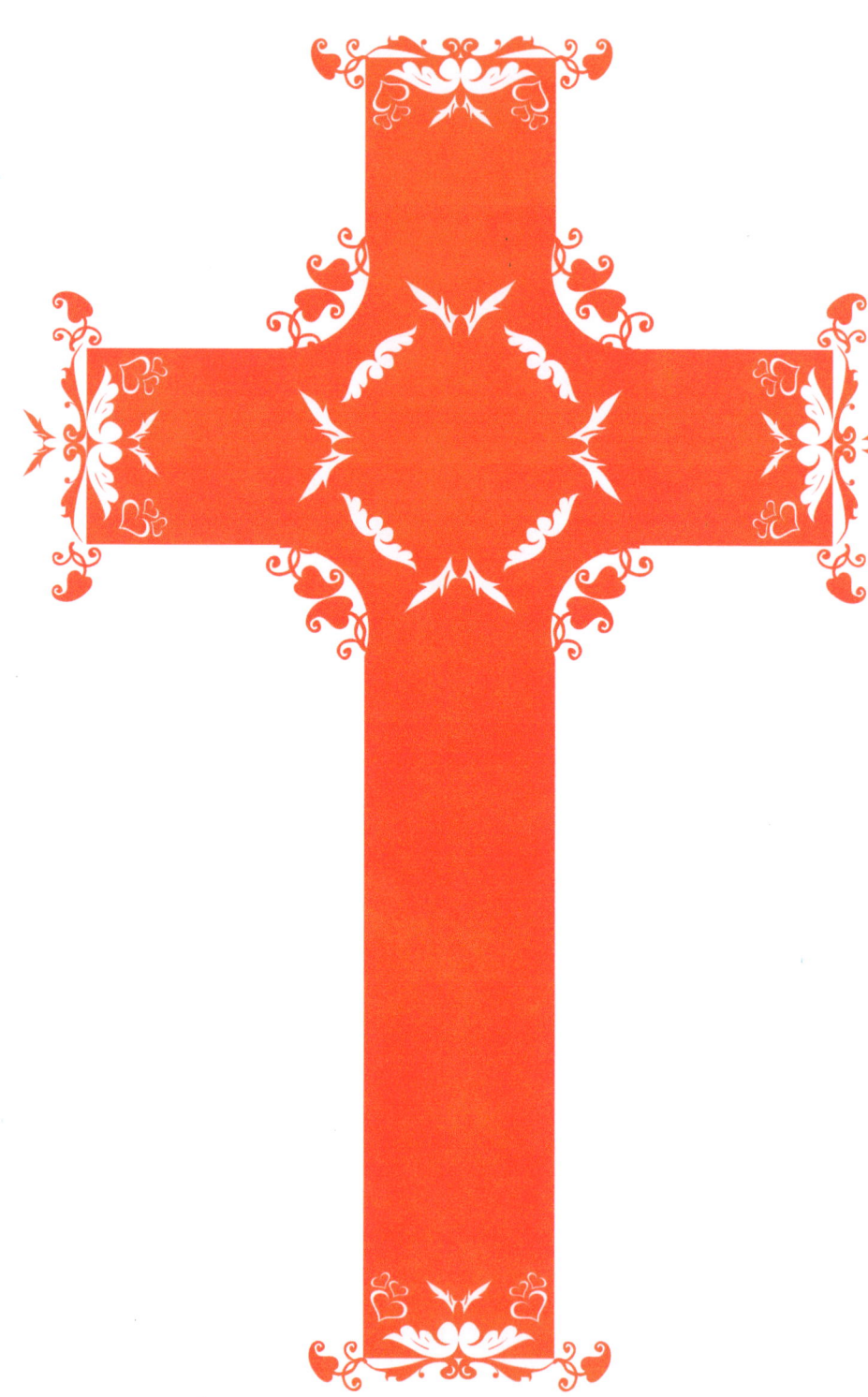

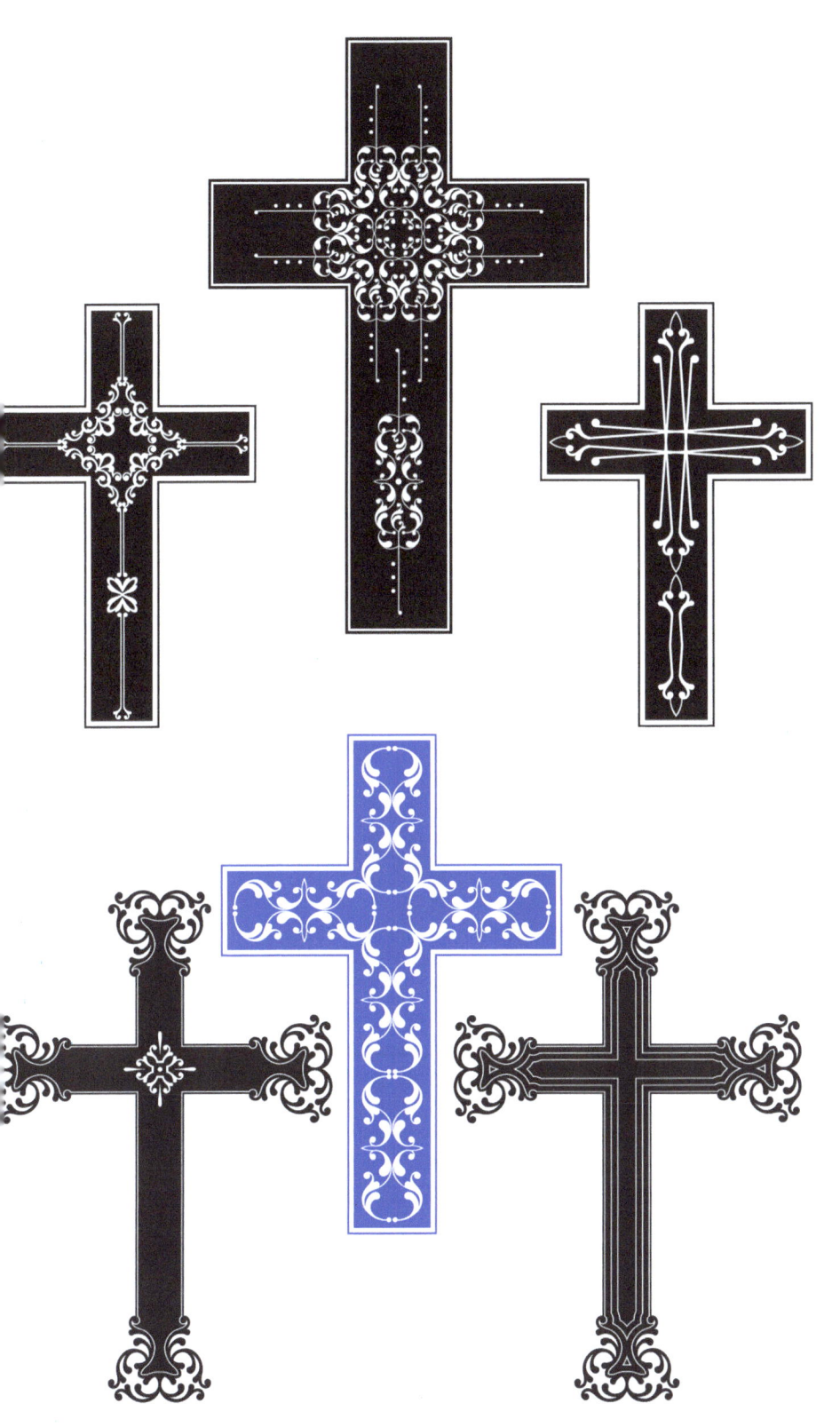

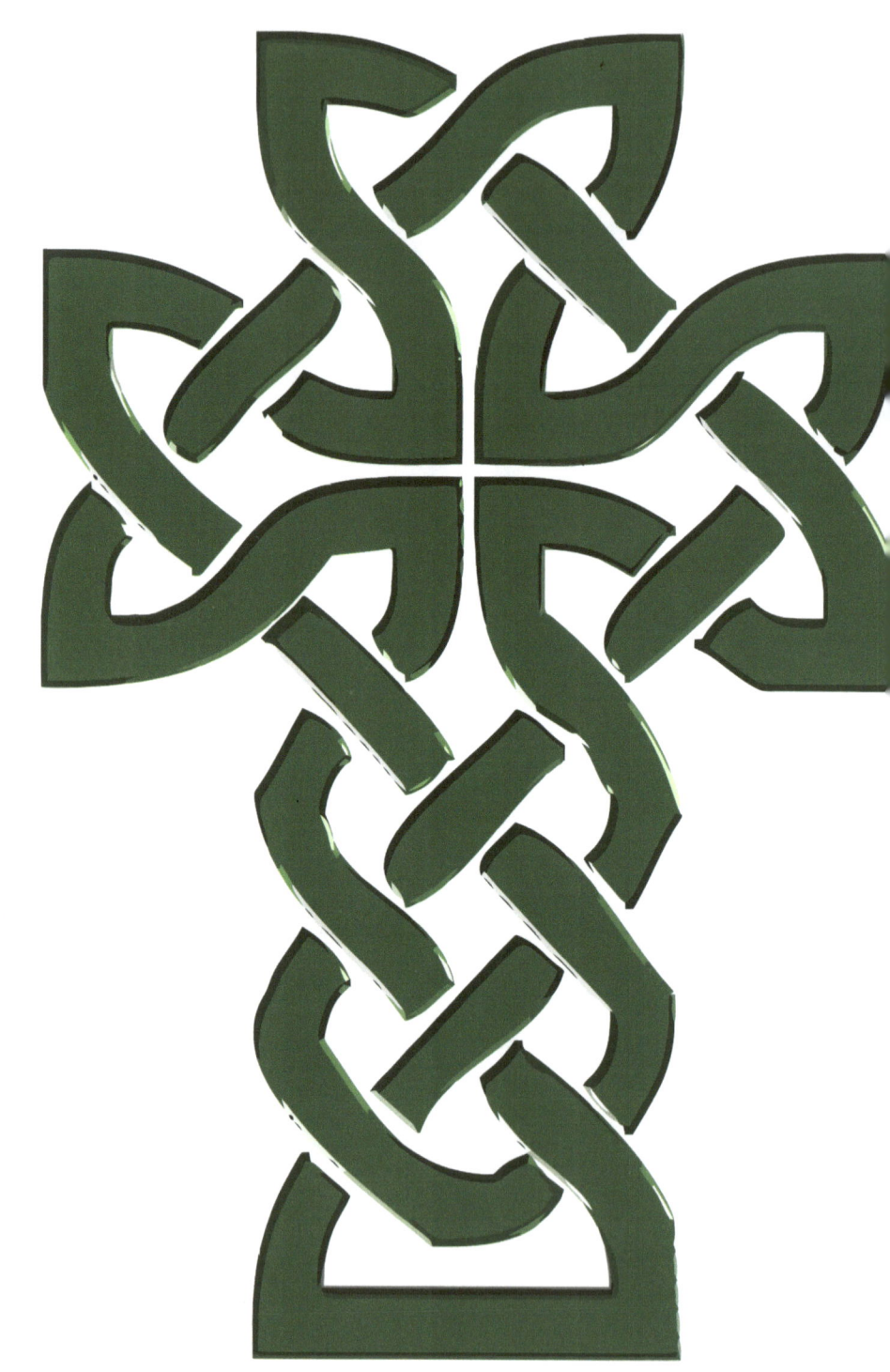

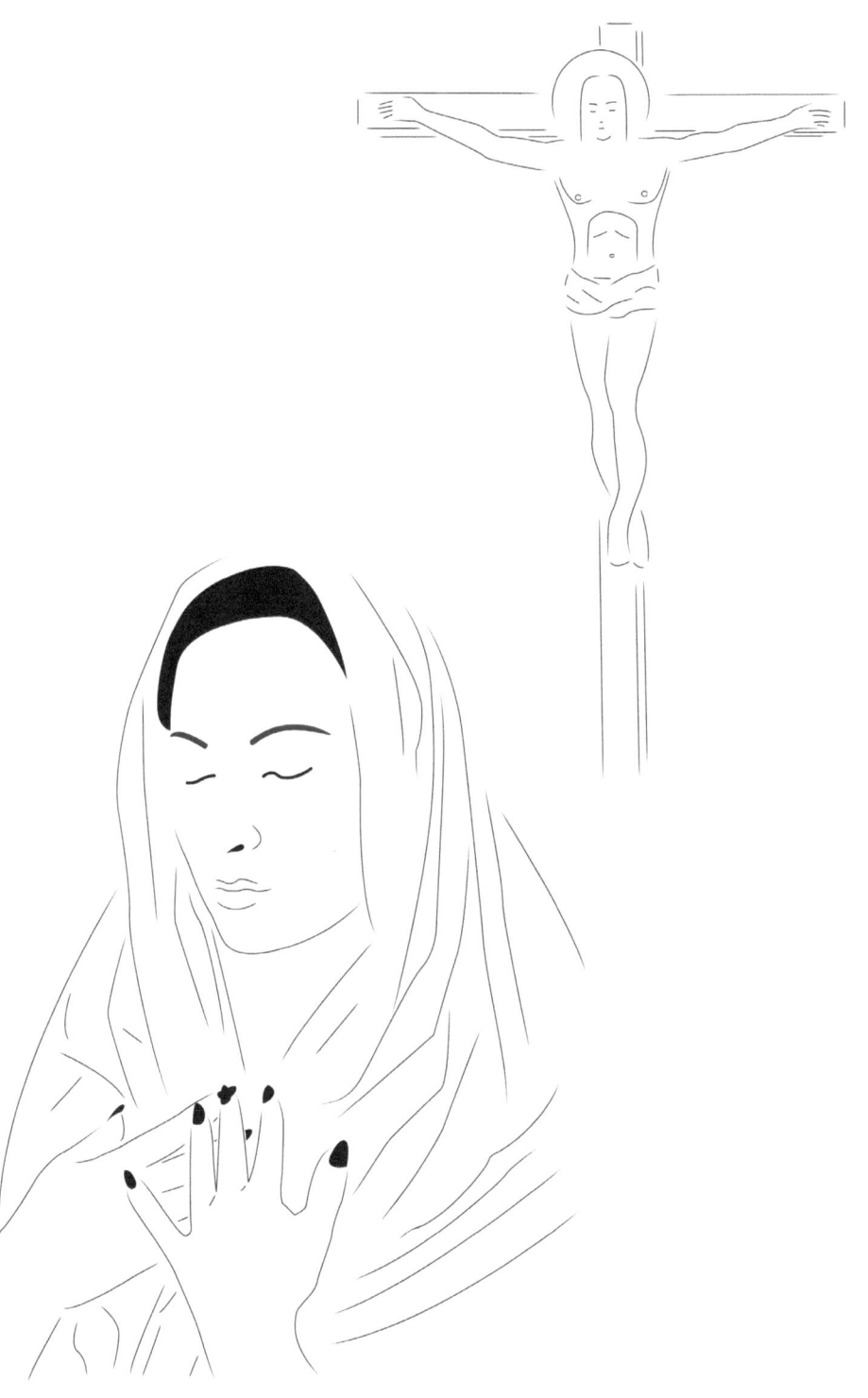

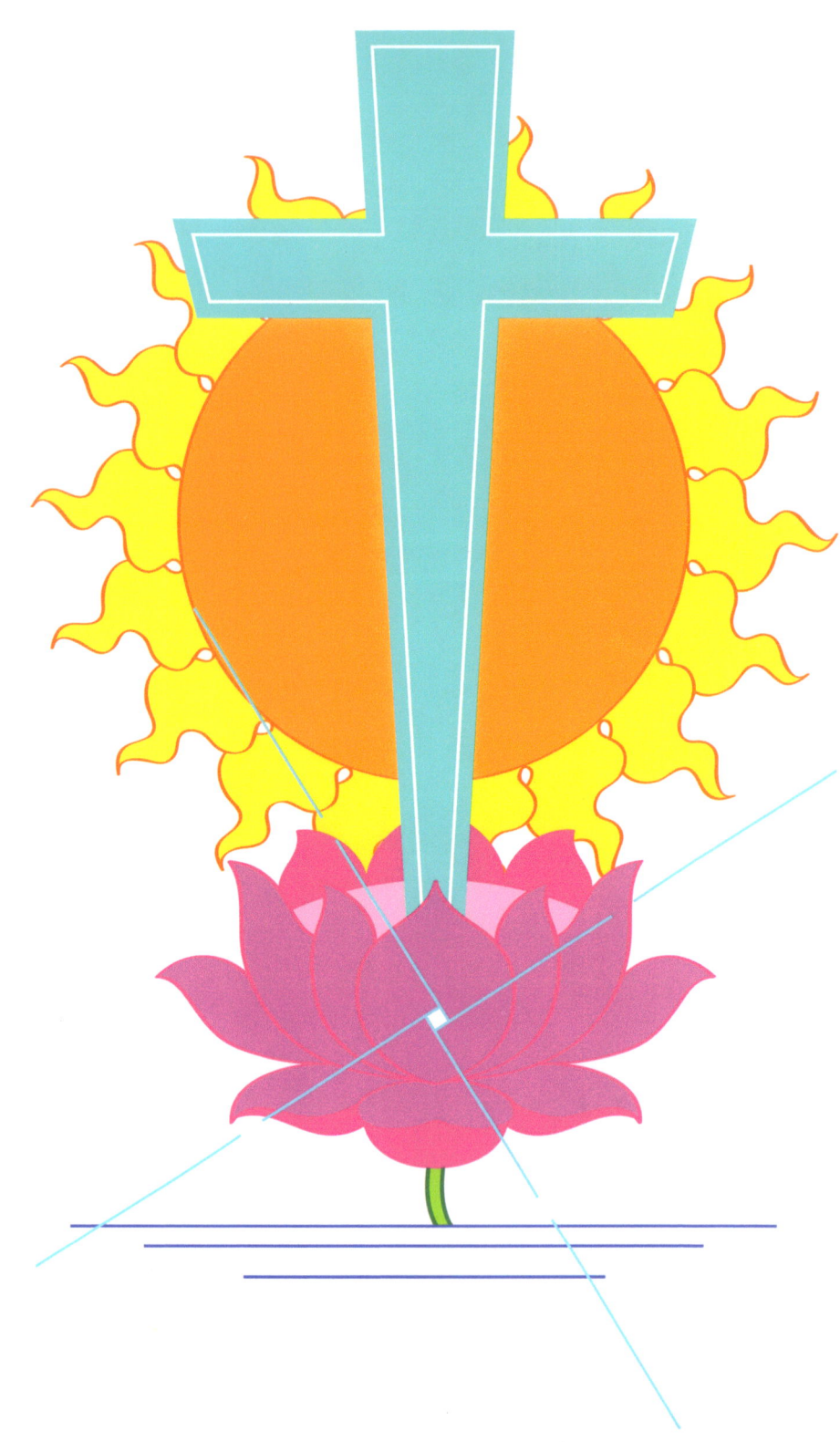

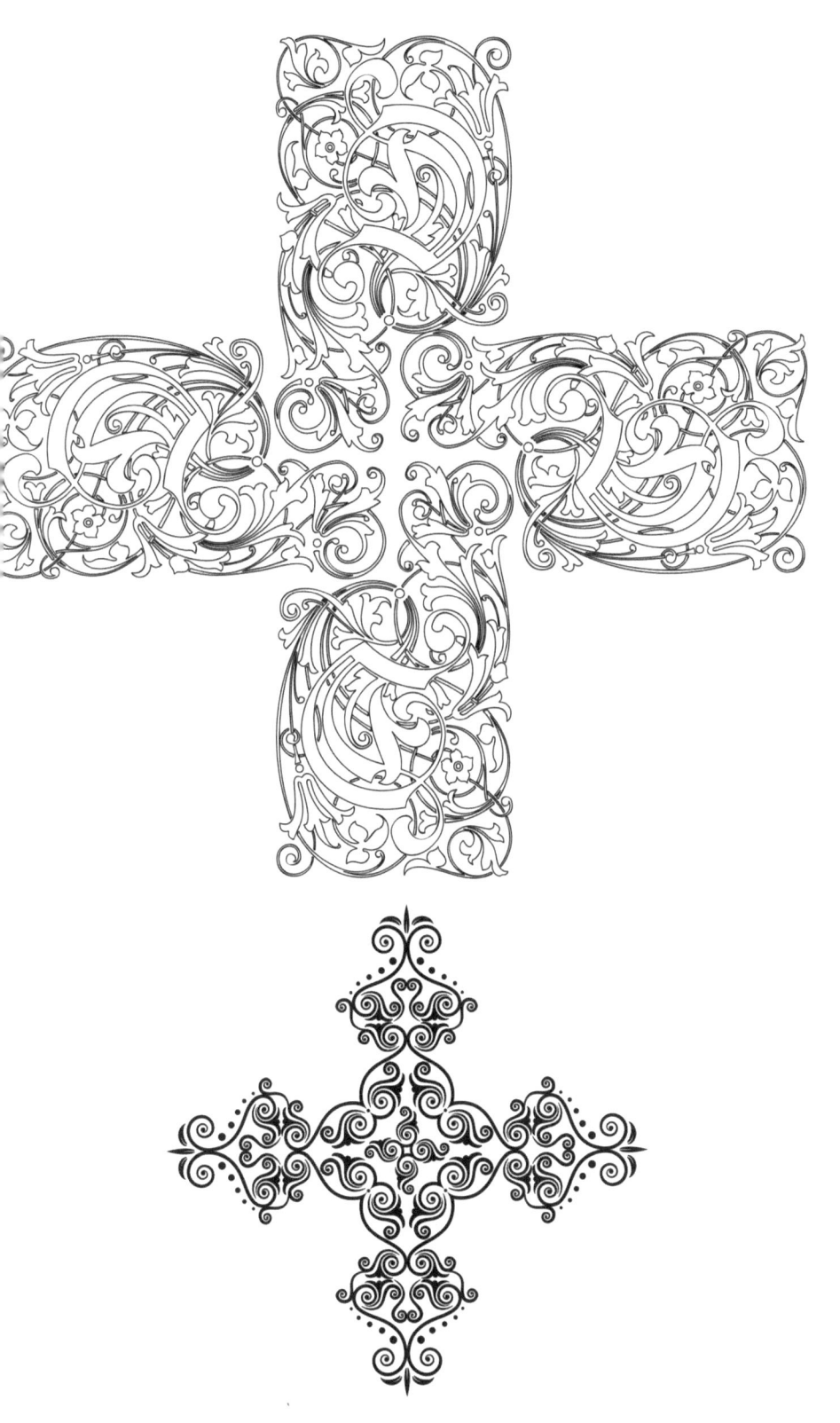

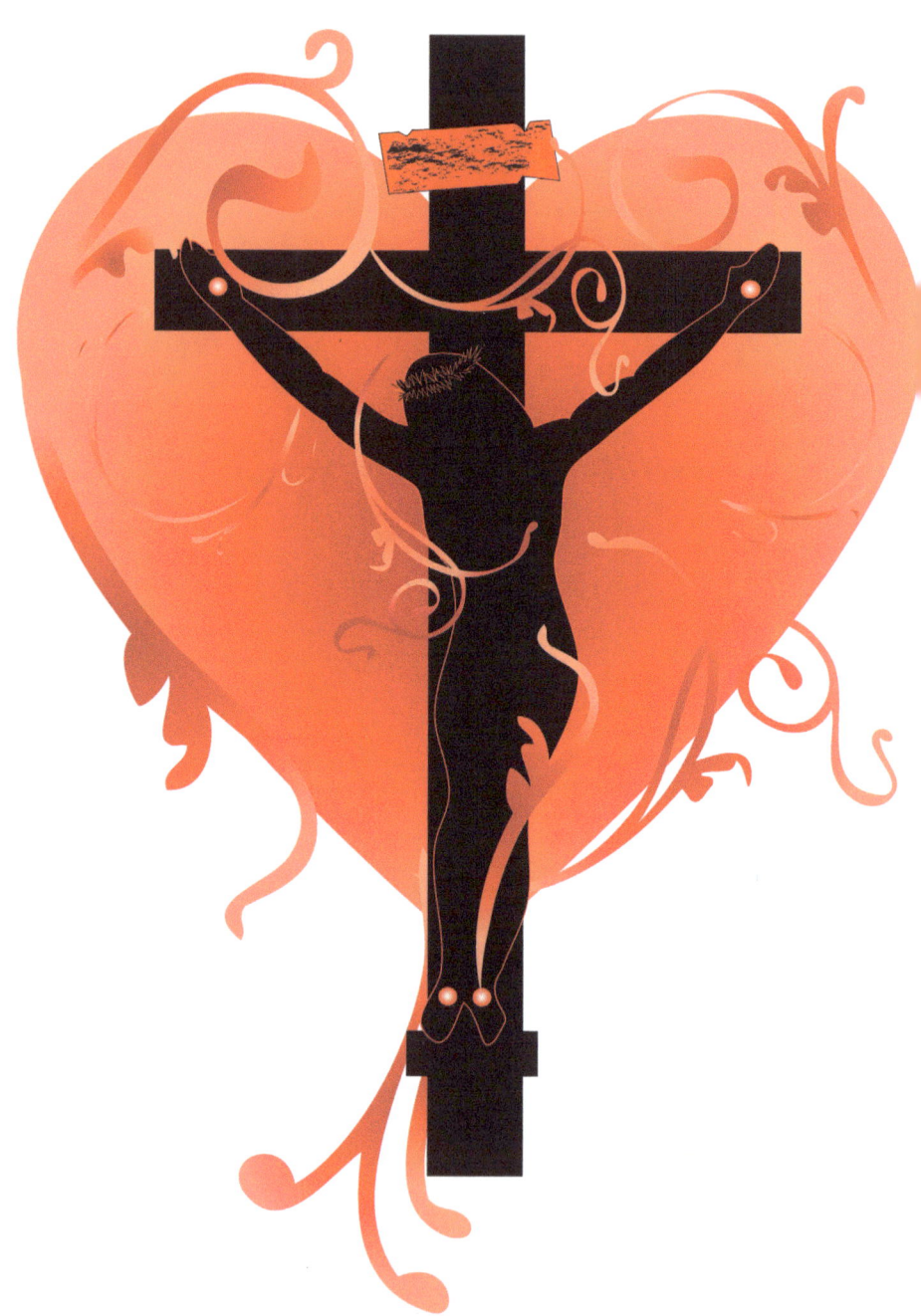

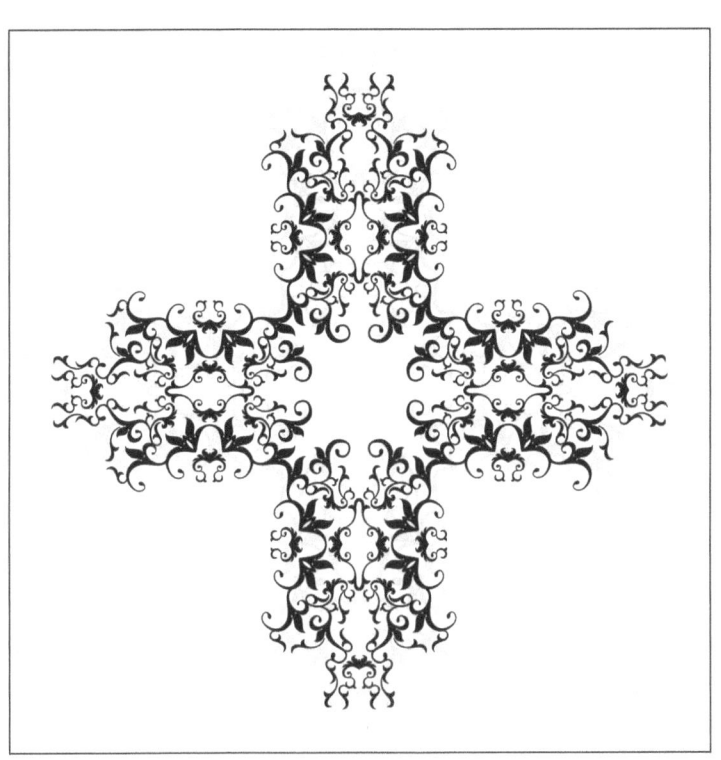

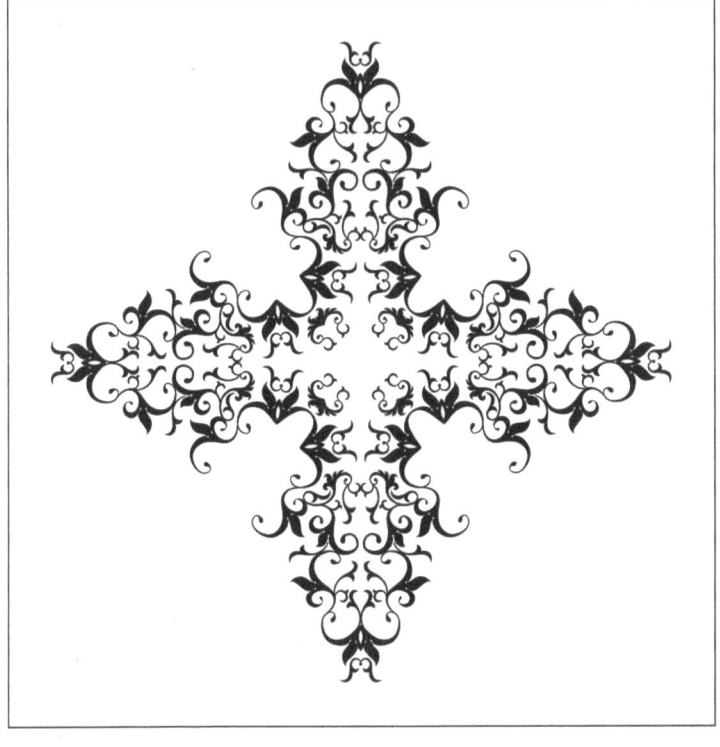

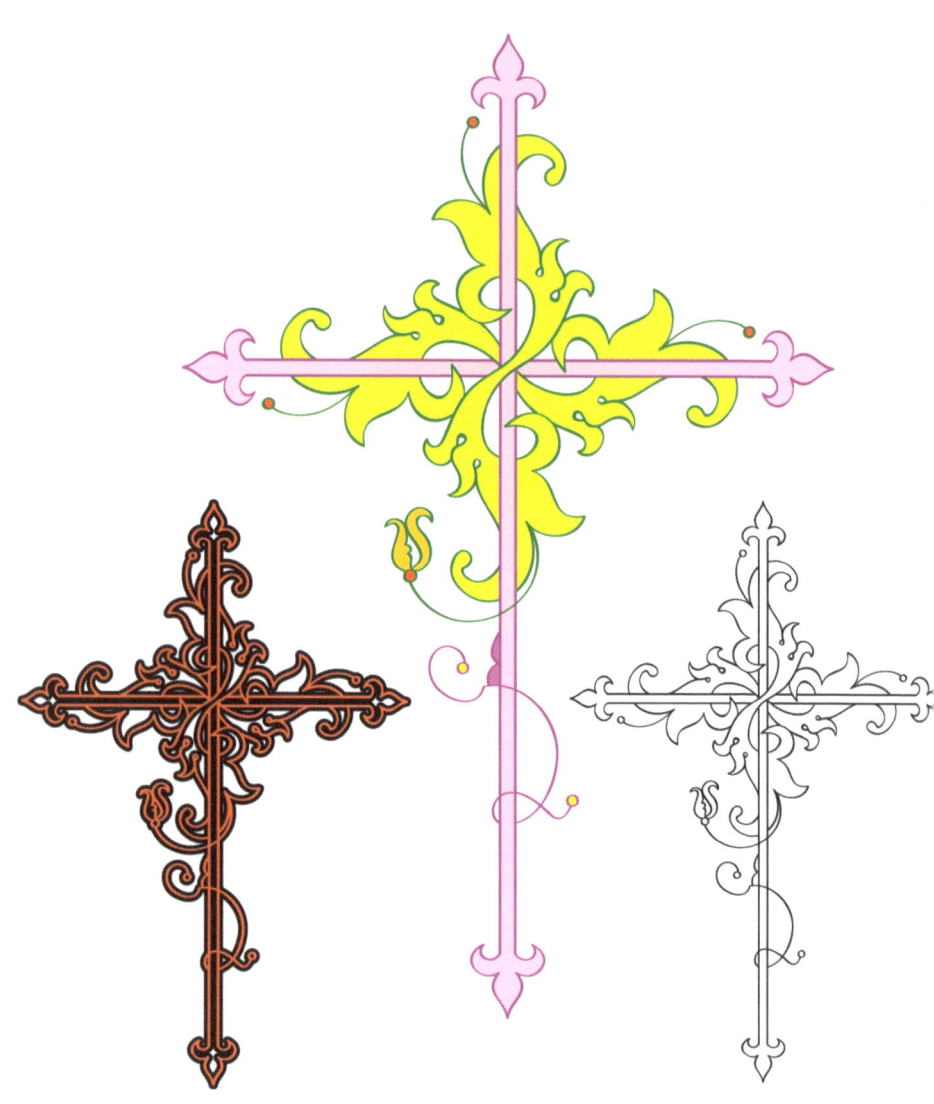

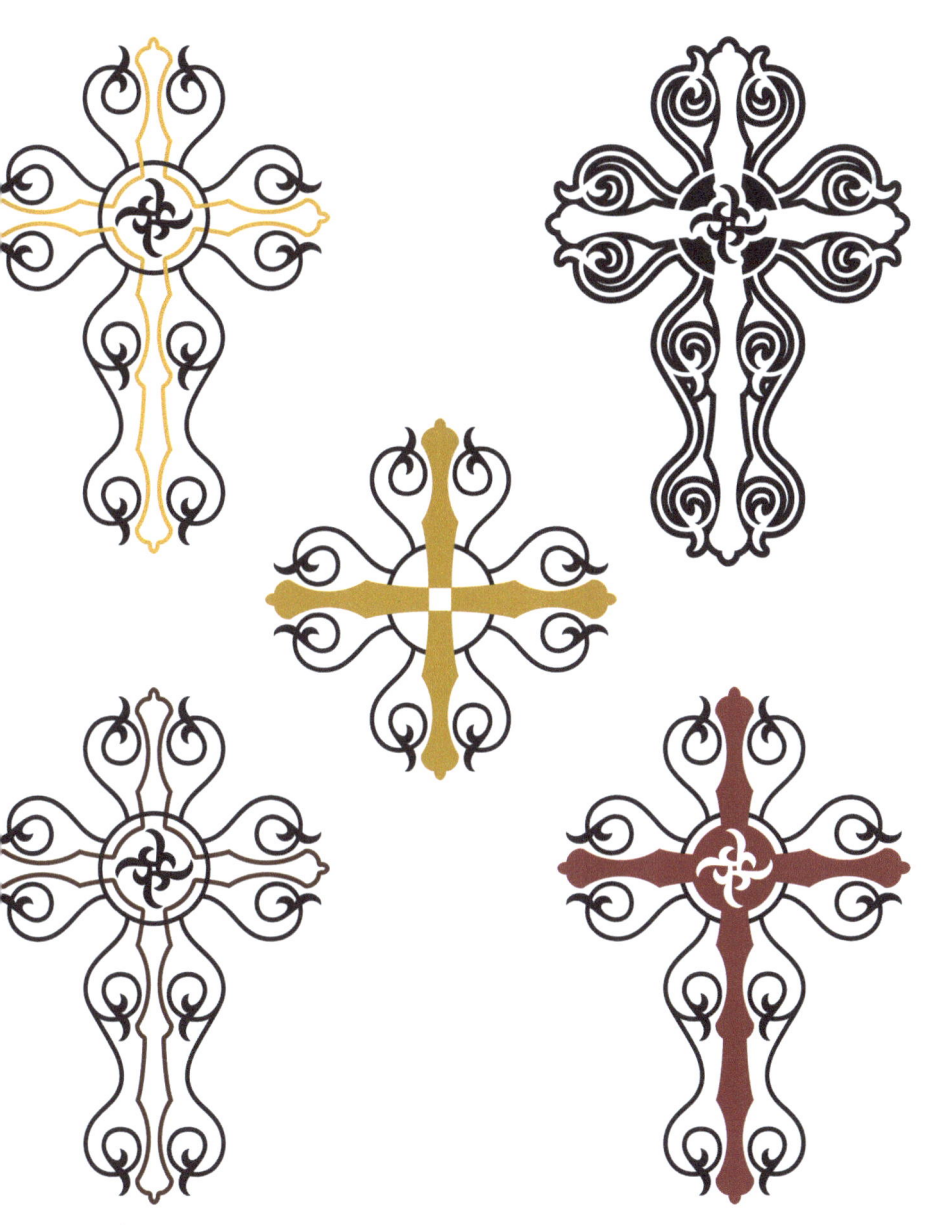

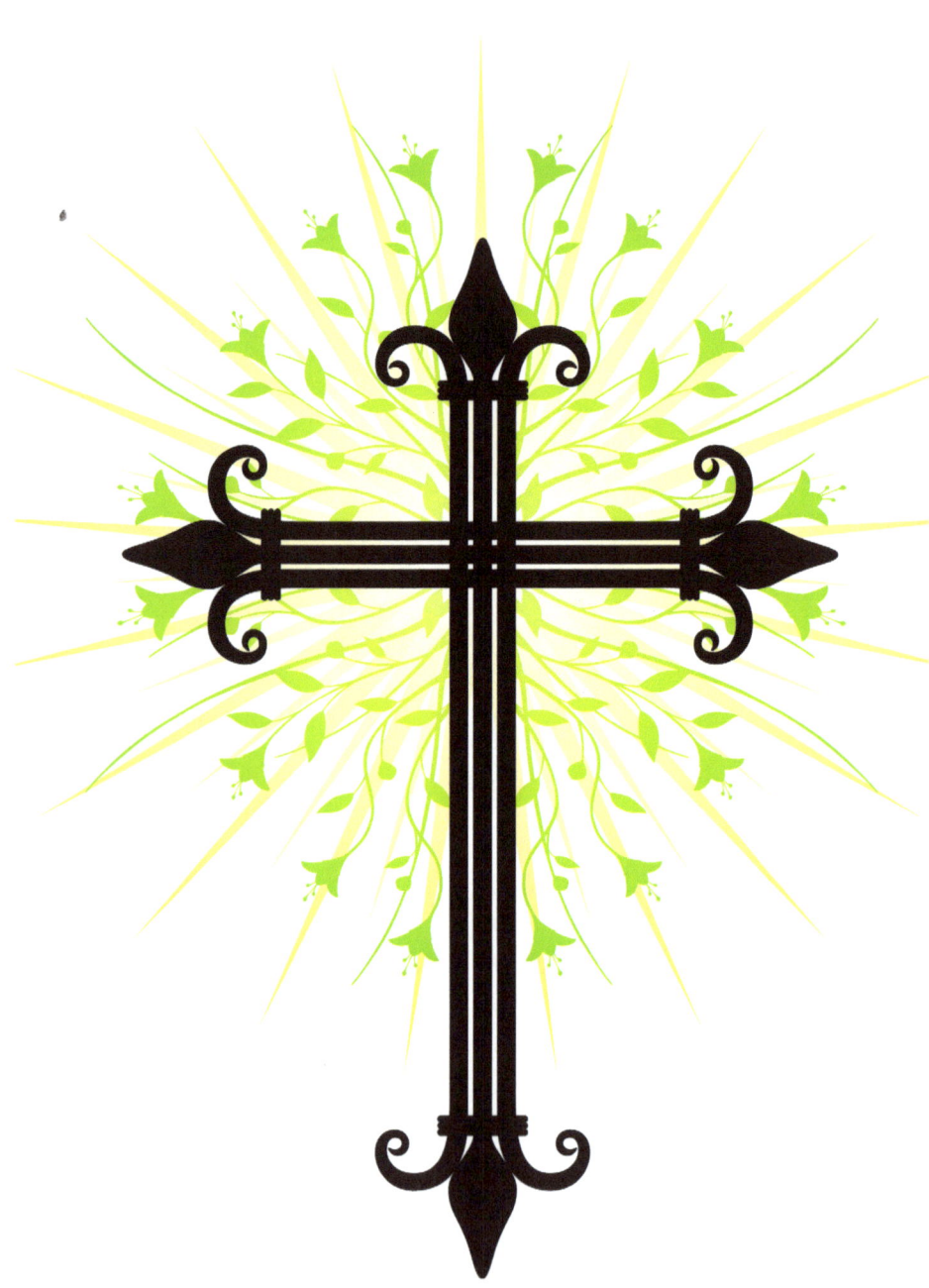

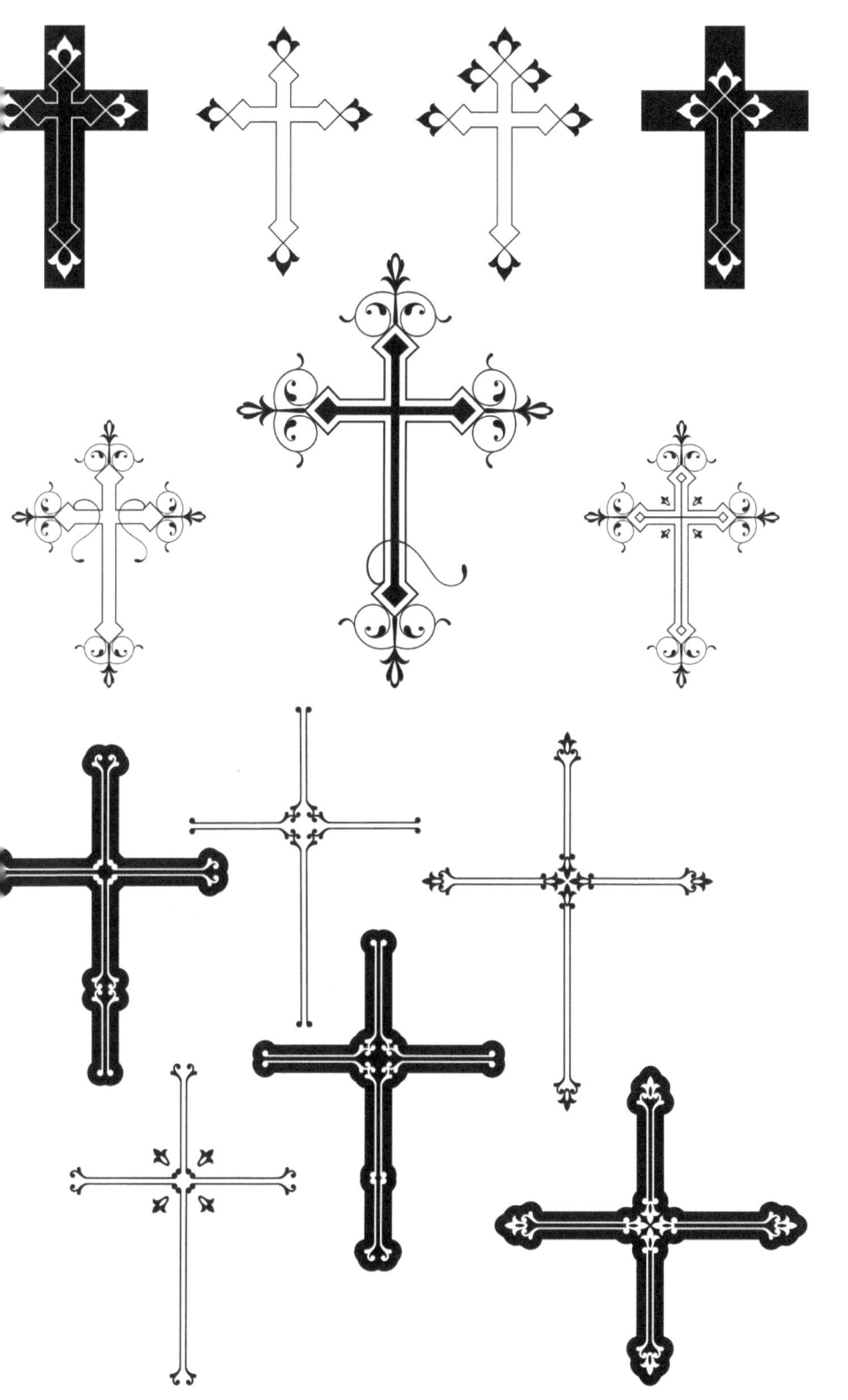

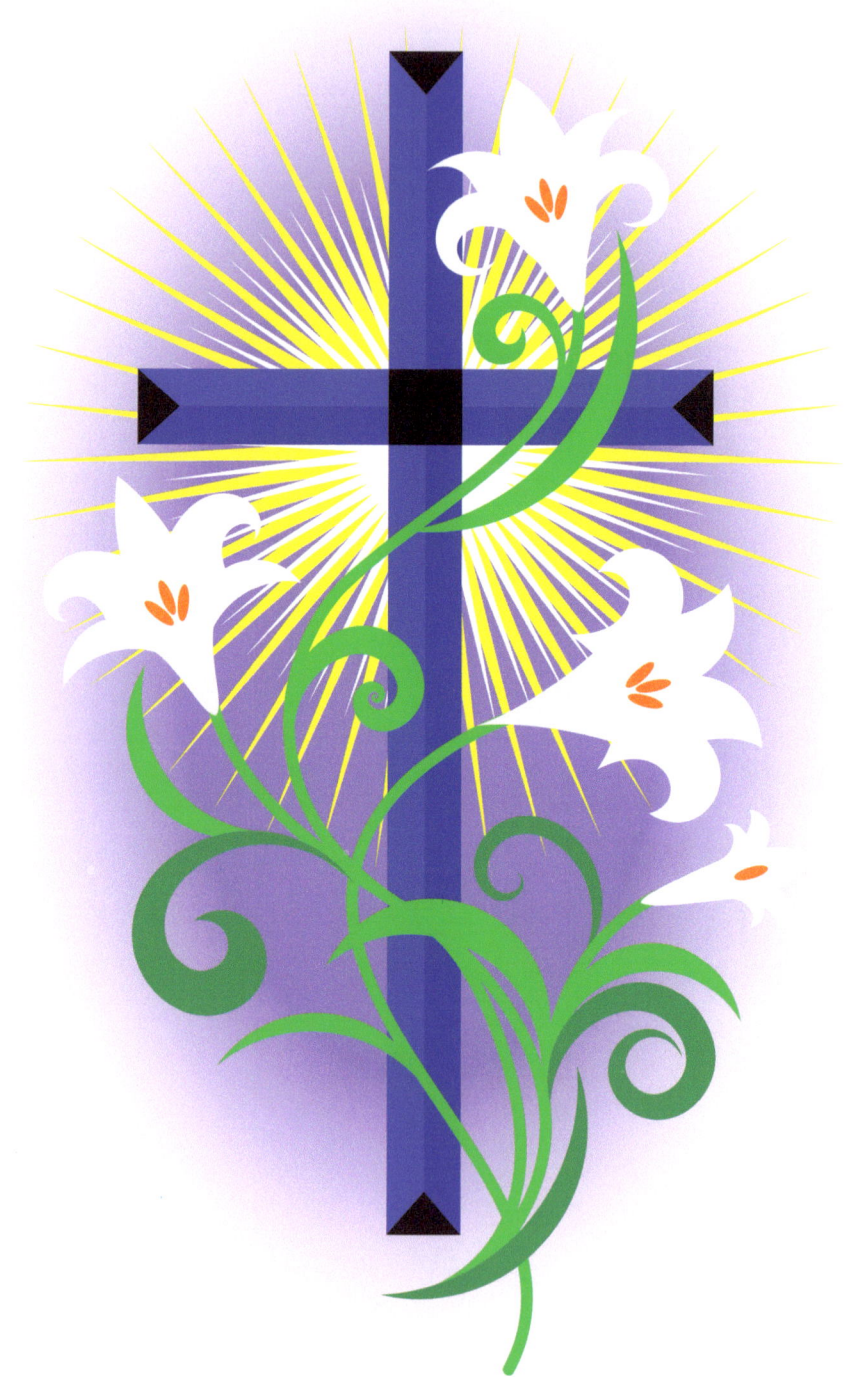

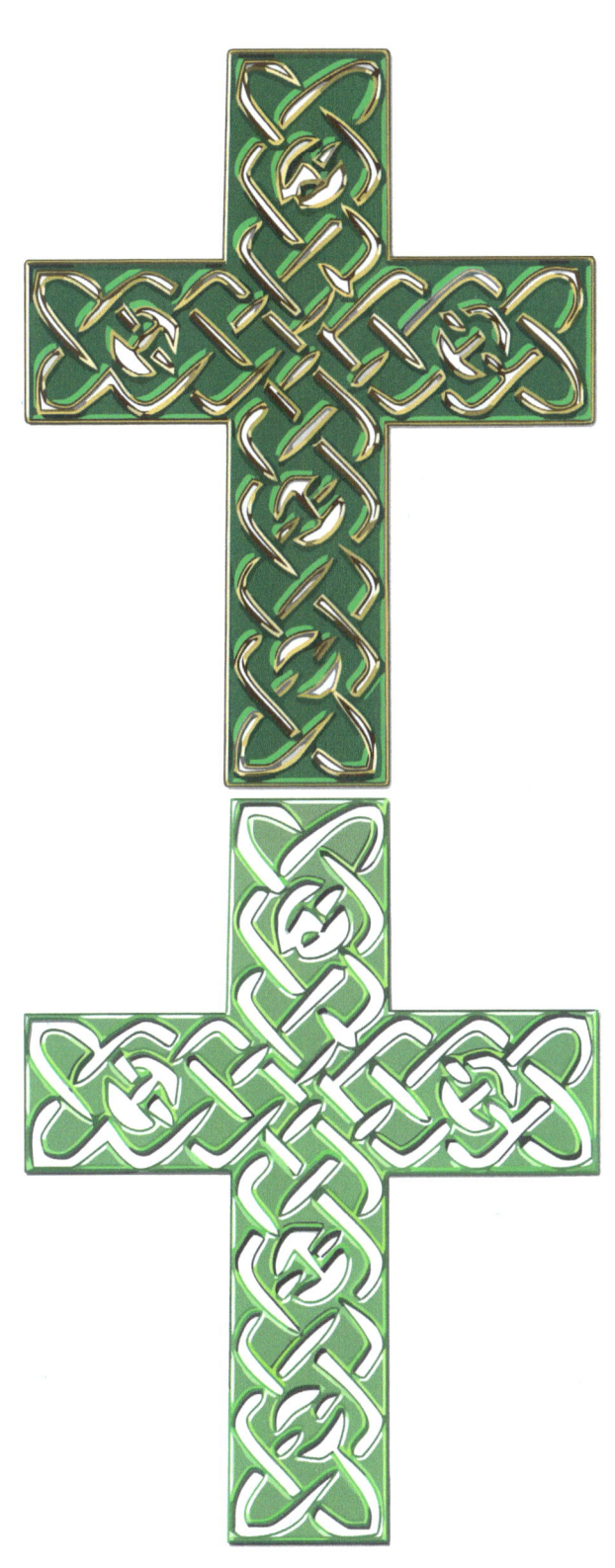

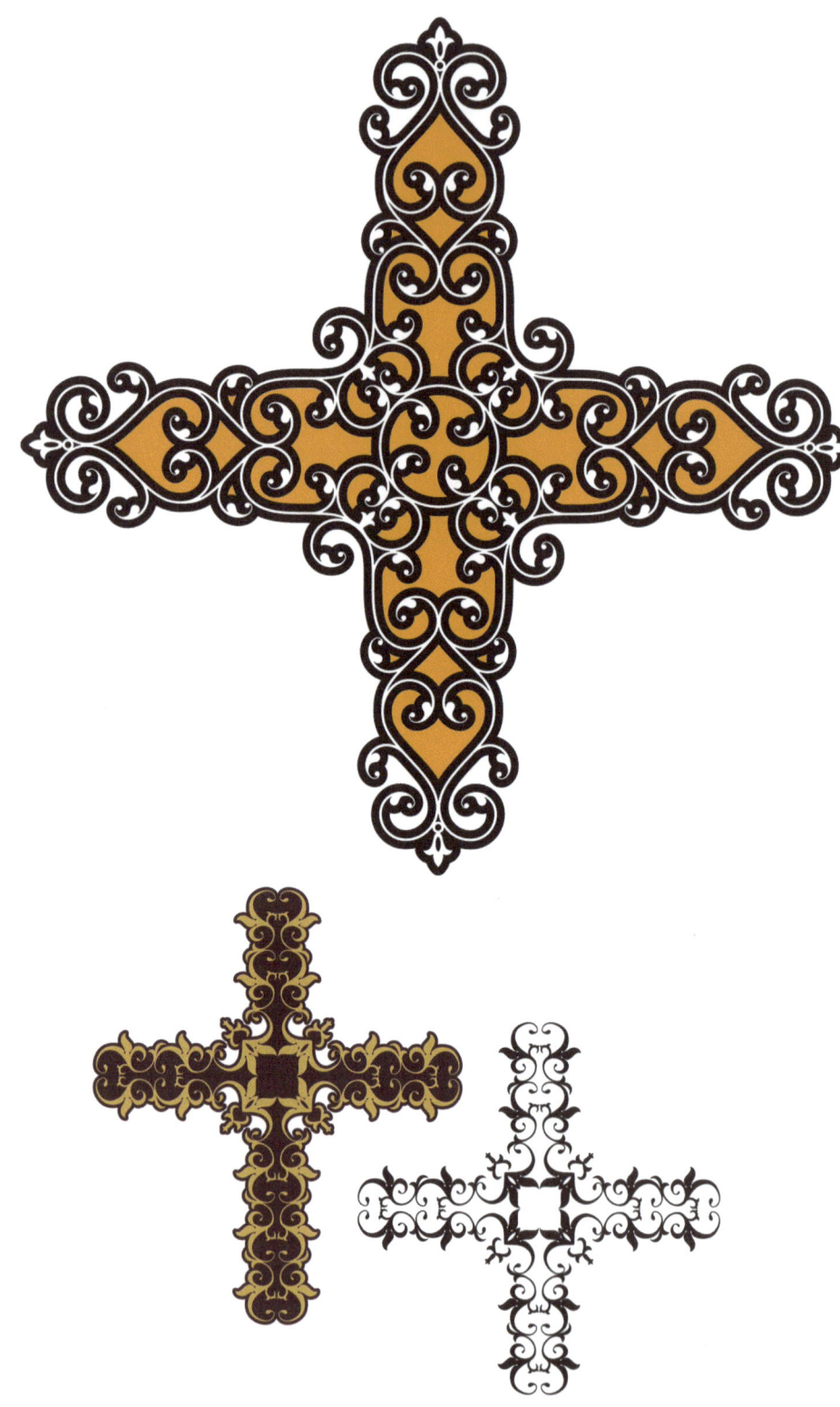

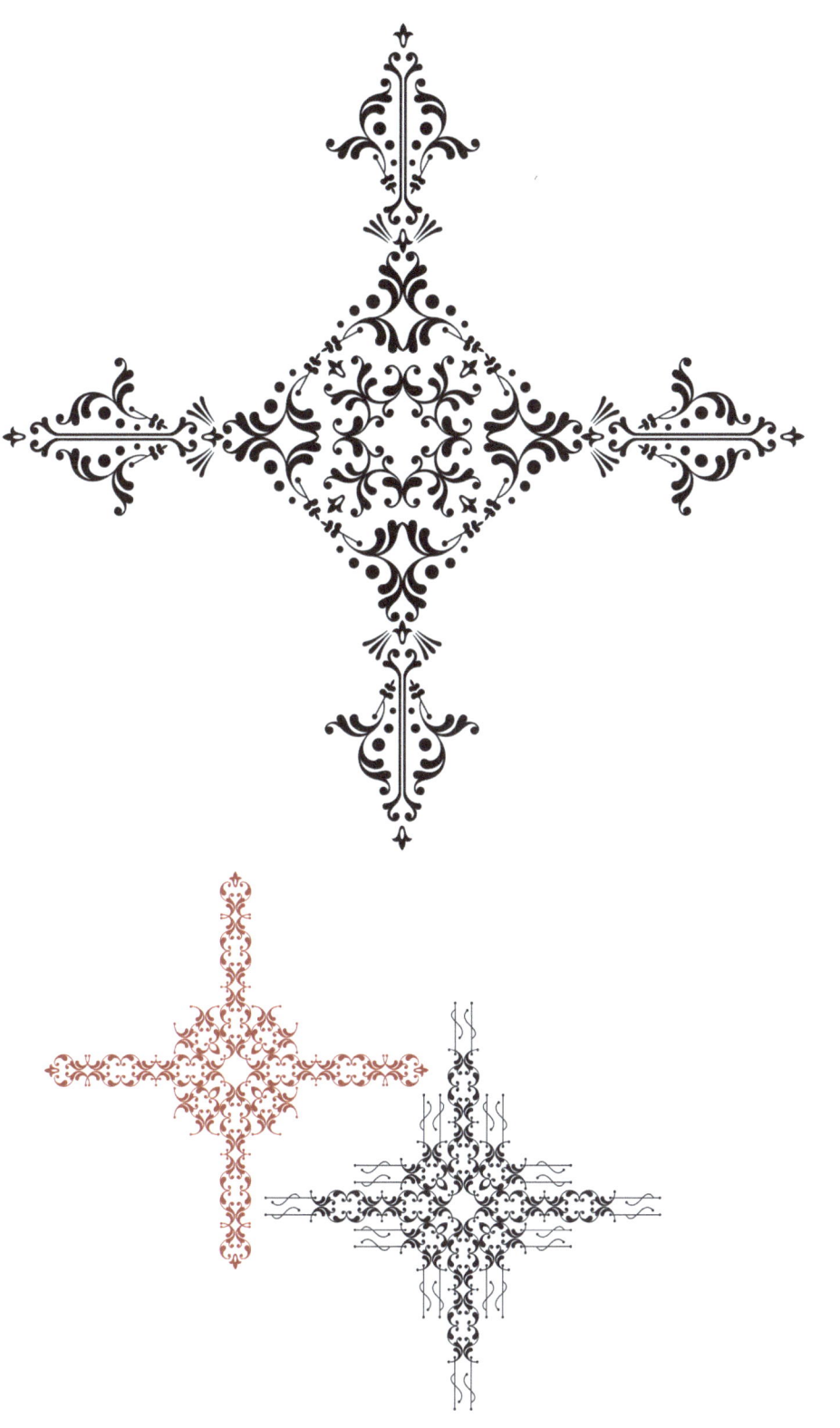

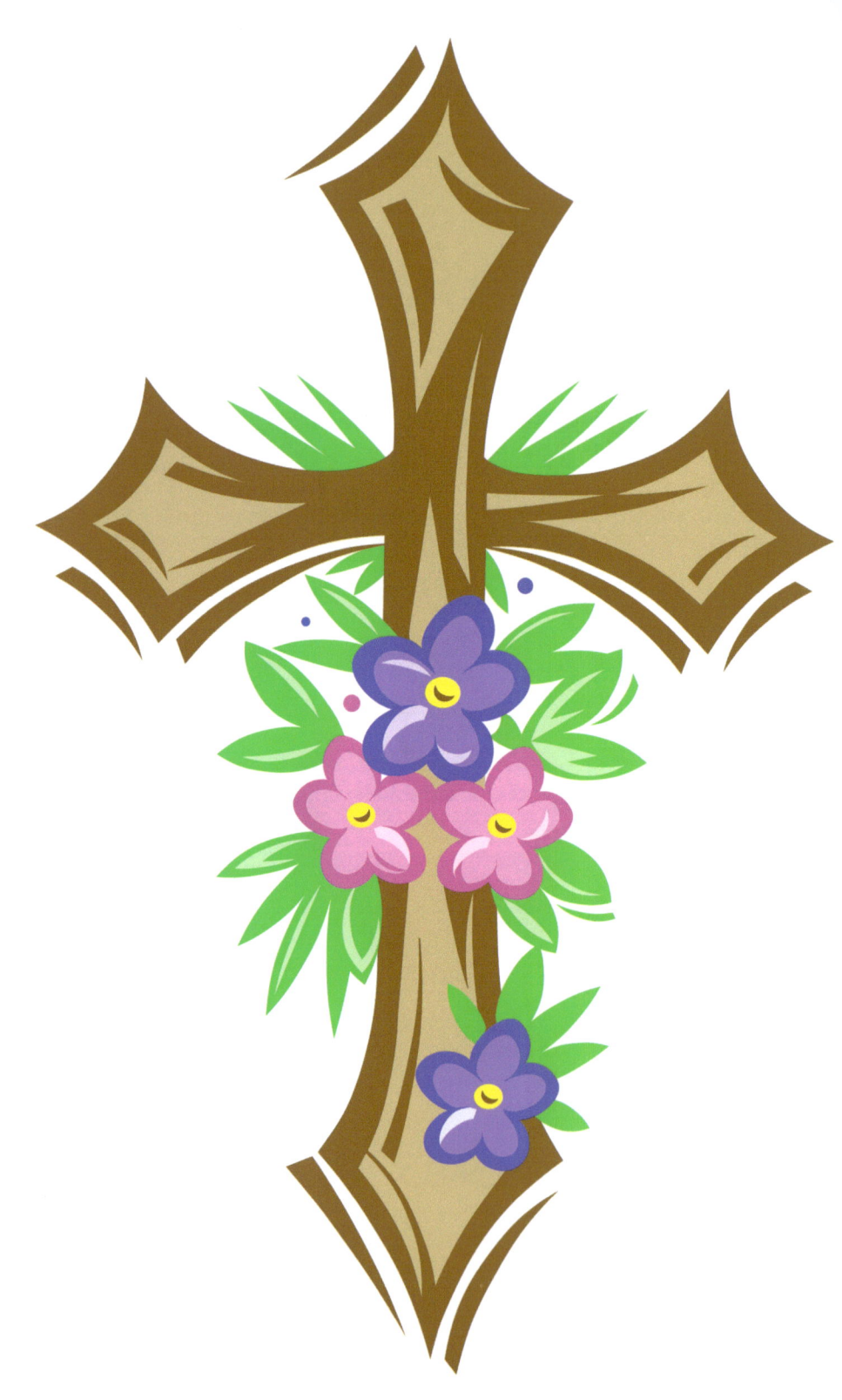

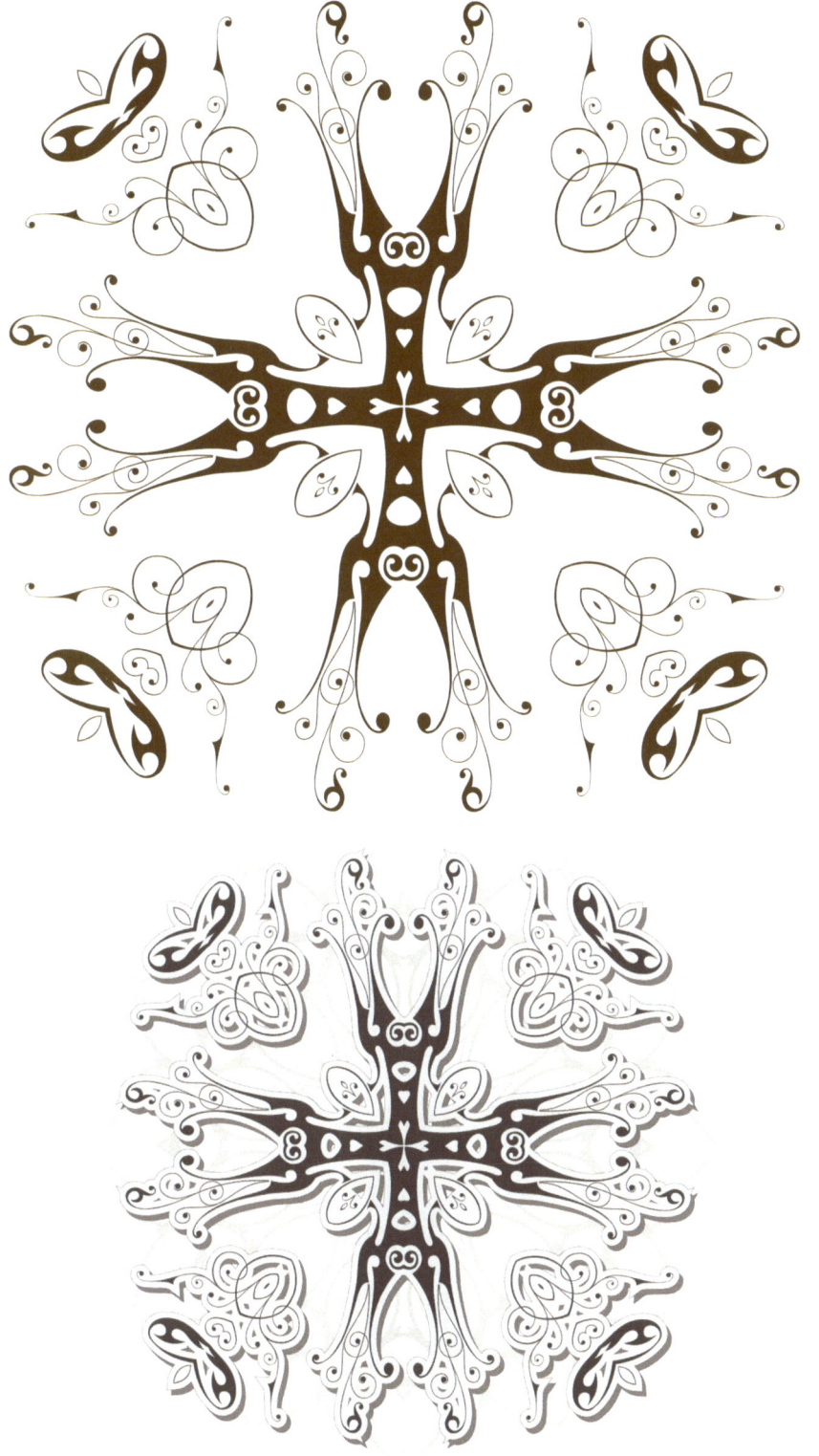

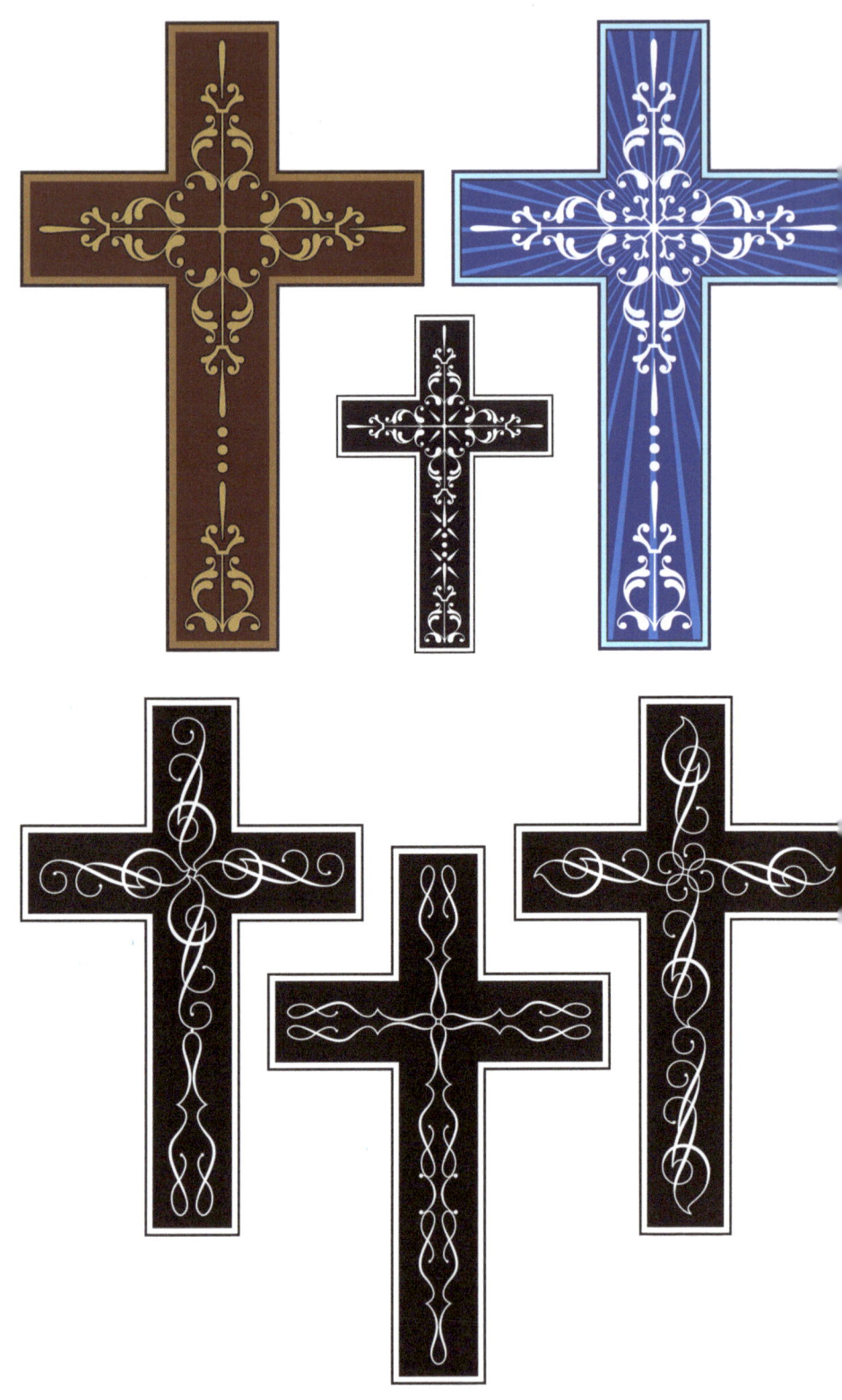

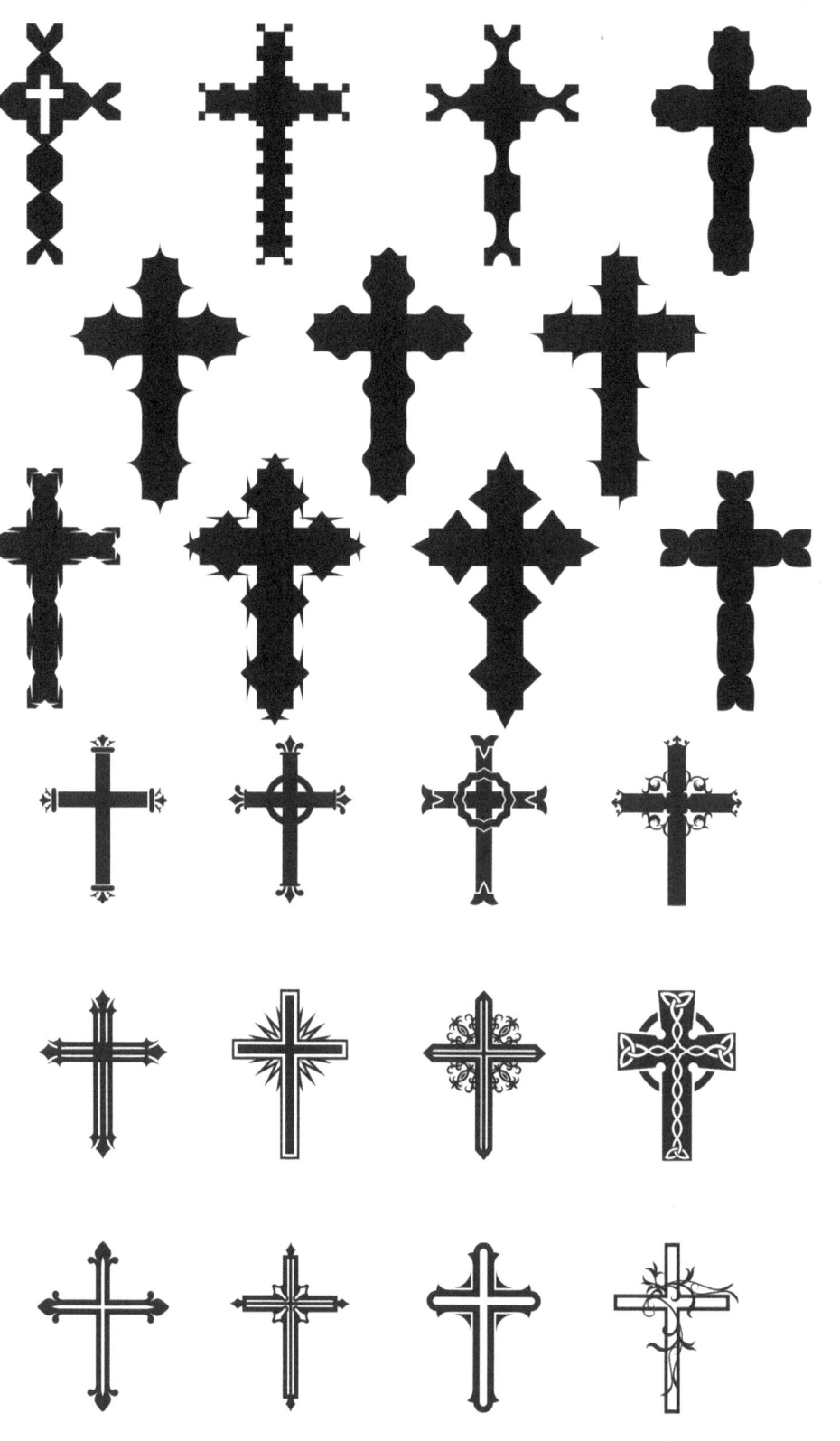

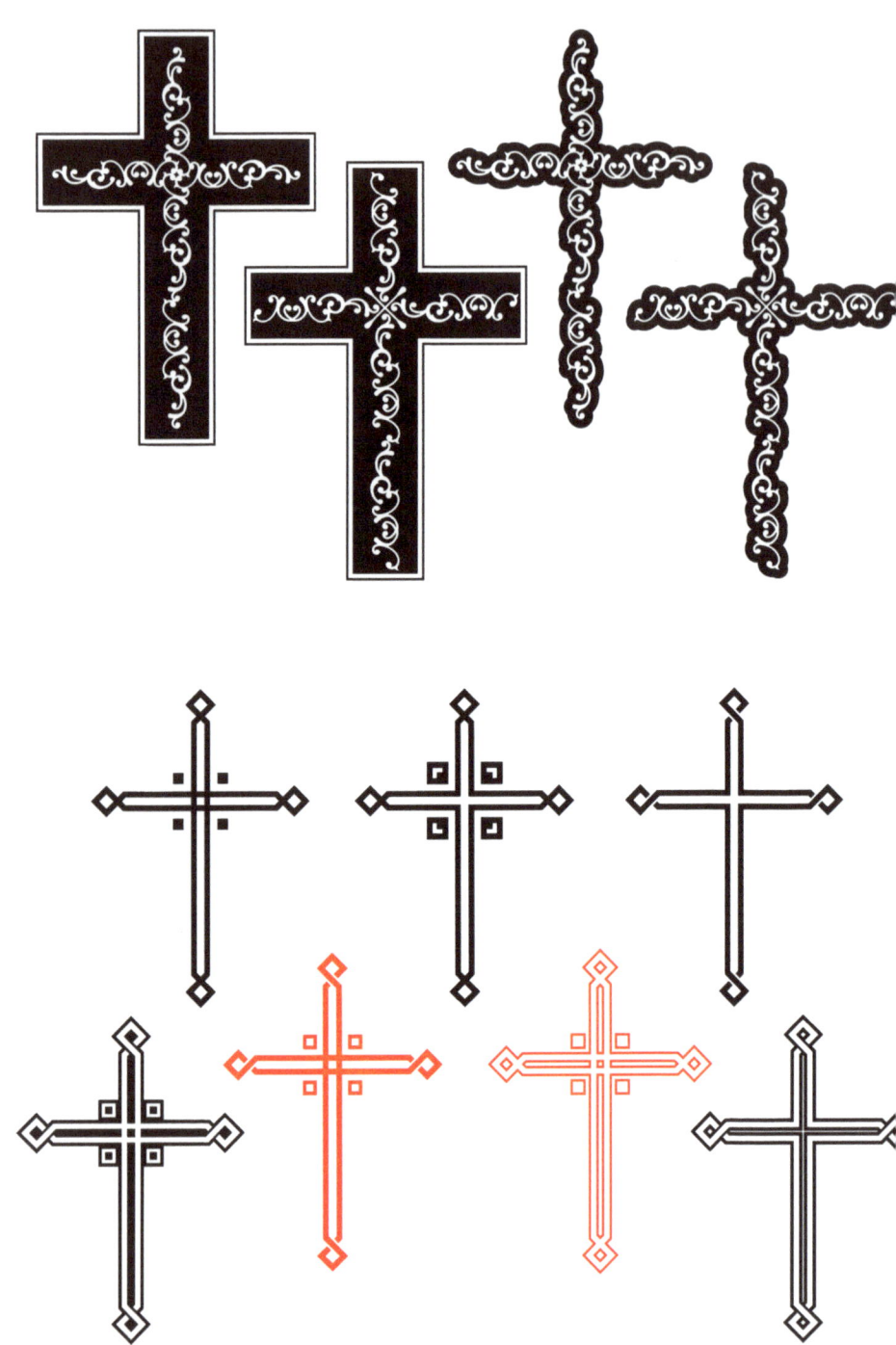

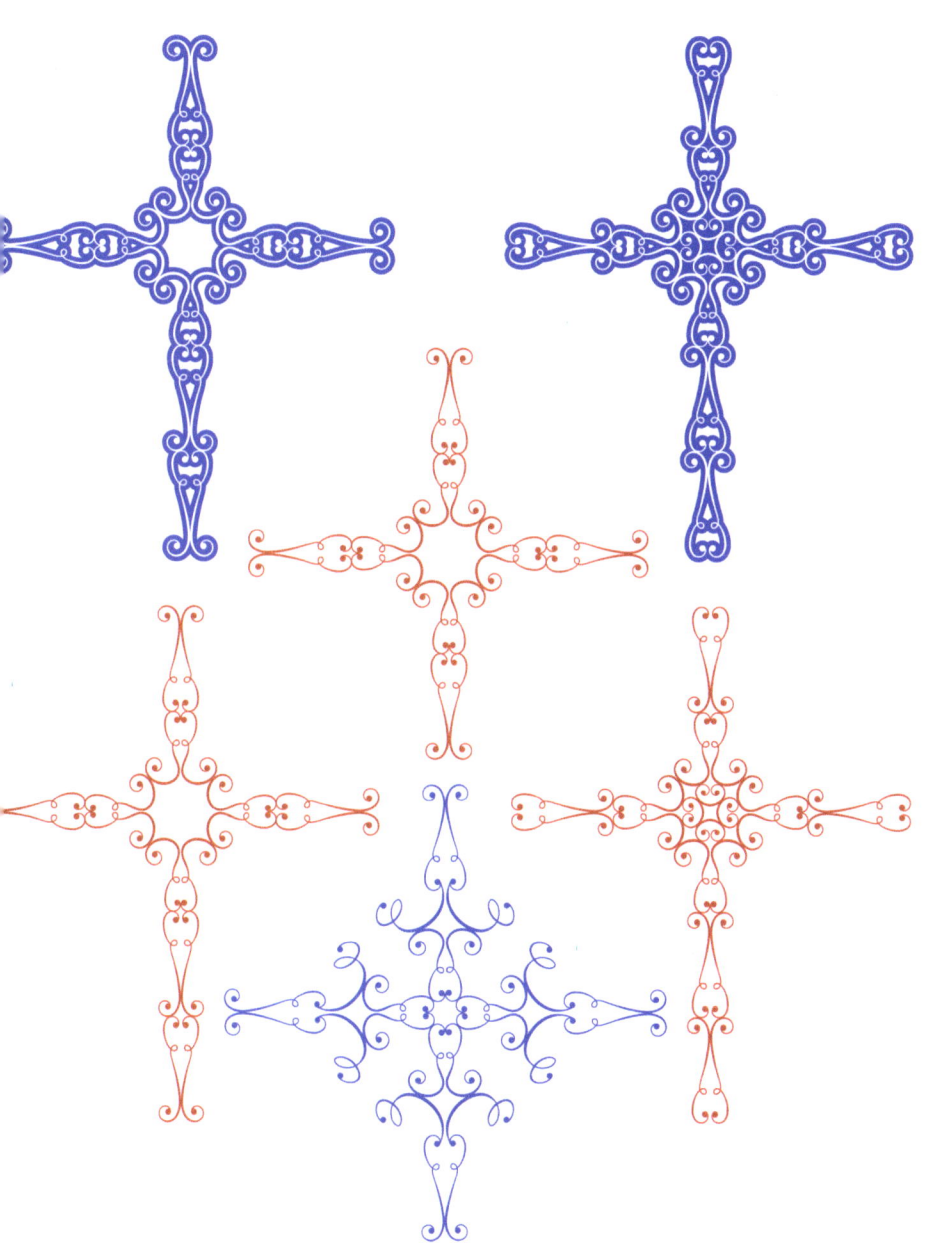

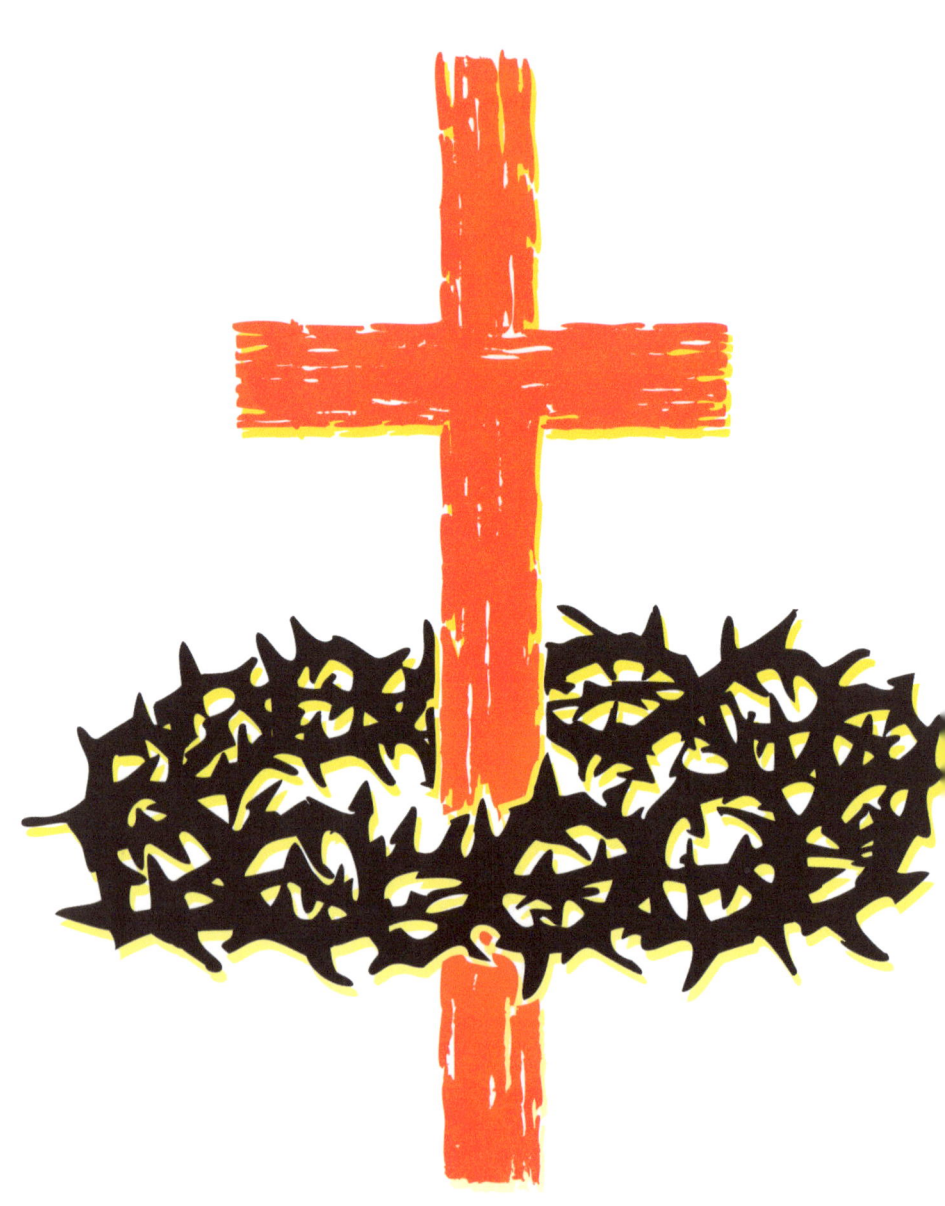

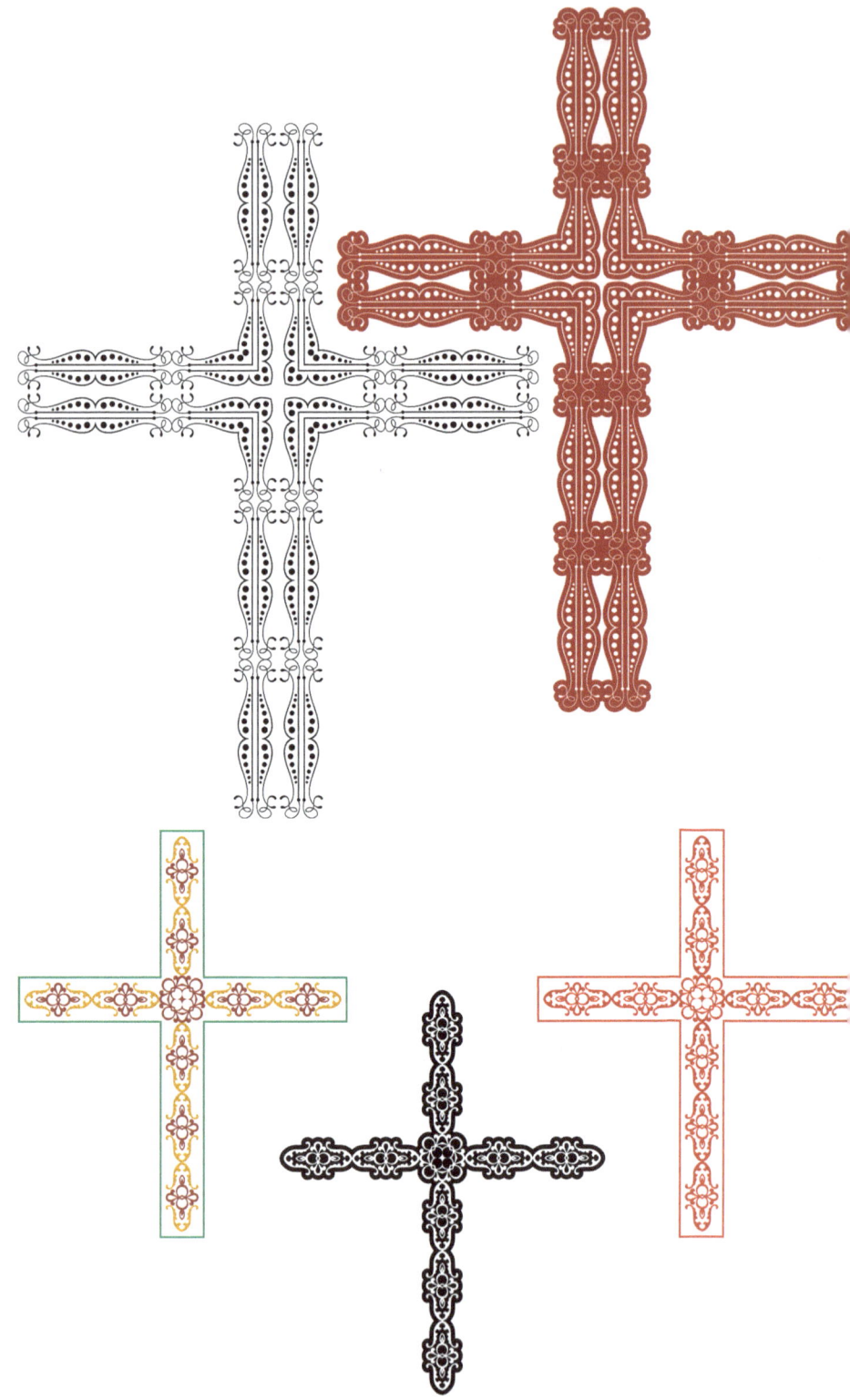

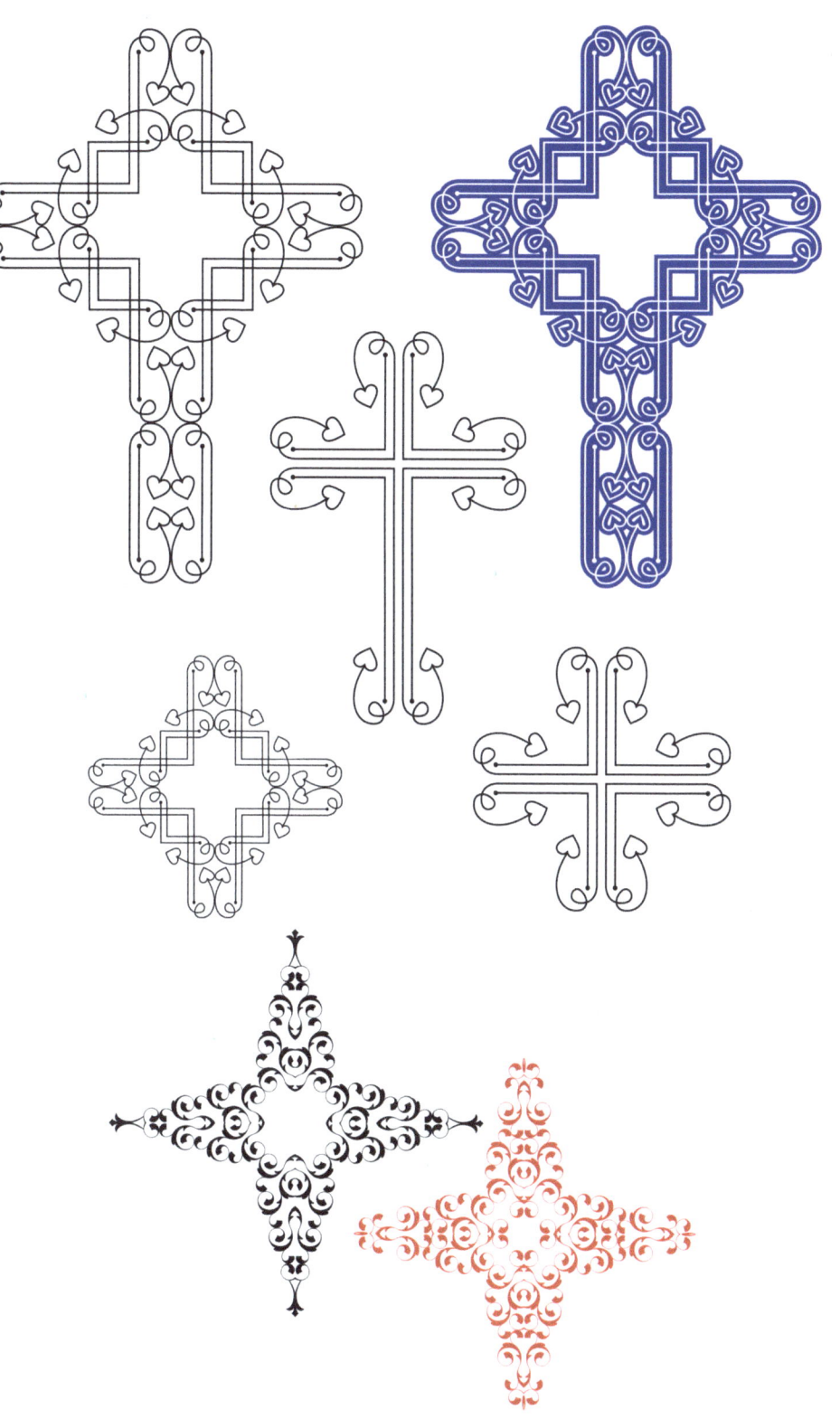

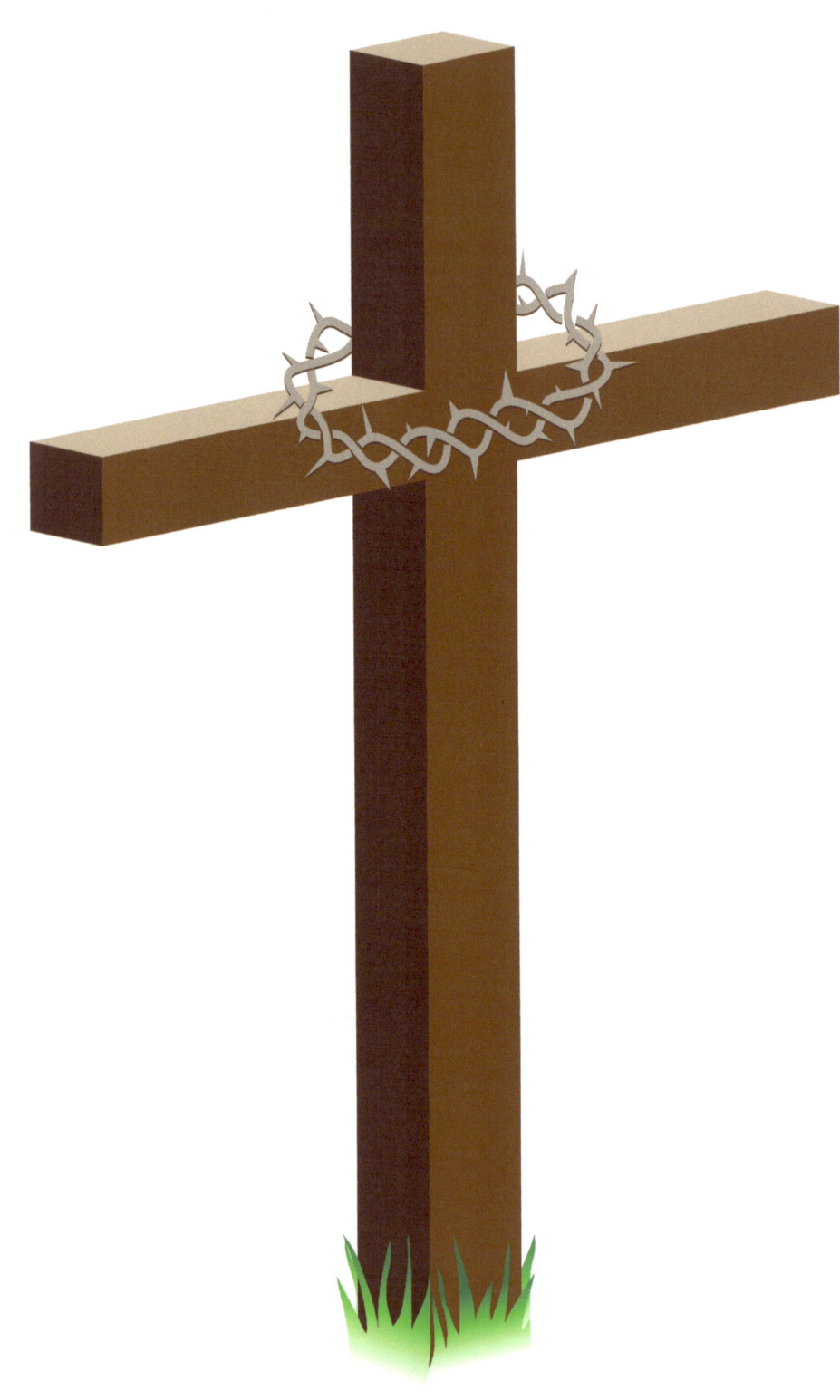

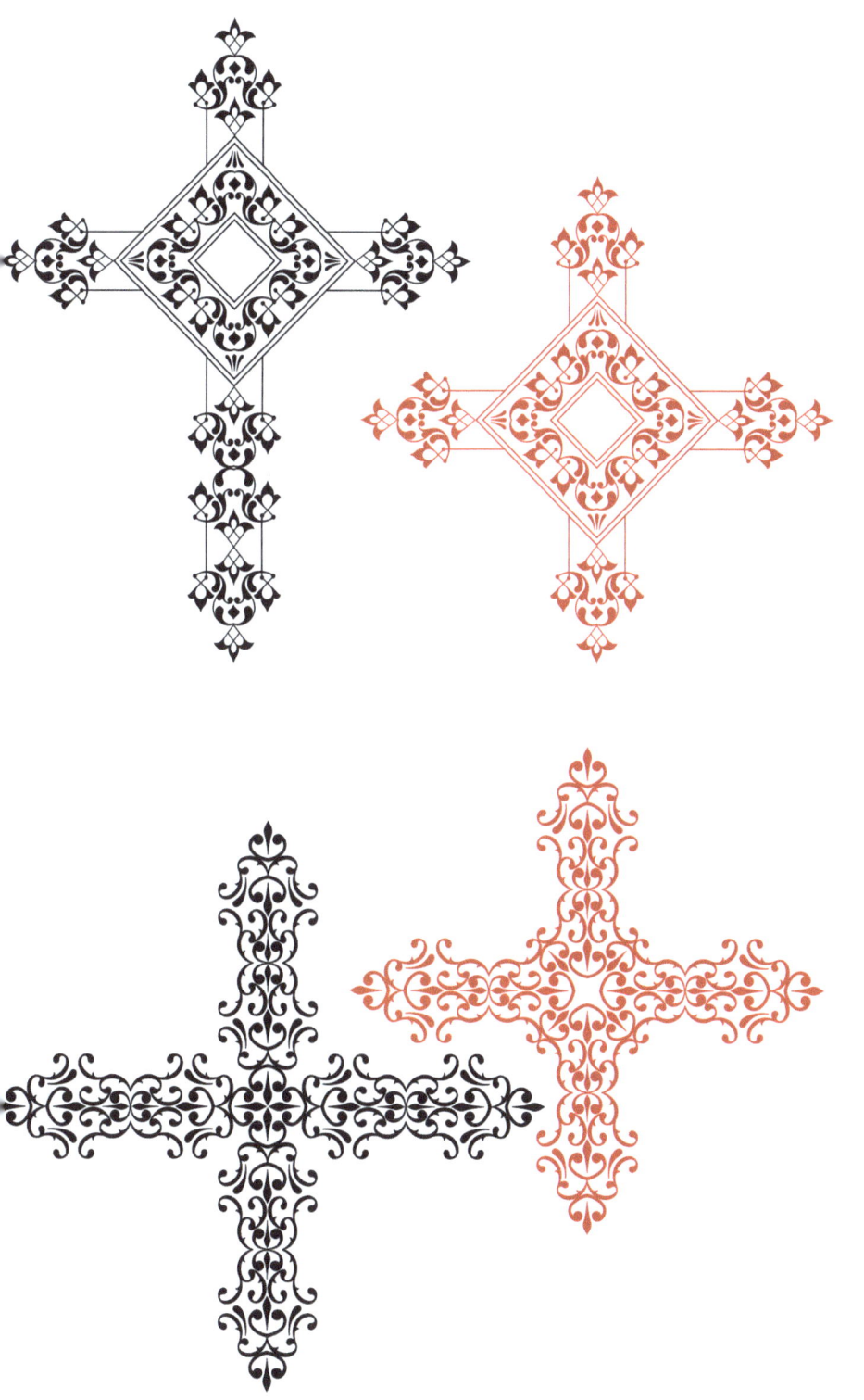

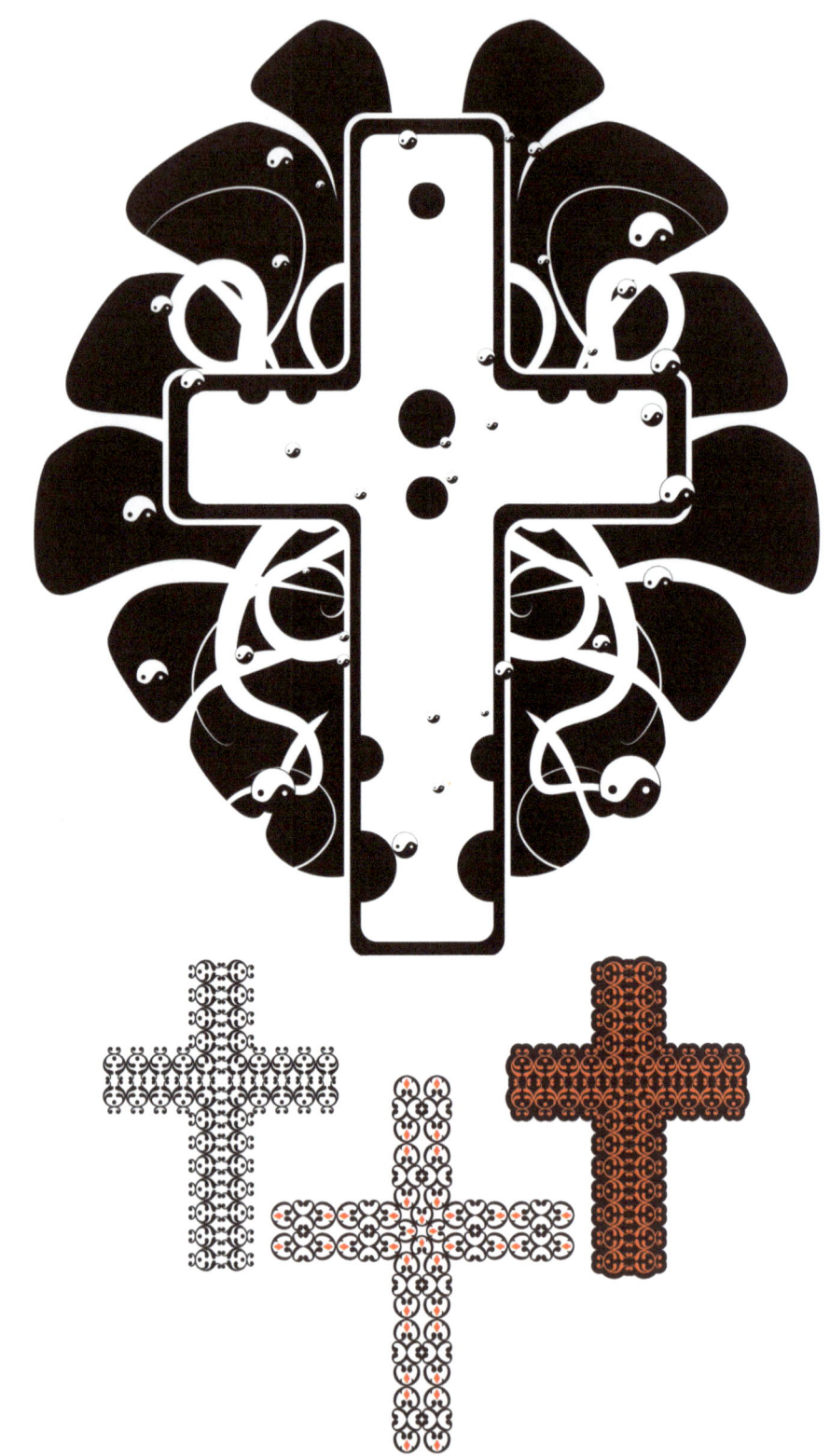

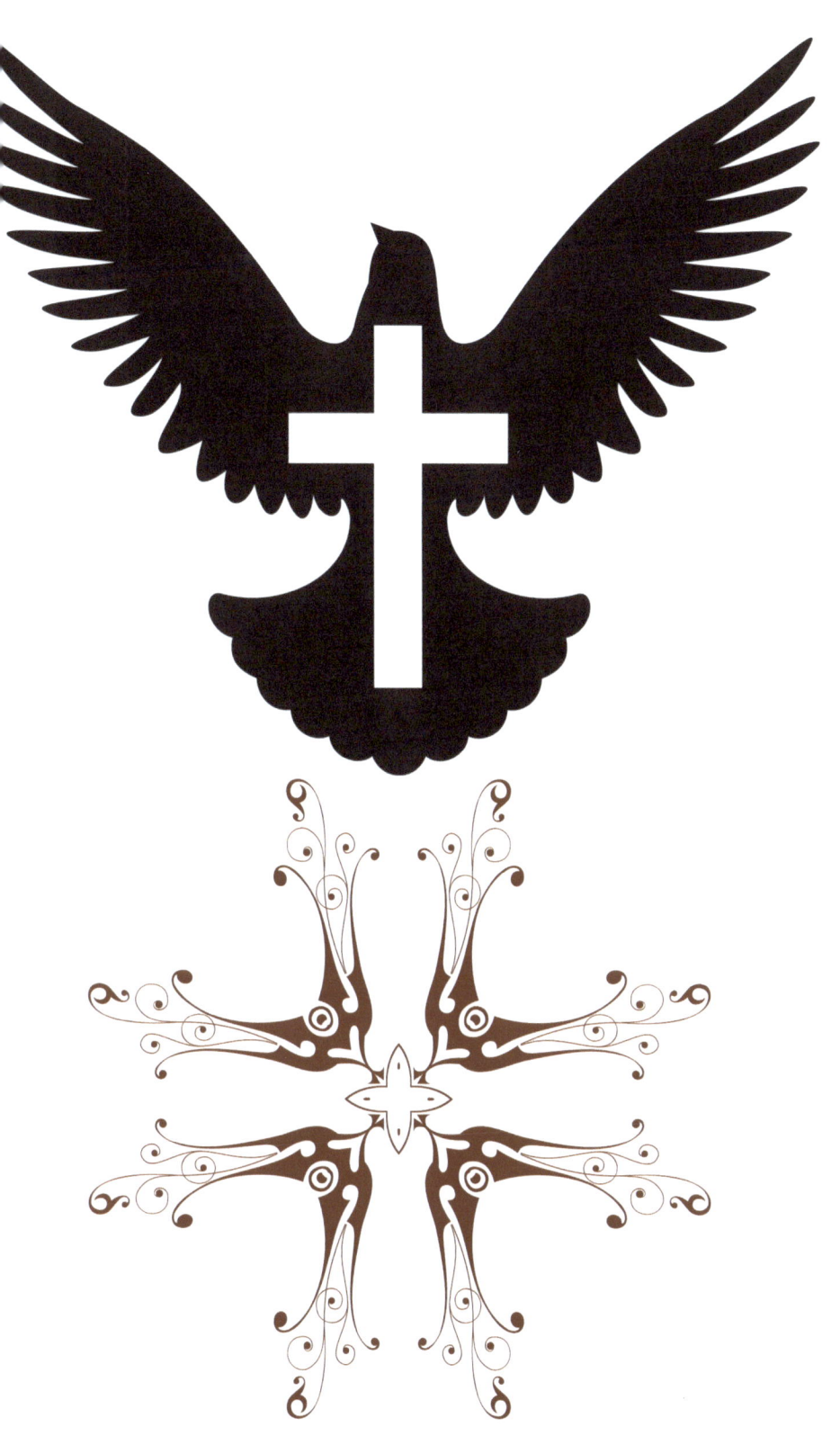

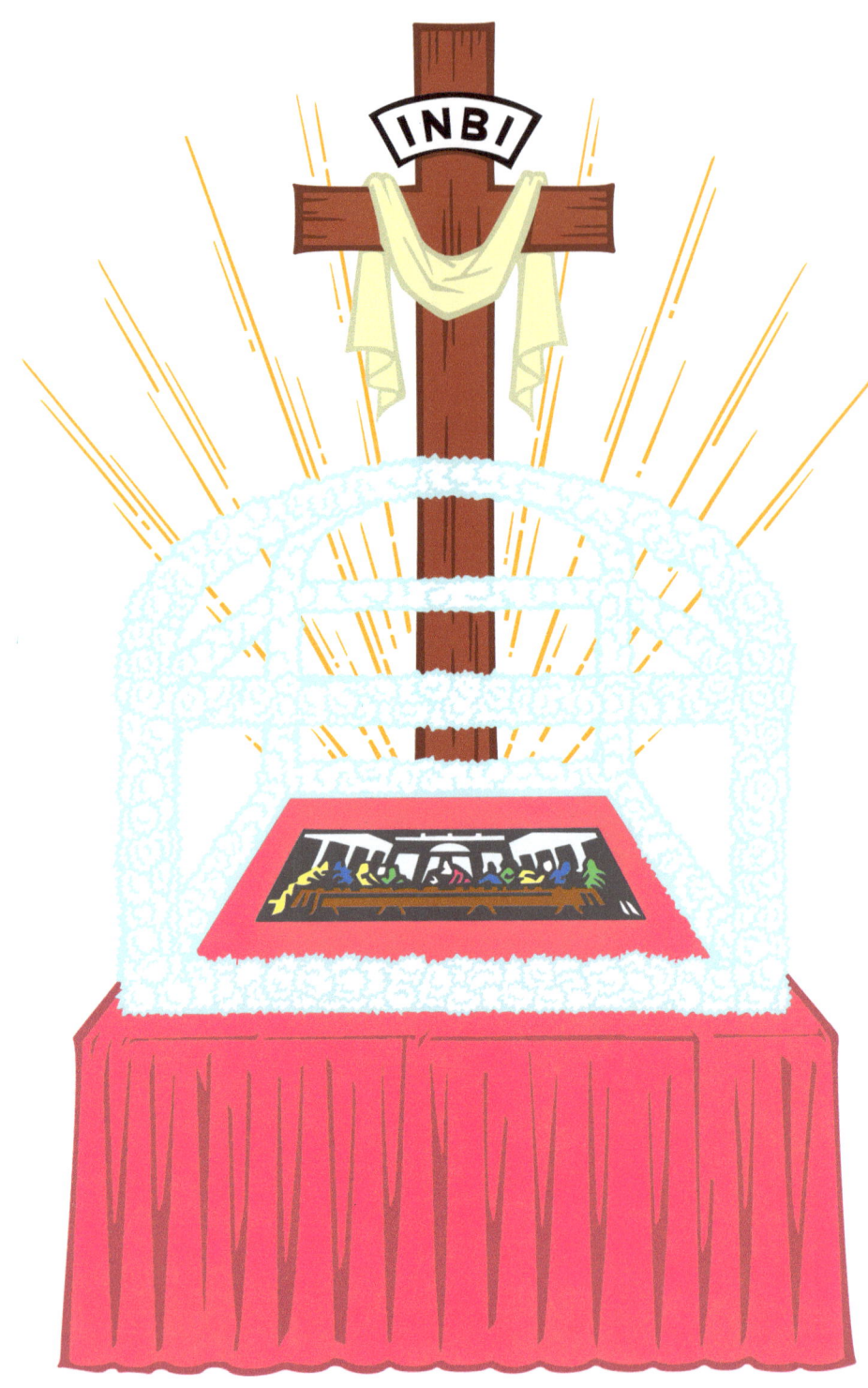

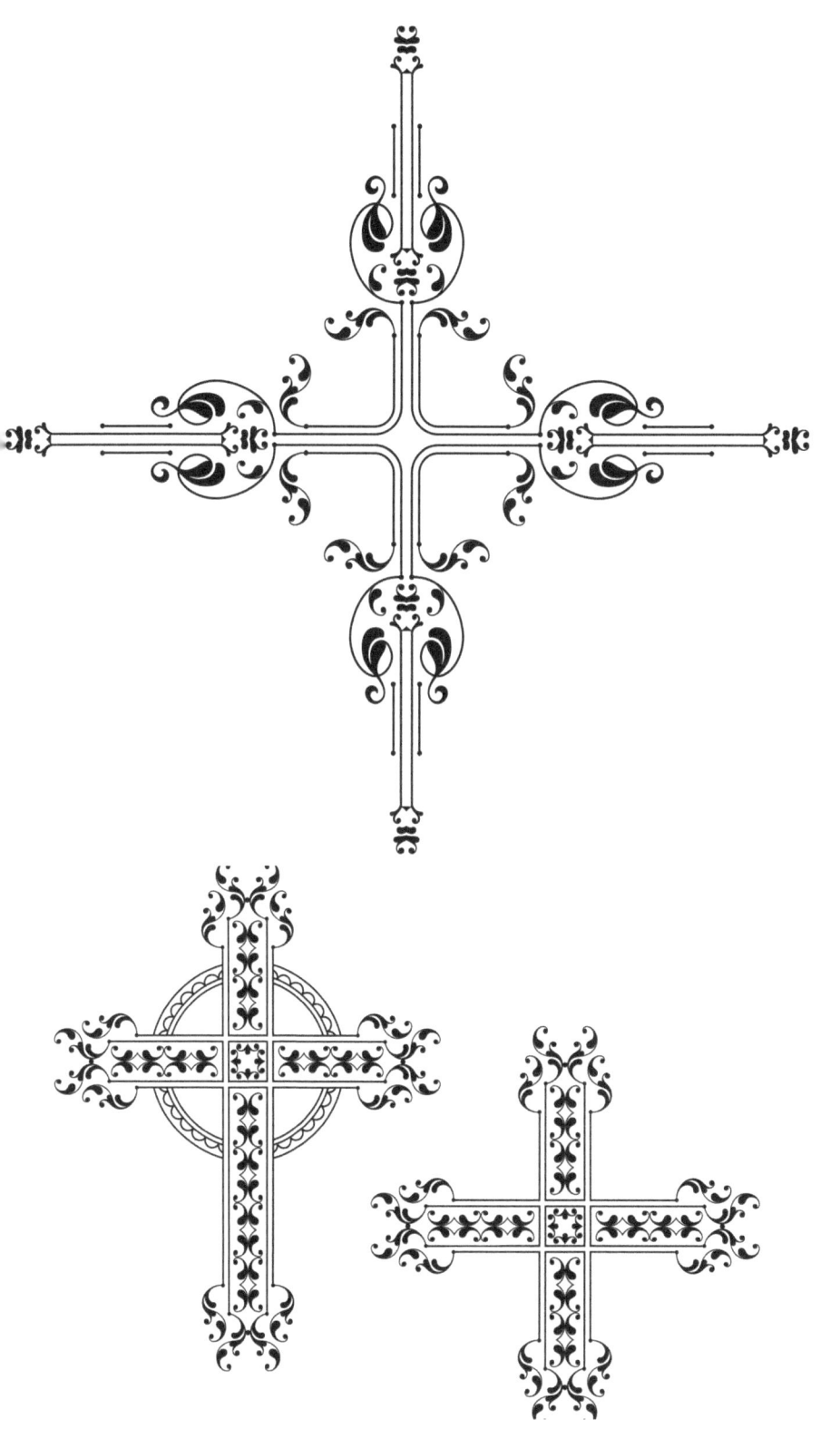

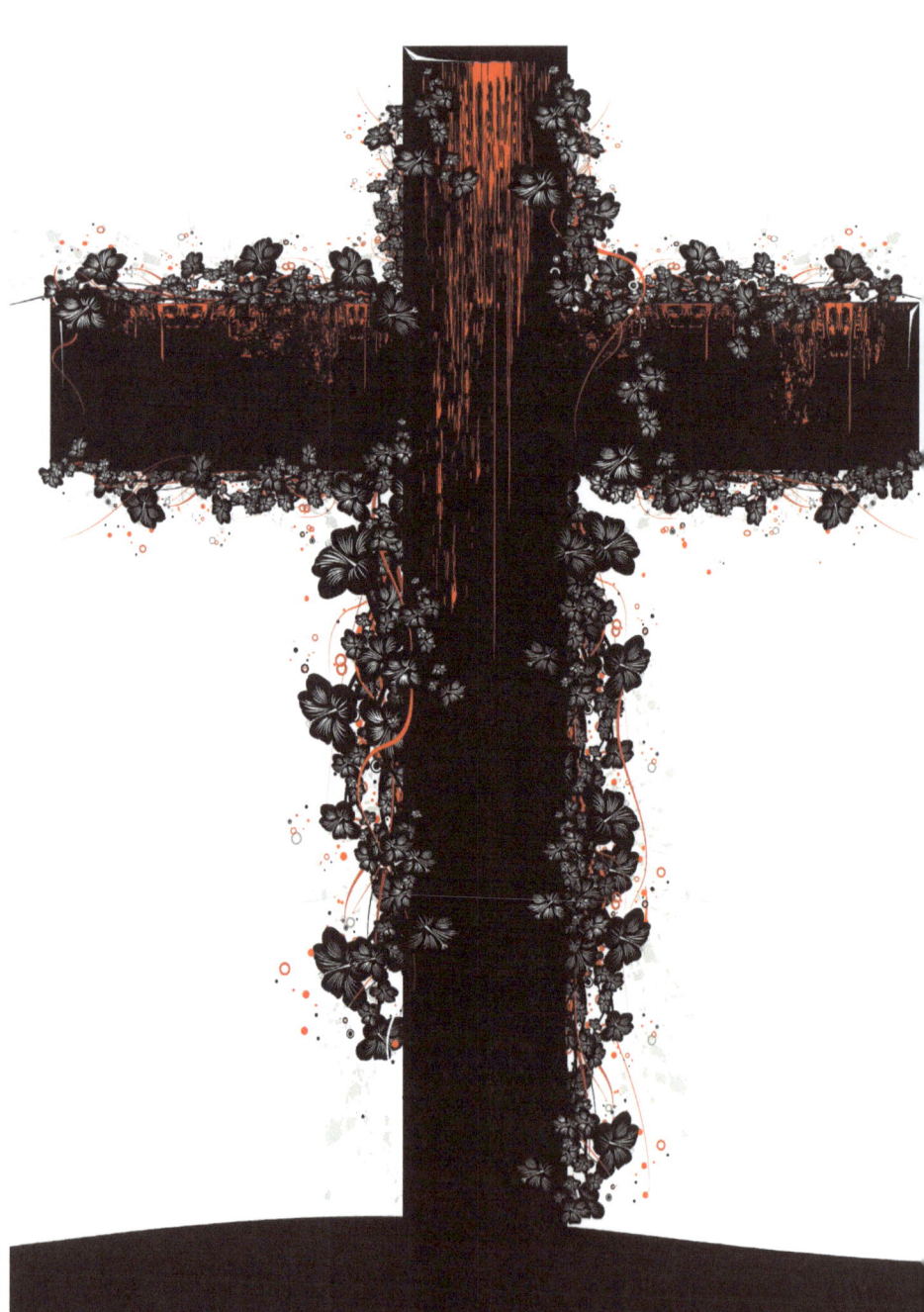

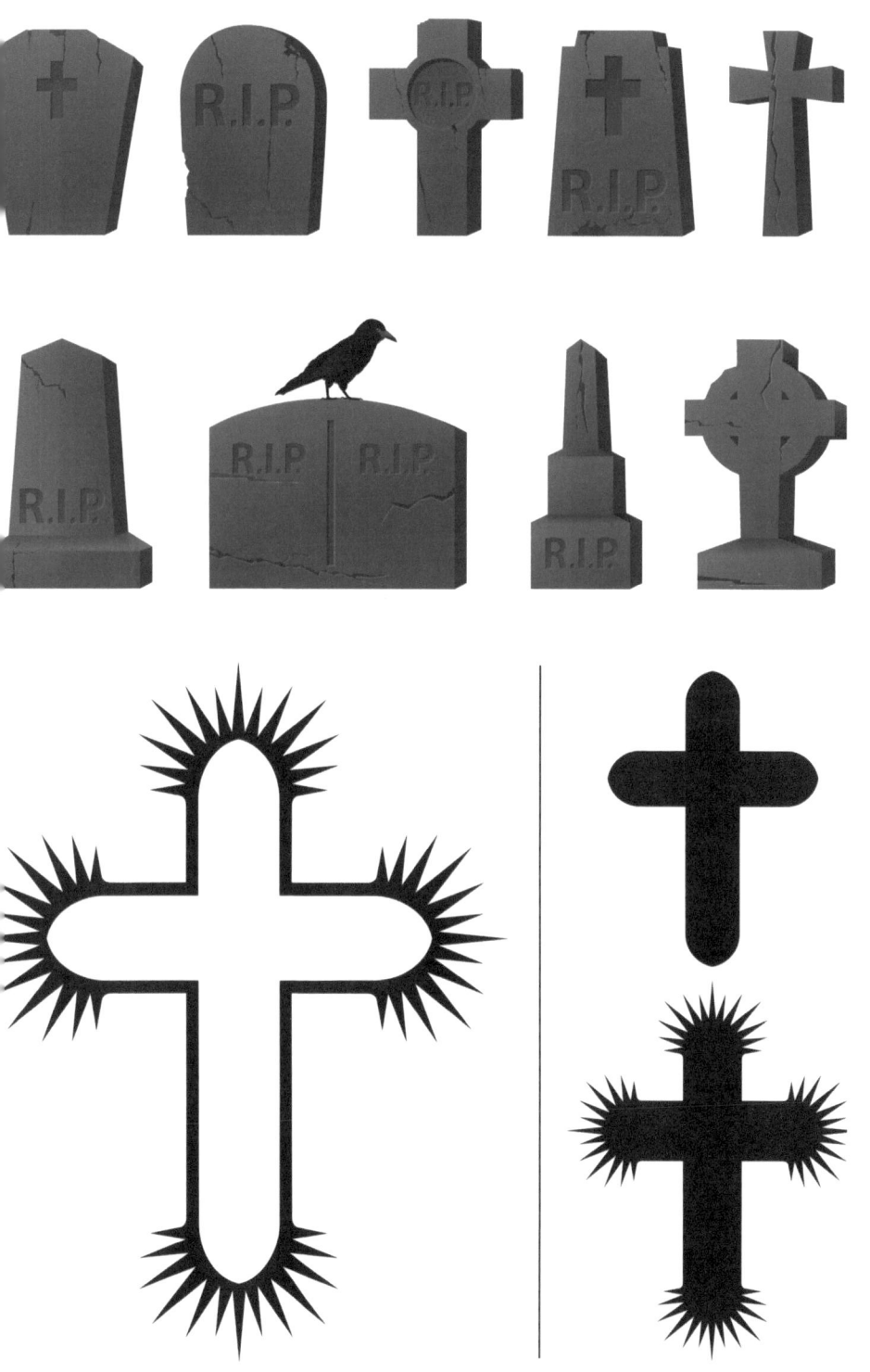

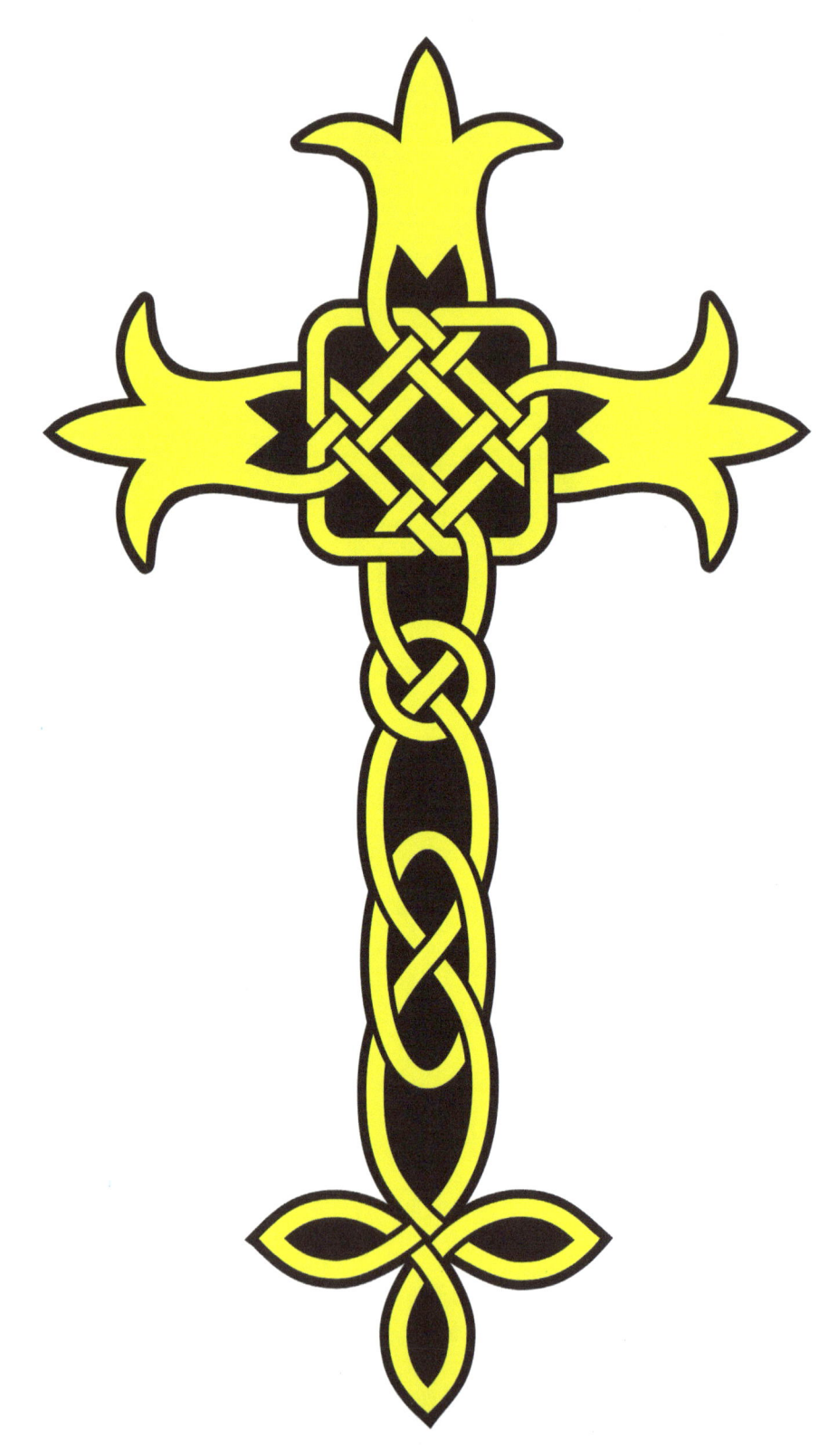

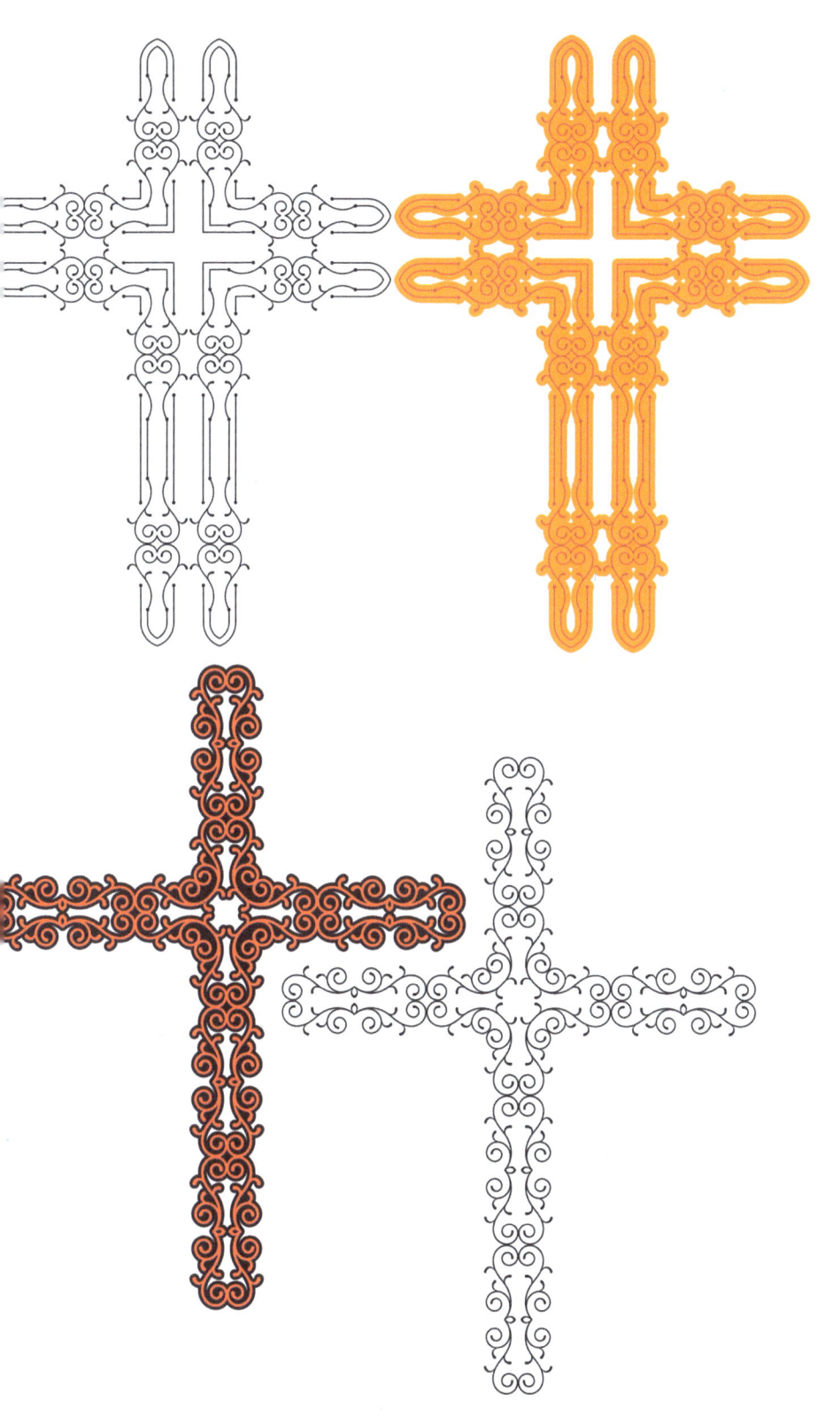

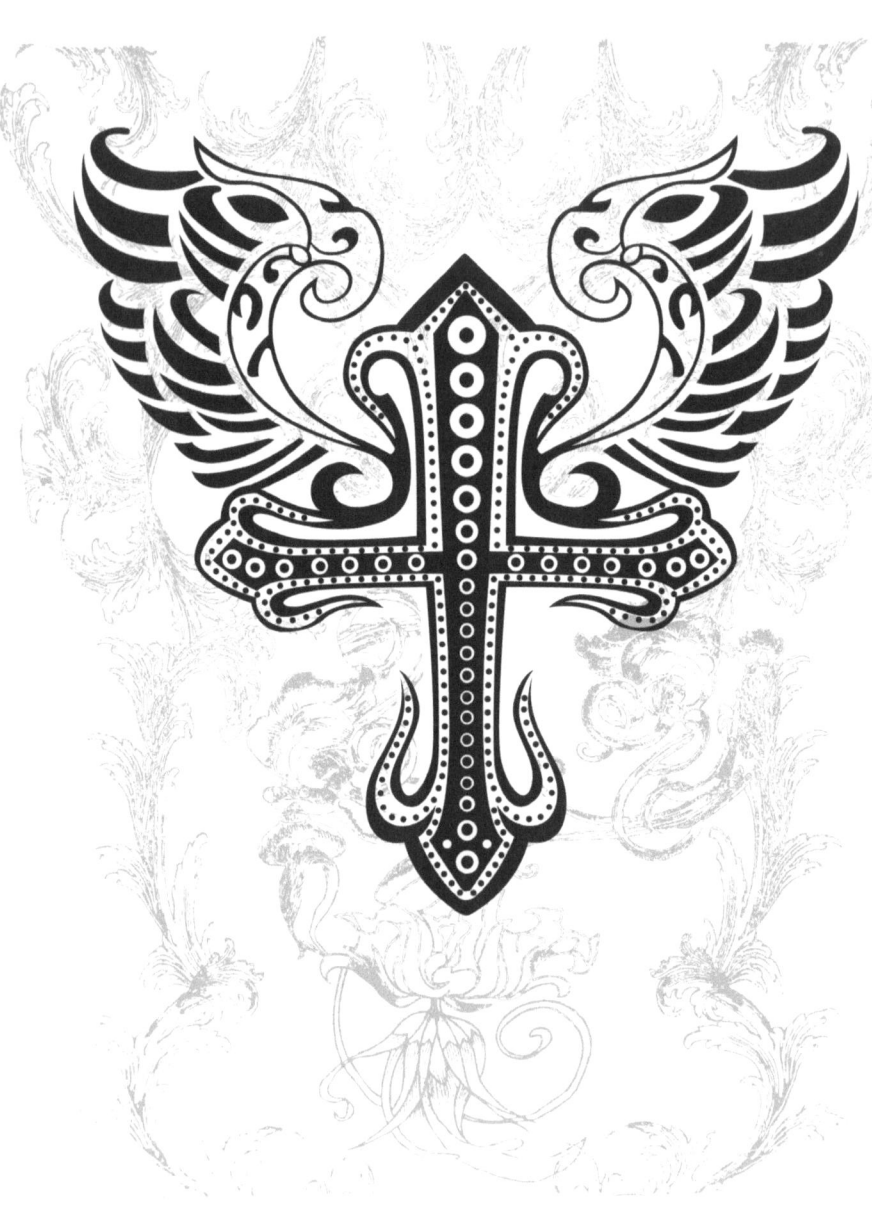

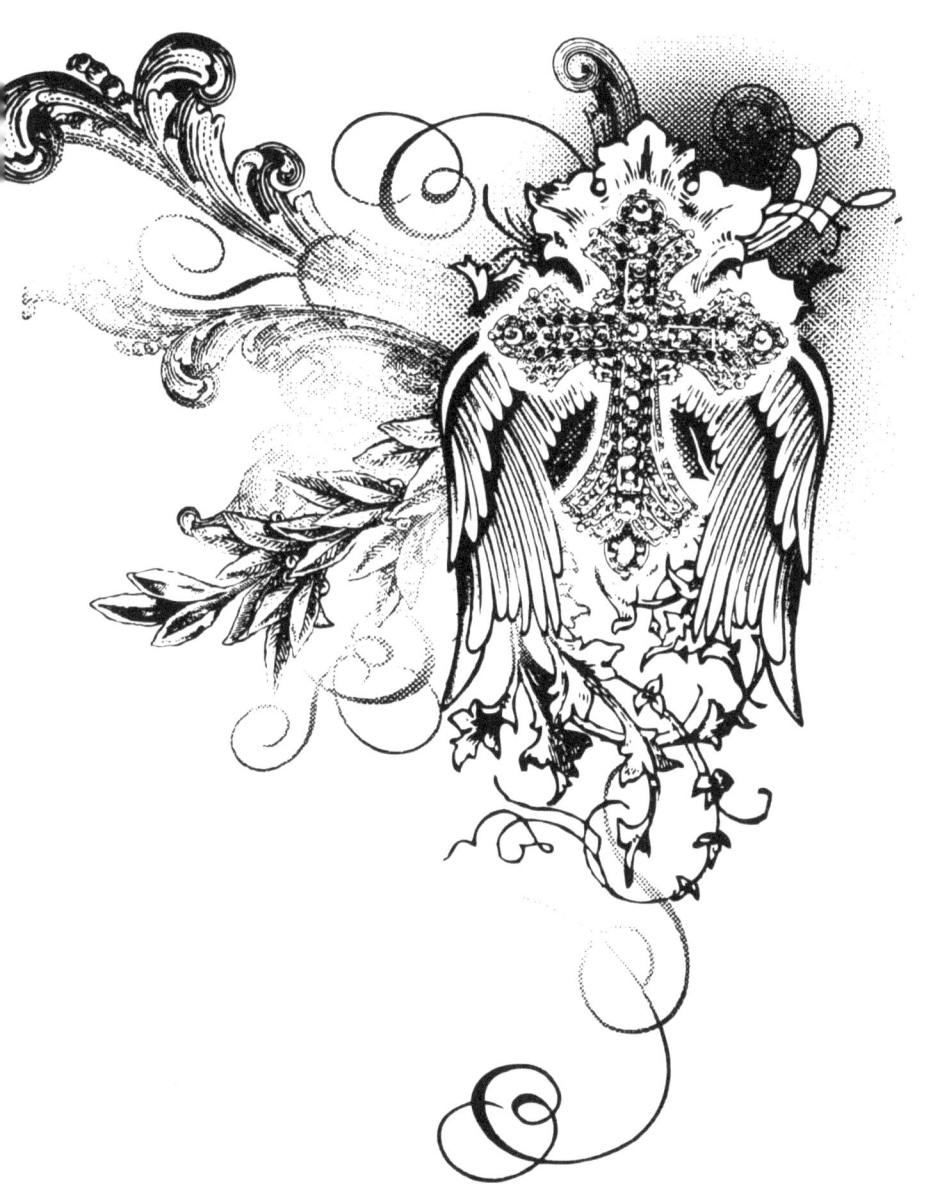

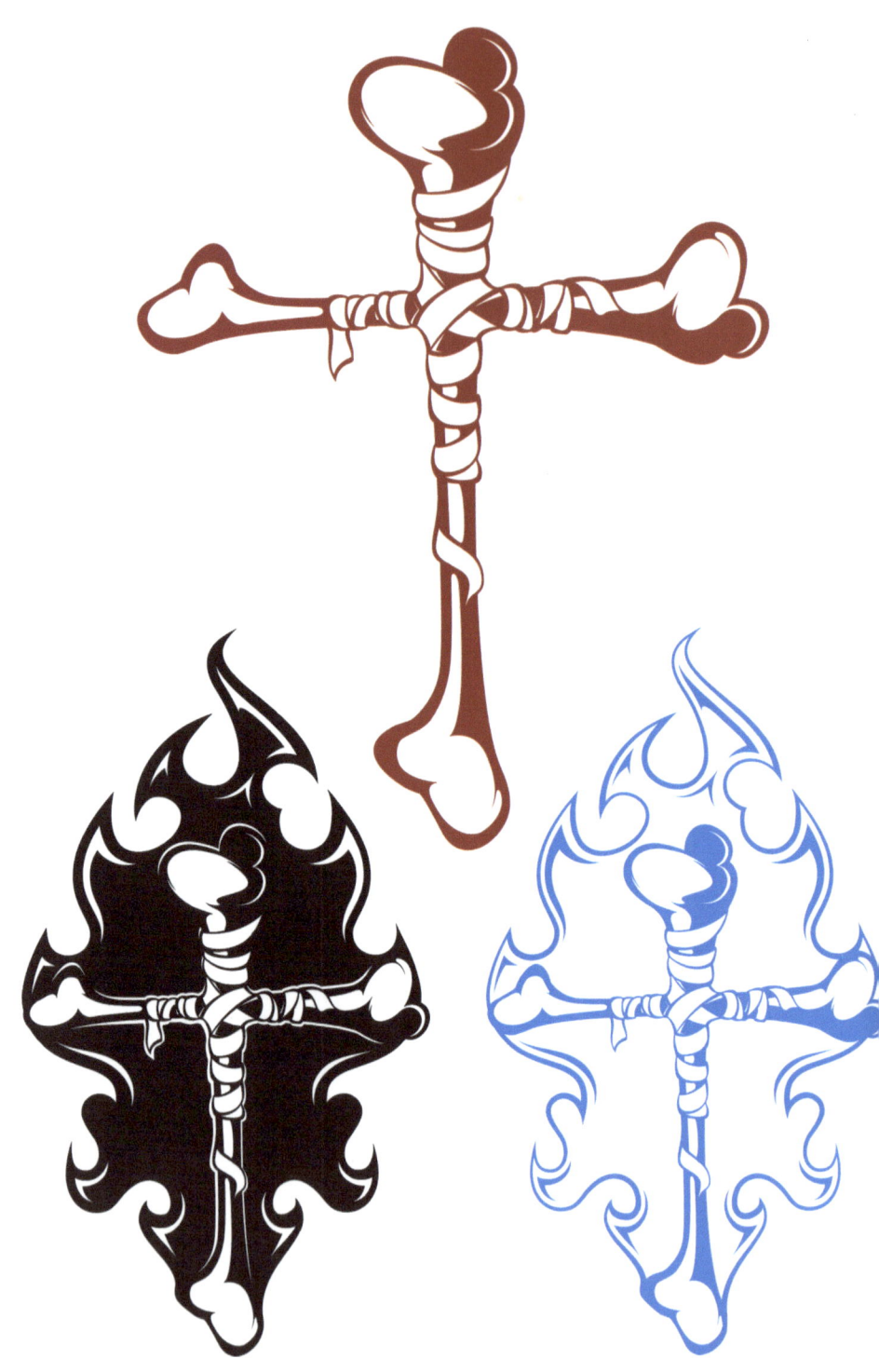

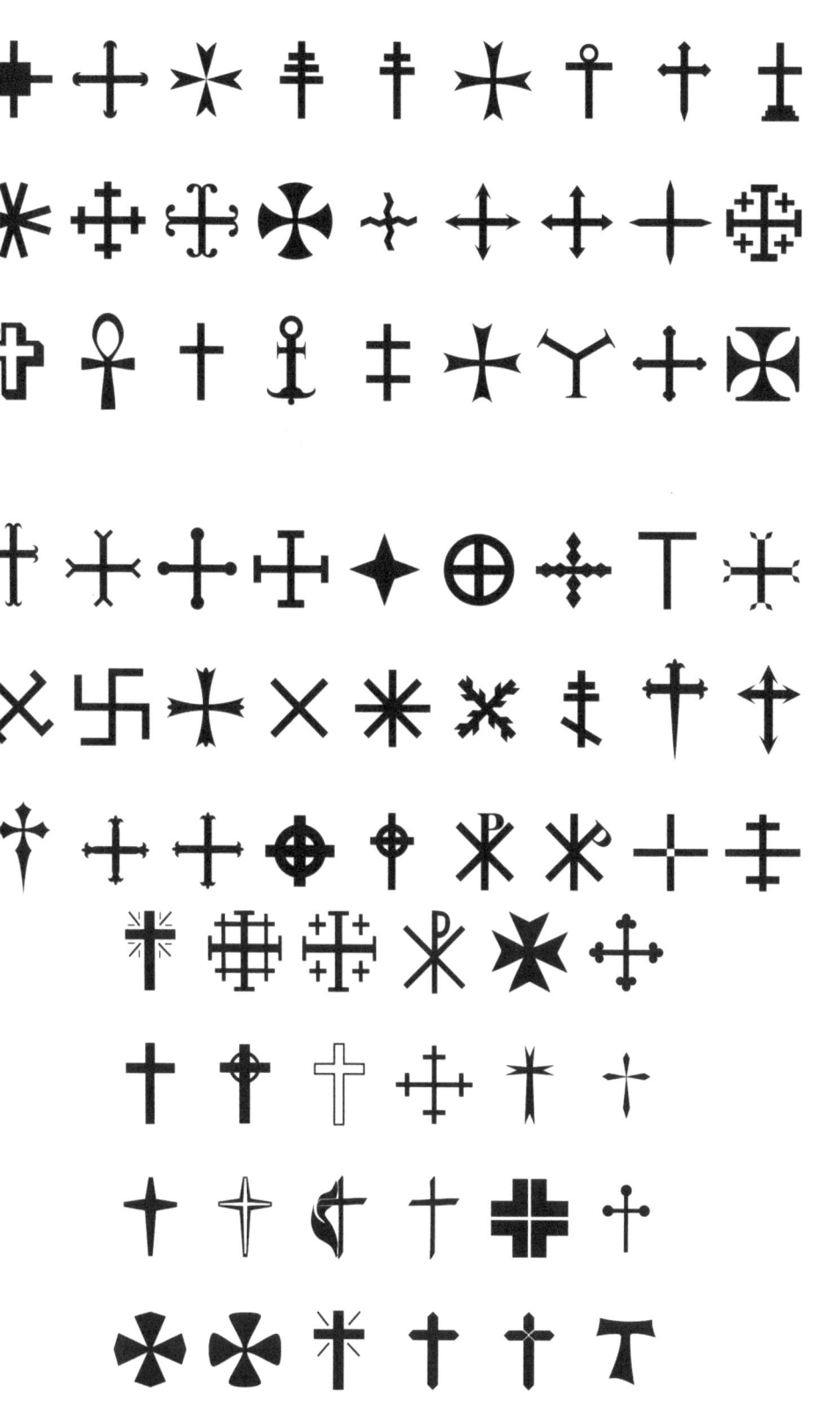

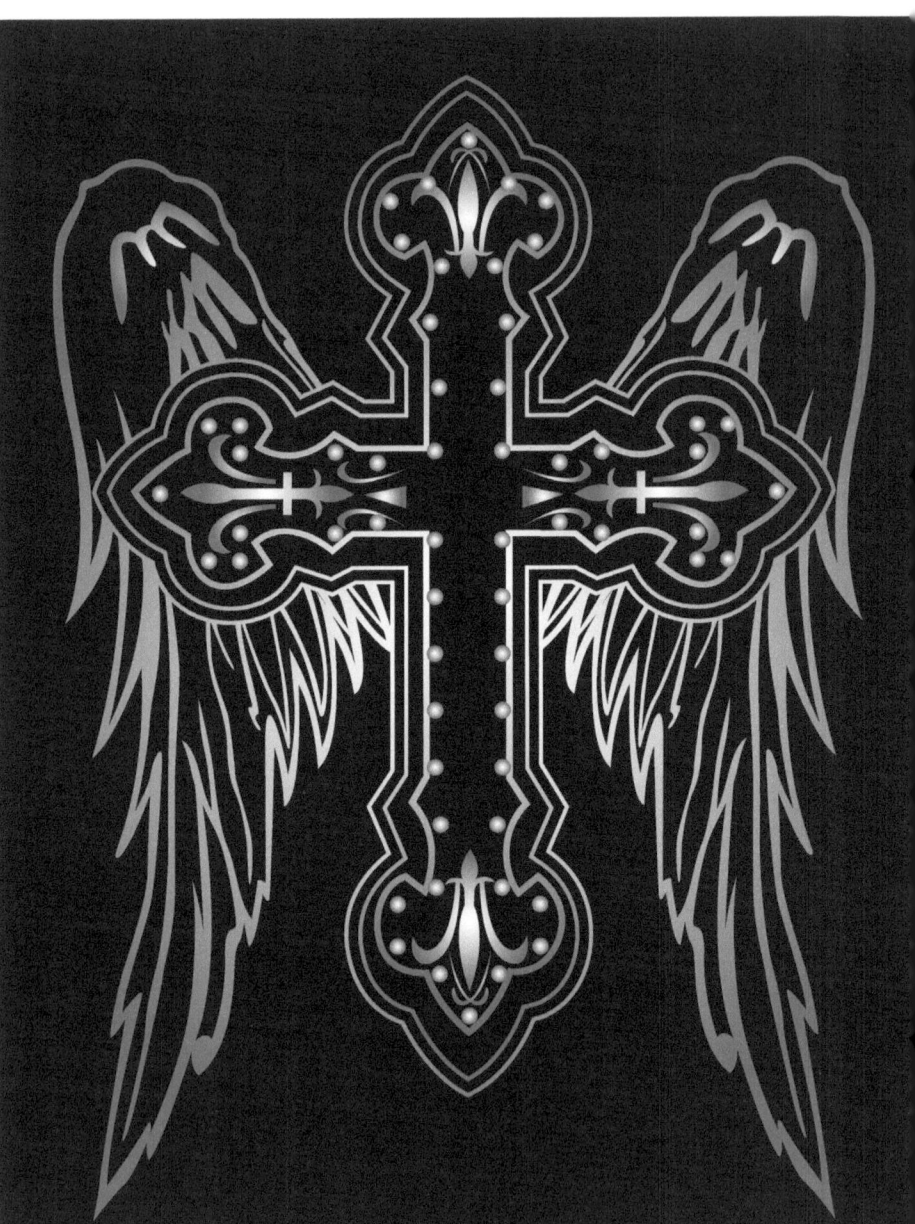

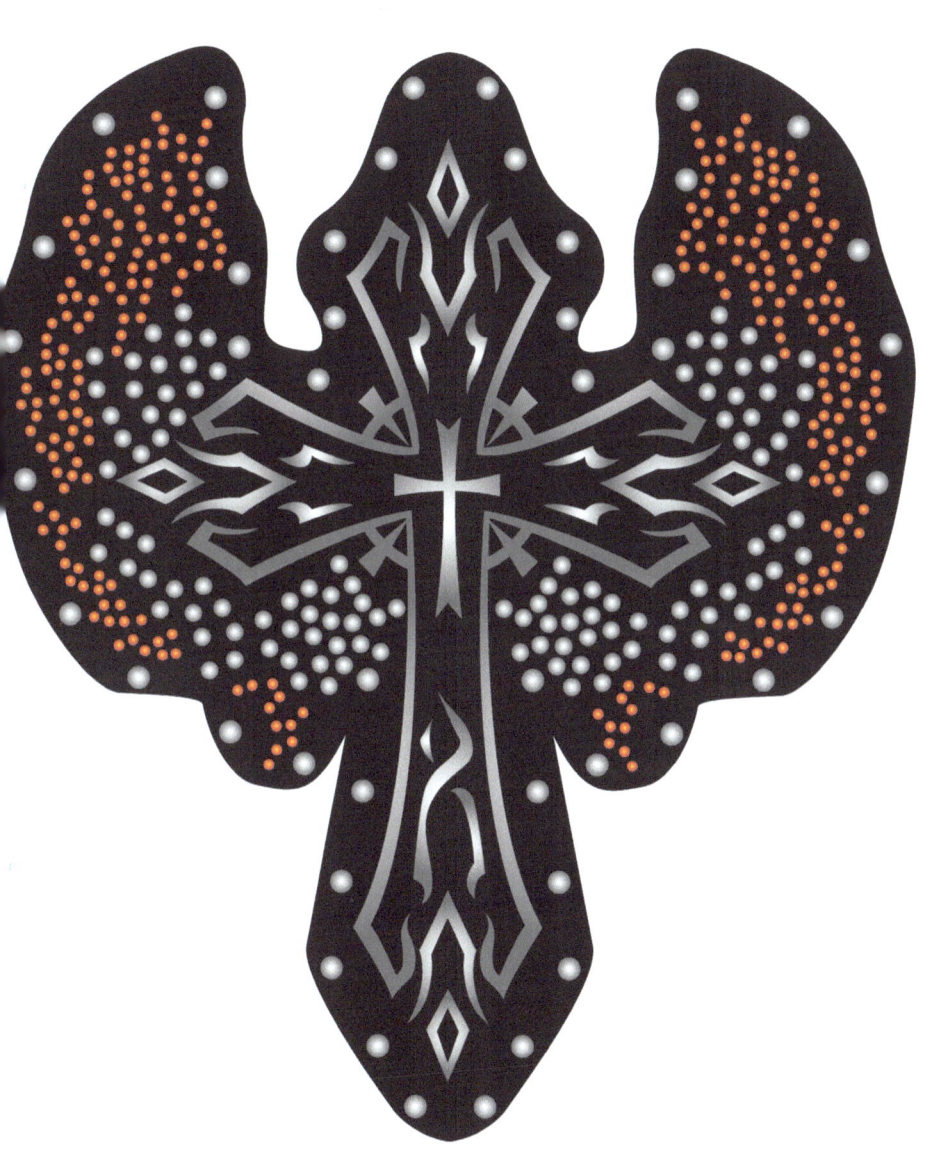

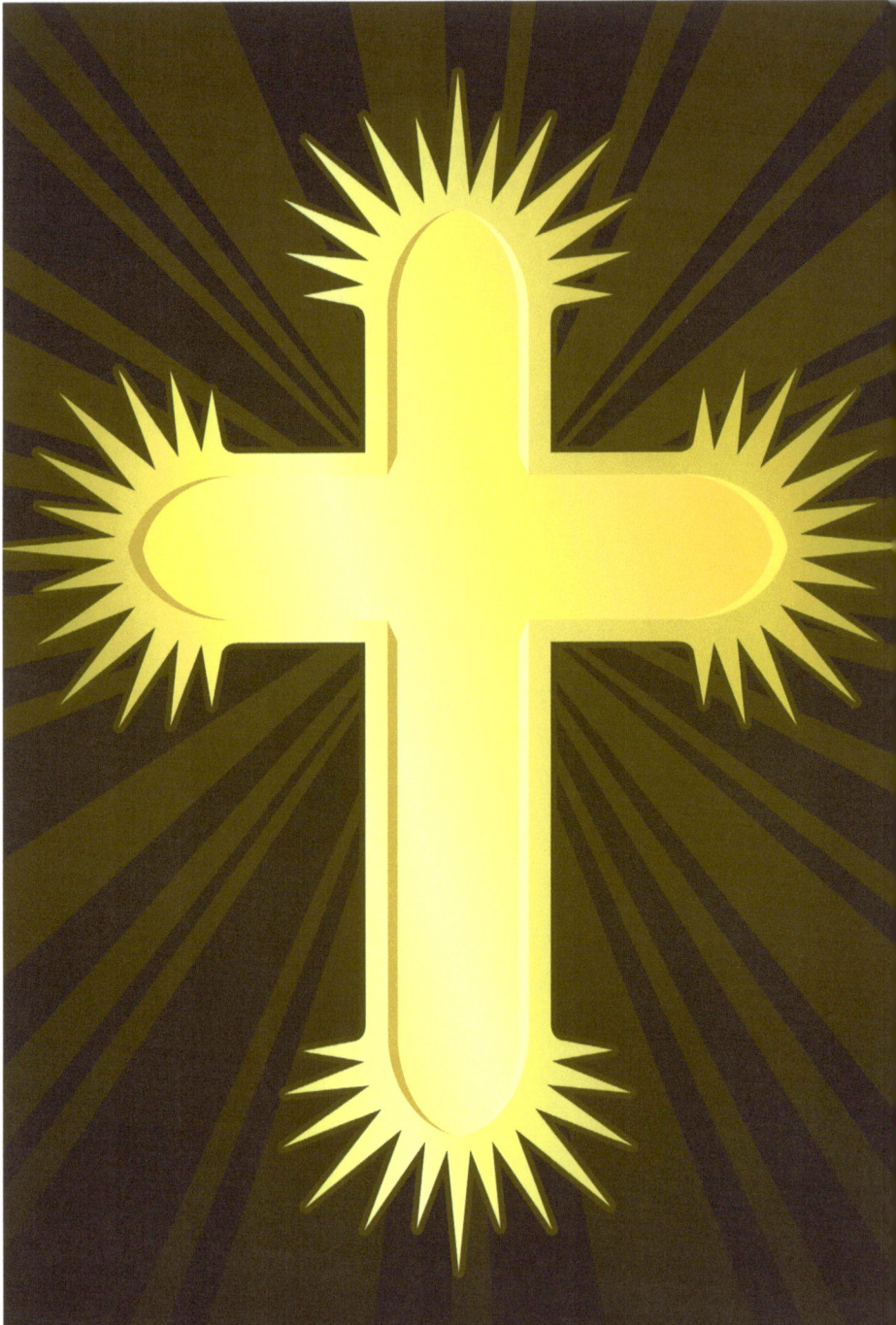

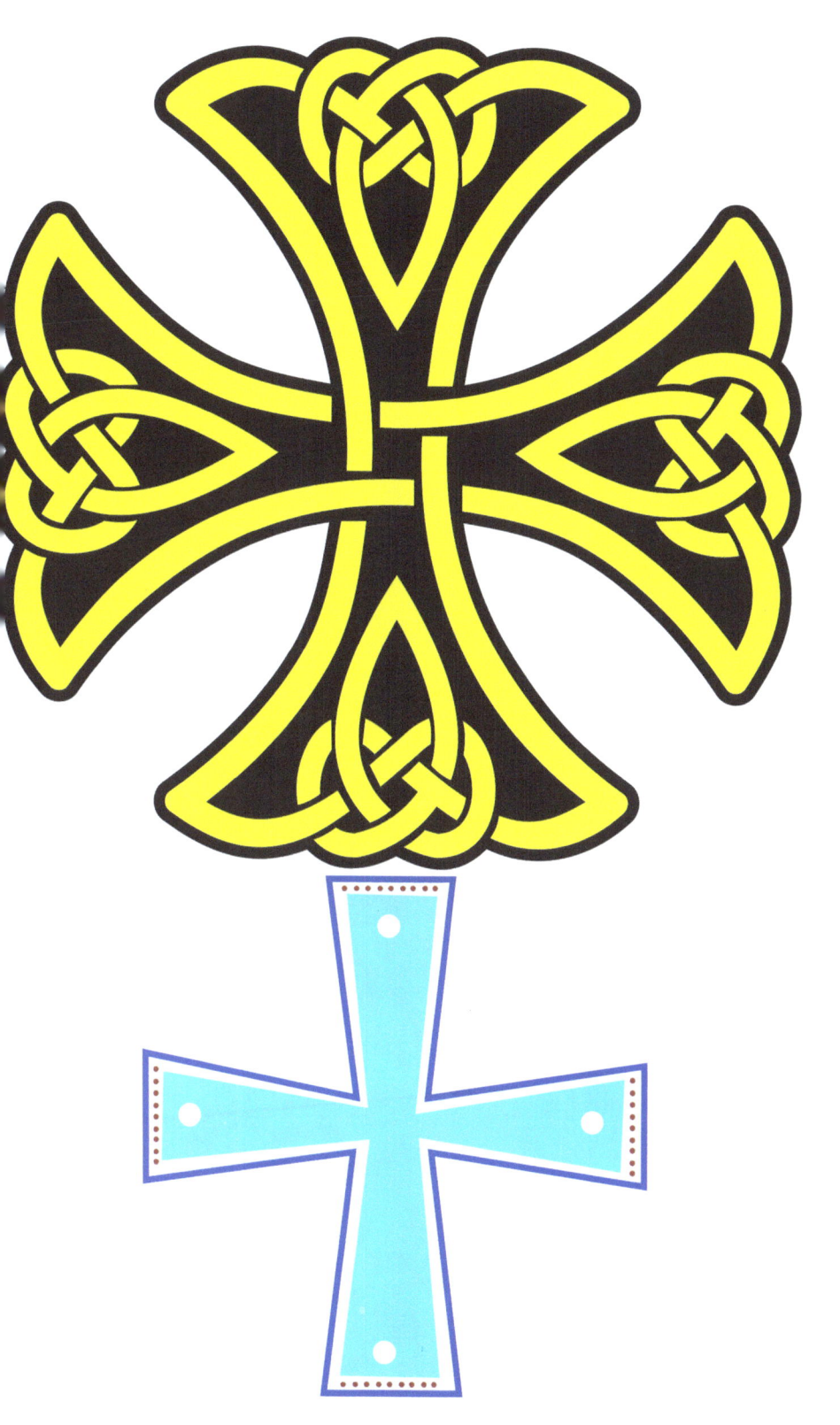

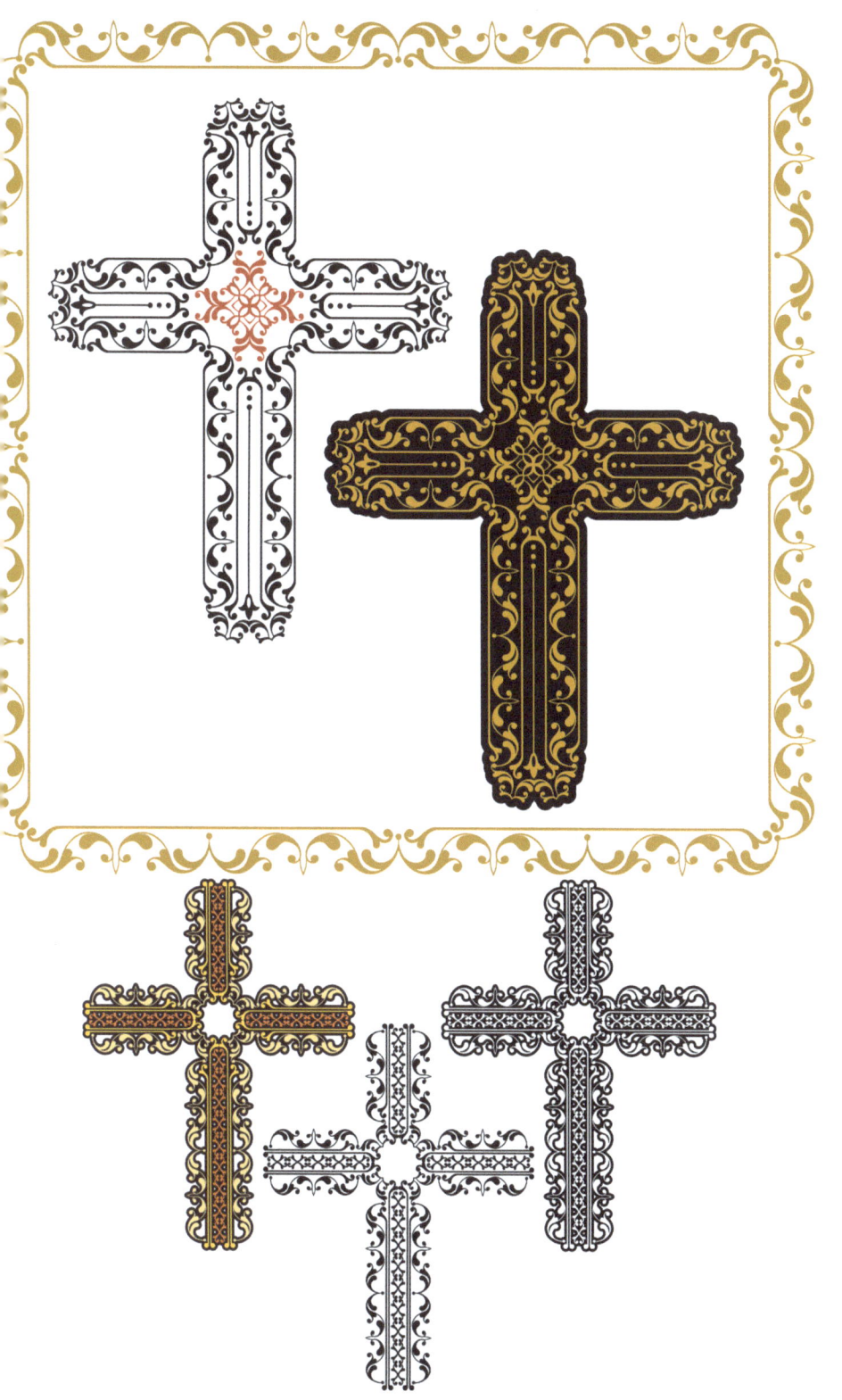

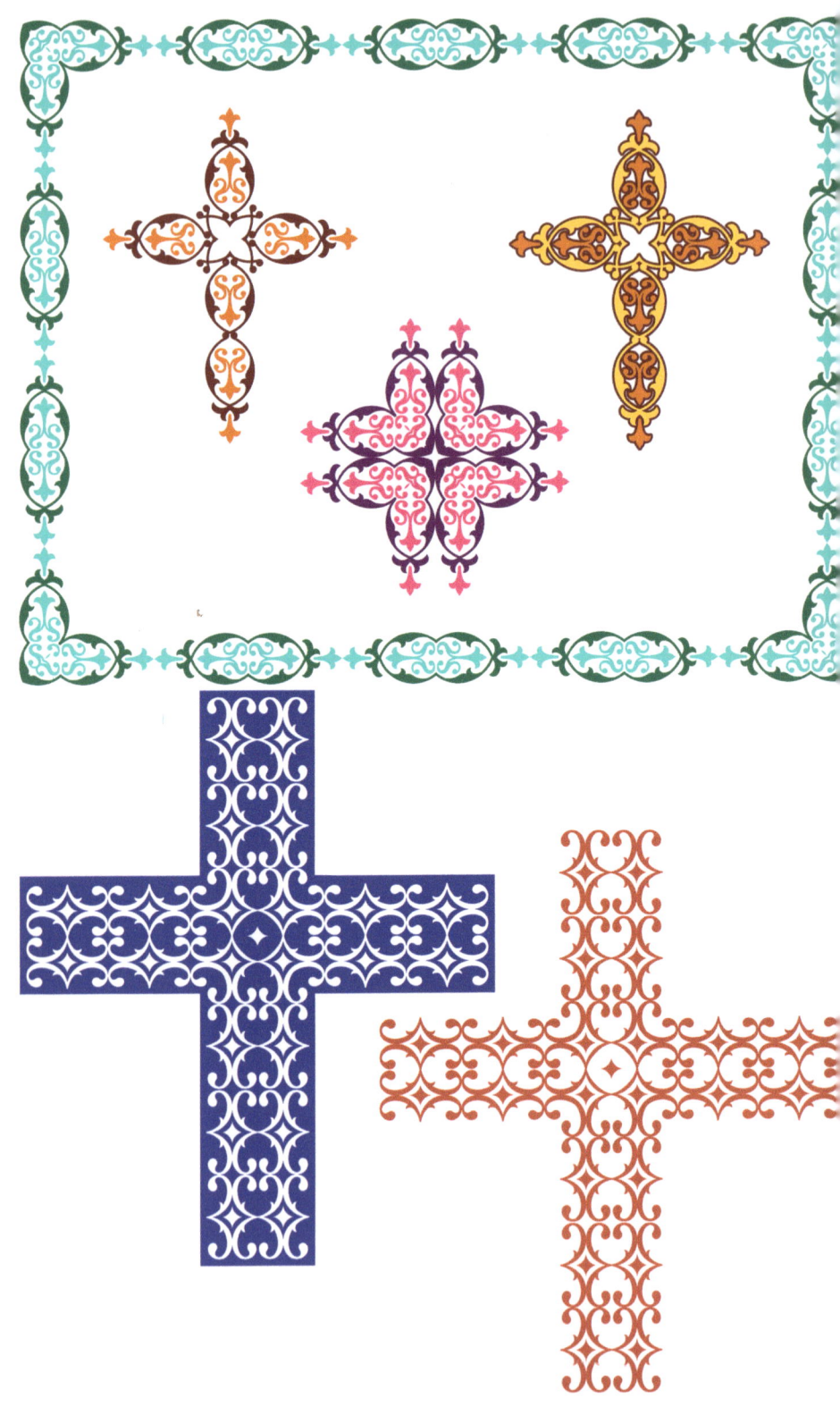

www.ingramcontent.com/pod-product-compliance
Lightning Source LLC
Chambersburg PA
CBHW040807200526
45159CB00022B/44